NEW ORLEANS

By the 1850s New Orleans
was already an established
city. The first St. Charles Hotel (domed building, left of
center), Gallier Hall and the
First Presbyterian Church (left,
foreground), and the first Odd
Fellows Hall (domed building
in foreground) are visible in
this 1852 view of the city as it
appeared from the top of St.
Patrick's Church. Courtesy,
The Historic New Orleans
Collection.

NEW ORLEANS

AN ILLUSTRATED HISTORY

TEXT BY JOHN R. KEMP

PICTURE RESEARCH BY JOHN H. LAWRENCE

"PRESERVING THE PAST" BY MARY LOU CHRISTOVICH

INTRODUCTION BY CHARLES L. DUFOUR

ADVISORY EDITOR, SAMUEL WILSON, JR., F.A.I.A.

AMERICAN HISTORICAL PRESS
SUN VALLEY, CALIFORNIA

Library of Congress Catalogue Card Number: 97-77010

ISBN: 0-9654754-6-8

Bibliography: p. 268
Includes Index

CONTENTS

New Orleans is a city rich in architectural treasures, one of the greatest being the Old City Hall—or Gallier Hall—designed by James Gallier in the 1840s. Regarded as one of America's foremost examples of the Greek Revival style, the hall is a spendid reminder of the energy and grace of the antebellum period. Courtesy, The Historic New Orleans Collection.

FOREWORD

New Orleans is, as it has often been remarked, the most "European" city of the United States. Founded by the French in 1718, ruled by Spain from the 1760s until 1803, and its population increased by influxes of German, Irish, and Italians as well as Anglo-Americans from other areas of the country, the city has retained a distinctive European atmosphere and a French *joie de vivre*. Although under the flag of Bourbon France for less than 50 of its first years, the French cultural heritage has been a dominant influence on its character. Until the middle of the nineteenth century, its newspapers were generally published in both French and English, laws were written in both languages, and legal documents and records of the early years are found in French probably more often than in English. During the Spanish period, Spanish became the official language for court records and other legal papers, but the language and customs of the people remained essentially French.

Of the buildings built during the French regime, only the old Ursuline Convent, designed in 1745, remains almost intact. The colonial city was nearly destroyed by the conflagrations of 1788 and 1794 and in its rebuilding, the architects and builders were almost all French—Guillemard, Andry, Lafon and Hilaire Boutte—and the architectural style of the new buildings was predominantly French. After the fires, the Spanish authorities enacted new building ordinances that required buildings to be of brick or of "brick between posts," covered with at least an inch coating of plaster or stucco. Roofs were to be of tile or slate, and flat or terrace roofs became common. The wrought-iron work of the Canary Islander Marcellino Hernandez, as seen in the balcony railings of the Cabildo, the Orue-Pontalba House (now the rebuilt home of Le Petit Theatre du Vieux Carre) and a few others, is perhaps the finest contribution of Spain to the architecture of New Orleans.

The noted architect, Benjamin H. Latrobe, observed in 1819 that "Americans are pouring in daily, not in families, but in large bodies. In a few years therefore, this will be an American town. What is good and bad in the French manners and opinions must give way and the American notions of right and wrong, of convenience and inconvenience, will take their place. ... One cannot help wishing that a *mean,* an *average* character of society may grow out of the intermixture of the French and American manners." Latrobe, as an English-born, American architect, regretted the changes being introduced by the incoming Americans with their red brick buildings in contrast to the picturesque French and Spanish stuccoed buildings of the colonial city. "We shall introduce many grand and profitable improvements but they will take the place of much elegance, ease and some convenience," Latrobe added.

The city has grown and changed over the more than two and a half centuries of its existence, and it has developed into a modern, thriving metropolis, the nation's second port. Its fascinating history has been recorded in many books, articles, paintings, and photographs. Over the years several publications devoted to the growth and to those who made it possible have appeared and form an invaluable source of information to those interested in the city's history. Among these were Jewell's *Crescent City Illustrated,* published in 1872; *New Orleans and the New South,* in 1888; *The City of New Orleans: The Book of the Chamber of Commerce and Industry of Louisiana,* in 1894; and *New Orleans, the Crescent City,* in 1903-04. Numerous guidebooks and surveys have provided additional information about this unusual city and the series, *New Orleans Architecture,* published by the Friends of the Cabildo, associates of the Louisiana State Museum, documents the city's distinctive architecture.

Not since the books named above, published between 1872 and 1904, has such a volume appeared that not only presents a concise history of the city, but also gives the history of many of the principal business concerns that have contributed to the city's growth and prosperity. In sponsoring this publication, the Preservation Resource Center adds another facet to its efforts to preserve the city's rich heritage of history and architecture.

Samuel Wilson, Jr., F.A.I.A.

Entitled Nouvelle Orleans, *this somewhat romanticized 19th-century painting depicts the city as it would look from a ship entering the port. Courtesy, The Historic New Orleans Collection.*

INTRODUCTION

New Orleans is *sui generis:* among American cities, it is one of a kind. A city geographically in the South—indeed, the Deep South—New Orleans is not a Southern city in the sense that Atlanta, Houston, and Dallas are Southern cities.

New Orleans, according to the 1840 census, became the third city in the nation, after New York and Baltimore, to reach a population of 100,000. Well into the 20th century, New Orleans continued to be the South's largest city; but it has since lost that honor, and in 1981 had fallen substantially behind other booming Southern cities.

During its long history, New Orleans had its share of picturesque rogues, clever rascals, and flamboyant demagogues. Corruption—long rooted in the political life of New Orleans—has often reached proportions of which Tammany Hall might have been proud. Yet for all of its foibles and failings, New Orleans is the envy of its richer and more aggressive sister-cities of the South. These cities, of course, will deny this vehemently.

Why should Atlanta, Dallas, or Houston envy New Orleans, all three of which outstrip her in many ways? It is simply because New Orleans has something that wealth cannot buy nor progress bring. New Orleans is a state of mind, a way of life. For charm, cuisine, and culture; for tradition, tomfoolery, and tragedy; for pestilence, plague, and politics; for floods, fires, and factions; for hurricanes and history, New Orleans has no rival in the United States.

Accordingly the history of New Orleans is colorful, complex, and always exciting, and in his text, John Kemp has capably exploited these characteristics.

Kemp gives a panoramic view of the history of New Orleans, narrating the story in admirable fashion from before Jean Baptiste Le Moyne, Sieur de Bienville, founded the city to the present and Mayor Ernest "Dutch" Morial. One will not find here an excess of details, for Kemp's goal was to survey New Orleans' past within designated limitations of space.

But the whole story is here. Kemp's style is smooth, clear, and direct. He has something to say and says it well; and he has given good pace to his narrative. That he has researched his subject in its many facets is readily evident. Kemp has delved deeply into existing secondary sources as well as using letters, newspapers, diaries, and interviews from which he has drawn skillfully.

The reader moves swiftly through the colonial period when New Orleans was the capital, first of French, then of Spanish, Louisiana. The Louisiana Purchase, the Battle of New Orleans, the lush era that followed the coming of the steamboat on the lower Mississippi, the rise of the plantation economy, and the boom days leading up to the Civil War are all well presented. So, too, is the Reconstruction period, with the carpetbaggers in command; and the rise of the Louisiana Lottery Company, which drained off millions of dollars annually from men, women, and even children. The author has a good, succinct description of the momentous segregation decision of the United States Supreme Court in the New Orleans case of *Plessy v. Ferguson.* When the doctrine of "separate but equal" received the blessing of the Supreme Court, the way was open for racial segregation in the South and

Kemp relates how black voters were disenfranchised by the "grandfather clause" written into the new Louisiana Constitution of 1898.

The history of New Orleans up to this point has been told by many writers in the past. But New Orleans' entry into the 20th century and the political history of the city between 1900 and 1925 has been treated, primarily, only in special studies rather than in narrative histories of the city. Kemp has told the story of Martin Behrman's 17 years in City Hall with clarity—no easy task considering the complexity of New Orleans' political wheeling-and-dealing in the rough-and-tumble era of Ring rule. The research he conducted for his biography of Behrman, published some years ago, has clearly stood him in good stead.

The rise to power of Huey Long, against the backdrop of the Great Depression, is deftly sketched in one of the most interesting sections of Kemp's narrative. Long not only held more power in his hands than any politician in Louisiana—before or since—but he also used power to achieve his goals without the slightest regard to niceties. His assassination cut short Long's already-meteoric rise on the national scene.

Kemp concludes his history with a survey of the decades from the end of World War II to the present. He ably describes the "Chep" Morrison years in City Hall and racial desegregation which was a stormy highlight of Morrison's career. He evaluates the city's progress during the administrations of Victor Schiro, "Moon" Landrieu, and "Dutch" Morial to end the story that really began 300 years ago (come April 9, 1982), when La Salle, standing on the bank of the Mississippi near the Gulf of Mexico, claimed Louisiana for Louis XIV.

Charles L. Dufour

In 1682 Rene Robert Cavelier, Sieur de La Salle, claimed for France the vast territory drained by the Mississippi River. He named it Louisiana in honor of King Louis XIV. Courtesy, The Historic New Orleans Collection.

CHAPTER I
"ROME AND PARIS
HAD NOT SUCH CONSIDERABLE BEGINNINGS"

The Mississippi River, the great divider of the United States into east and west, was born at the conclusion of the Ice Age, when melting glacial water etched a great valley southward across the continent to its point of escape into the Gulf of Mexico. Today the river rises from small streams that feed Lake Itasca in northern Minnesota, flowing 2,350 miles and draining — with its tributaries — all or part of 31 states, accounting for more than a third of the total runoff of the continental United States.

As the Mississippi cascades and winds its way toward the Gulf, it travels from a temperate to a subtropical climate and from an elevation of about 1,400 feet to sea level at its mouth. The upper Mississippi flows through central Minnesota from lake to lake, cutting through glacial debris at such descriptively named towns as Grand Rapids and Little Falls. During the winter the river is often clogged by ice and thick, hazardous fogs settle on the cold waters of the unfrozen parts during warm spells. Below St. Paul, Minnesota, the river valley widens and the grade decreases as the river becomes a major spillway for the continental ice sheet stretching northeast and northwest.

The Mississippi's major tributary, the Missouri — more than 2,000 miles itself — joins 17 miles north of St. Louis, Missouri. Here the river width increases to 3,500 feet and when the Ohio River joins at Cairo,

Illinois, the river expands to 4,500 feet. The lower Mississippi meanders in great loops across broad alluvial plains dotted by marshes, oxbow lakes, and remnants of the river's former channels. Natural levees, built up from sediment carried and deposited in times of flood, border much of the river, making it higher than the surrounding areas. Breaks in the levees often flood the bottomlands.

Below the confluence of the Mississippi, Arkansas, and Red rivers, the Mississippi enters a birdsfoot-like delta, fanning out and into the Gulf through small and large distributaries (such as the Atchafalaya River and Bayou Lafourche). The main stream continues southeast through the delta, entering the Gulf through several mouths including Southeast and South passes.

The present delta has been built outward by sediment carried by the main stream during the last five centuries. Geologists recognize three earlier deltas, and believe that the river is in the process of abandoning its present course — diverting through the Atchafalaya River — perhaps even in the face of man's greatest technological skills employed to contain it. For here is clearly seen the true power — and indifference — of the river: in a posture of perfect neutrality, the river takes no responsibility for New Orleans, nor for the other cities along its banks, essential though it was and is for their vitality. The stream has been one of the key participants in a compelling drama which, although the setting was only the place where the Mississippi meets the sea, has had worldwide effects and engaged the imaginations of some of modern history's most significant thinkers and doers.

Europeans had been aware of the Mississippi River Valley since the early 1500s, but no attempt had been made to colonize it. The first European to discover the mouth of the Mississippi was probably Alonso Alvarez de Pineda during his exploration of the northern Gulf Coast in 1519. He called the great river the Rio del Espiritu Santo. In 1527 Panfilo de Narvaez, a wealthy Spaniard living in Cuba, set sail from Spain to take possession of Florida and any other land he might want. After a series of disasters and desertions, Narvaez and his small fleet left from the western coast of Florida for Mexico. Soon after sailing past the mouth of the Mississippi, a storm wrecked the

fleet. The few survivors wandered on foot through the swamps and forests for almost 10 years before reaching a Mexican settlement. An account of Narvaez's tragedy, and more important, a description of the coastline, was written later by one of the survivors, Alvar Nunez Cabeza de Vaca.

Another Spaniard, Hernando de Soto, who was intrigued by Vaca's account of the Gulf Coast, landed at Tampa Bay in May 1539. But Soto's expedition was doomed to failure, just as his predecessors' had been. After three years of misery and wandering through present-day Florida, the Carolinas, Alabama, Tennessee, Arkansas, Missouri, and Louisiana, Soto died in May 1542, somewhere on the Mississippi near Arkansas.

While the Spanish were the first to see the mouth of the great river, it was the French — already a formidable presence in the Great Lakes area — who first attempted to settle the Mississippi. In 1682 Robert Cavelier, Sieur de La Salle, became the first known European to reach the mouth of the Mississippi by descending the river. On April 6, after almost two months of traveling, exploring, and visiting with Indian tribes along the way, La Salle and his followers reached the mouth of the river with its brisk currents and vast grassy wetlands. On the morning of April 9, a cross was erected on a chosen spot and after honor was paid to God and the king, La Salle took possession of the territory named for Louis XIV, ". . . as far as its mouth at the sea, or Gulf of Mexico, and also to the mouth of the River of Palms, upon the assurance we have had from the natives of these countries, that we are the first Europeans who have descended or ascended the said river."

It was an acquisition with few parallels in world history, one which caused historian Francis Parkman to remark on the irony of "a feeble human voice inaudible at half a mile" claiming "the fertile plains of Texas; the vast basin of the Mississippi, from its frozen northern springs to the sultry borders of the Gulf; from the woody ridges of the Alleghenies to the peaks of the Rocky Mountains — a region of savannas and forests, sun-cracked deserts, and grassy prairies, watered by a thousand rivers, [and] ranged by a thousand warlike tribes."

Determinedly, La Salle returned to France to organize a new expedition to plant a colony at the mouth of the Mississippi. At that location, he thought he would be able to reap the riches of the interior as well as that in the nearby Spanish shipping lanes.

La Salle and the settlers left France for Louisiana in July 1684. But by accident or by decision, the three small ships bypassed the Mississippi and ended up on the beaches near present-day Galveston, Texas. Two of the ships were lost and the third left the settlers stranded on the beach and returned to France. Three years later, with his dream of a Mississippi colony shattered, La Salle decided to return to Canada. On foot and without charts, the explorer and a small party left the settlement for their long journey. After weeks of wandering, La Salle was killed by his own men. A few survivors made their way back to Canada, but those settlers staying behind at the Texas settlement vanished, falling victim either to Indians or to the Spanish.

During the early 1690s prominent Canadians unsuccessfully urged Louis XIV and his ministers to build a colony in Louisiana. The famous Italian-born explorer Henri de Tonti sent his own request for a Mississippi colony to the king in October 1697. But Tonti's suggestion, like the others, was ignored. The pressure from Canada persisted, however, and finally gained the interest of Louis Phelypeaux, the Comte de Pontchartrain and minister of marine for Louis XIV. France had several good reasons for colonizing Louisiana: namely, to protect and expand her colonial possessions; to contain westward movement by the British on the Atlantic Seaboard, for they had already established trade contacts with the Indians along the Mississippi River; and finally, to serve as a base for raids on the prosperous Spanish sea trade passing through the Gulf.

The French government dispatched Canadian Pierre Le Moyne, Sieur d'Iberville, with his younger brother, Jean Baptiste Le Moyne, Sieur de Bienville, and five small ships on September 24, 1698, to establish a permanent settlement in Louisiana.

On January 24, 1699, Iberville and his expedition anchored off Santa Rosa Island near the mouth of Pensacola Bay. The Spanish, however, had beaten the French to the area with the establishment of a settlement at Pensacola a month before. The Spanish commandant went out to meet the French. He was cordial to the Frenchmen, but refused to let the intruders enter the bay. Iberville raised anchor and sailed west to Mobile Bay, where he set up a temporary base at Dauphin Island. From the island the explorers sailed further westward, exploring the barrier islands of the Mississippi Sound. Iberville decided to set up his new base at Ship Island and dispatched his younger brother, Bienville, to explore the mainland.

On February 13 Bienville and a small party reached the coast where they encountered a handful of Biloxi Indians who fled at the approach of the white men. Bienville's men were able to capture a few of the sickly ones who could not run fast enough. The Frenchmen offered their infirmed guests the comfort of grass mats to sleep on, but the mats caught fire during the night and the Indians were dispatched to the Great Spirit. Bienville's party later captured a woman of the Biloxi tribe and the same day the Frenchmen came upon a Bayagoula (also spelled Bayougoula) raiding party en route to attack the Mobile Indians. From the Bayagoulas, Bienville learned of a great river, called the Malbanchia, located about a hundred miles to the west. With this Bienville hurried

The Louisiana Territory and its principal river, the Mississippi, dominate this early 18th-century map of North America by Guillaume de L'Isle. (THNOC)

ROME AND PARIS HAD NOT SUCH CONSIDERABLE BEGINNINGS • 13

The Canadian-born Le Moyne brothers, Pierre, Sieur d'Iberville, and Jean Baptiste, Sieur de Bienville, entered the mouth of the Mississippi to explore the lower Mississippi Valley and investigate the possibility of colonizing the area. Pierre is on the left, Jean Baptiste is on the right. (THNOC)

back to Ship Island and Iberville.

On February 27 Iberville set out with two *traversiers* and his men to find the Mississippi. After five days of enduring blinding rain and high winds and seas, the Frenchmen found the river on March 3. But Iberville wanted definite proof that he had rediscovered La Salle's river.

Moving upstream the explorers encountered an Indian hunting party that guided them to the Bayagoula village. Here Iberville learned that Tonti had left a letter with the Mougoulachas Indians when he had descended the river in 1686 looking for La Salle's ill-fated expedition. Upon reading the letter, Iberville found the assurance he wanted and wrote, "There is no doubt that the Mississippi is the Malbanchia."

Iberville had fulfilled part of his mission: to rediscover the Mississippi. Now, he turned his attention to the second part of his instructions — building a settlement to protect the Mississippi from other European explorations. Consistent with this purpose, Iberville decided to build Fort Maurepas on Biloxi Bay about a hundred miles northeast of the mouth of the Mississippi.

In May 1699 Iberville made the first of several voyages to France bringing supplies and new settlers to the struggling colony. Iberville warned the king, and his advisors who had opposed the Louisiana venture, that unless France established a strong colony there, "the English colony which has become very consid-

erable will grow in such a manner that in less than one hundred years, she will be strong enough to seize all America and drive out all other nations."

Iberville's fears evidently were not unfounded, for the British had already dispatched an expedition to scout a site for a colony on the Mississippi. On September 15, 1699, Bienville and a small band of Frenchmen were paddling on the Mississippi in two small canoes when they encountered the English corvette *Carolina Galley* at anchor in the river. Bienville approached the ship, told her captain she was in French territory, and ordered him to leave. Should the Englishmen refuse, Bienville said, he would use force. The bluff worked and the 12-gun corvette weighed anchor while its captain threatened to return with a greater force. Bienville, his five men, and two canoes were, of course, in no position to force the ship to leave. But the bend in the river, some dozen miles below present-day New Orleans, where Bienville sent the British downriver shaking their fists, is still known today as English Turn *(Detour des Anglais* or *Detour aux Anglais)*.

When Iberville returned to the colony and heard of the British expedition, he quickly ordered the building of Fort de Mississippi on the first high spot above the mouth of the river. This cypress-log fort with four cannons and fifteen men was the first French post in what is now the state of Louisiana. By 1707, however,

the little fort, that was to have defended France's claim to the Mississippi, had been abandoned.

Direct confrontation with the English, however, was the least of the Frenchmen's problems. With English traders pushing westward from the Atlantic Coast, several Indian tribes — including the Caddos, Tunicas, and Muskhogeans, as well as the Choctaws and Chickasaws — were caught between the two European powers vying for dominance in North America. For the French, maintaining diplomatic relations with the Indians was a constant, and not always successful struggle in the face of English intrigues among the tribes. When the numerous tribes were not busy raiding each other, they were killing either Frenchmen or Englishmen depending on which colonial power was exerting the most pressure at the time. During peaceful periods, they provided food for the settlers, hides for the fur trade, and wives for lonely frontiersmen. For many generations the Indians of southeast Louisiana provided foodstuffs for the markets of New Orleans, including fish, game, and one of the seasonings they introduced to Creole cookery: file, used so often in gumbos.

Iberville's strategy with the Indians, es-

pecially the antagonistic Chickasaws, was to convince them of British intentions to enslave them and take their lands. Bienville went one step further in his attempts to keep the powerful Chickasaws in line, by threatening to arm the Choctaws, the Illinois, the Mobilians, and other tribes and encouraging them to make war on the Chickasaws. To further ensure their peaceful cooperation, Iberville wrote to the vicar general of the bishop of Quebec imploring him to dispatch missionaries to live among the Choctaws and Chickasaws.

Nor were the English and the Indians the only problems the French colonists encountered in their Louisiana colony. Critical food shortages constantly reminded the Le Moyne brothers of their dependence on supplies from France and the goodwill of the Indians. Complicating matters further, the early settlers — mainly frontiersmen — were far more interested in trapping and trading than in planting crops. Food shortages in 1709 and 1710 were so severe that the colonists survived on Indian corn, and at one point, Bienville sent many of his soldiers to live among the Indians for survival.

Diseases — especially malaria and swamp fever — also caused terrific losses among the colonists. When Iberville returned from one of

A detail of a map by Thomas Jeffreys from the 1770s shows the site of Fort de la Boulaye, which once stood southwest of Lake Borgne. The fort was an early Mississippi River settlement. (THNOC)

his trips to France in 1701, he found Fort Maurepas decimated by disease, prompting him to gather the survivors, take them to Mobile River, and establish Fort Louis de la Mobile (later moved and renamed Fort Louis de la Louisiane) 55 miles from the mouth of Mobile Bay. Iberville himself died of yellow fever he contracted in Havana in 1706, leaving Bienville as the acting governor of the Louisiana Territory.

For all of these reasons, the early Louisiana settlements remained thinly populated. The most serious barrier to establishing a viable colony, however, remained that of enticing women to reside in the wilderness and raise families.

Despite a shipment of young women to the colony in 1704, the population steadily decreased. That year the population consisted of 180 men, 27 French families with 10 children, 11 Indian slave children, and 4 priests. Four years later it was only 122 men, 24 colonists, 25 children, 28 women, and 80 Indian slaves. Conditions were so adverse, it was reported, that even some French soldiers had deserted to

the English in the Carolinas.

Under these circumstances the colony was of minimal value to France, a situation that the ministry of Louis XIV finally set about remedying and which, in turn, led to the founding of New Orleans. Ironically, it was internal conflict between the French and the French-Canadians at Fort Louis that finally prompted royal intervention.

Bienville, in command since the death of Iberville in 1706, had been having personal problems with commissary Nicolas de La Salle and Father Henri Roulleaux de La Vente, the pastor of the Mobile settlement. Both La Salle and Father de La Vente loathed the Le Moyne brothers and sent numerous letters to their superiors complaining about Bienville, whom the priest called a "rogue." The Canadians, La Salle wrote, "are shiftless and libertines who care only to run the woods." Bienville, in return, leveled his own charges against the commissary and priest. La Salle, he said, constantly tried to undermine the commandant's authority; while the priest, he said, illegally conducted marriage ceremonies between white men and

Among the Indians Iberville had to contend with in the early 1700s were the Choctaws, shown here dressed as warriors carrying scalps. Drawing by A. De Batz. Courtesy, Smithsonian Institution, National Anthropological Archives.

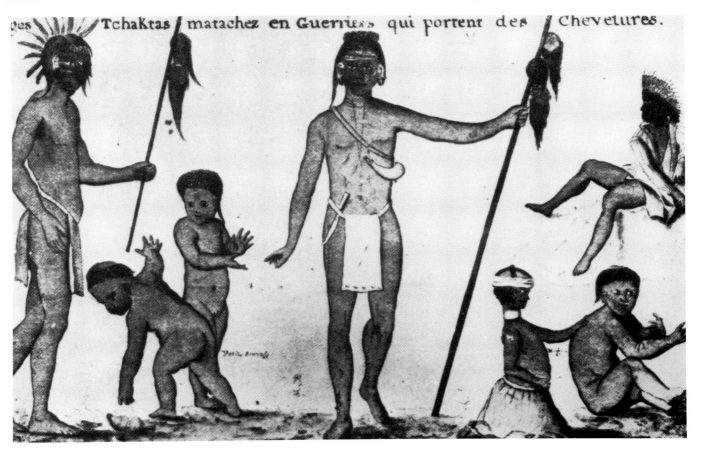

des Tchaktas matachez en Guerriers qui portent des Chevelures.

Indian women. He also charged the priest with baptizing children naked in the outdoors, which, he said, resulted in the deaths of several youngsters.

After months of charges and countercharges sailing between France and Louisiana, the French ministry decided to make a change. Louis XIV removed both Bienville and La Salle from office. As replacements, Nicholas Daneau, Sieur de Muy was sent to be governor and Jean-Baptiste-Martin d'Artaguiette d'Iron to be commissary. Daneau de Muy died on the way over and d'Artaguiette arrived in early 1708, immediately setting about investigating the charges leveled by all parties. A month later, d'Artaguiette wrote Pontchartrain not only exonerating, but actually praising Bienville for his efforts under difficult circumstances. Most of all d'Artaguiette pressed the king to realize the importance of Louisiana to France. Its location on the Gulf of Mexico and the Mississippi River was ideal for commerce and the exploitation of the vast and immeasurably wealthy interior of North America.

In 1712 the king, unhappy with the negligible growth in the crown colony and his treasury depleted by the War of Spanish Succession (1701–1714), granted Antoine Crozat a 15-year exclusive charter to Louisiana. Crozat, a wealthy French merchant, was not new to the business of colonial trade. He held stock in the Guinea Company, with its profitable African trade, and in the Asiento Company which carried on a lucrative slave trade between Africa and the New World. Under the terms of the charter, Crozat gained all commercial rights to "Louisiana" south of the Illinois district possessed by the Crown including all the area between Mexico and the Carolinas. Crozat could mine and export ores and precious stones; control all trade in the colony; have full use of all Crown-owned buildings and property in the colony; and the exclusive right to import slaves from Africa. In return Crozat was to colonize and develop the region under the laws, edicts, and ordinances of France.

Crozat was particularly interested in mining the colony and establishing trade with Mexico. So in 1710 he appointed Antoine de La Mothe Cadillac, who supported Crozat's ideas on commerce, to replace Bienville, who favored an agricultural colony, as governor. Cadillac arrived in 1713, carrying a letter from the Crown

instructing him to investigate La Salle's earlier charges against Bienville. This initiated a feud between the two men that lasted Cadillac's entire term in Louisiana and that eventually resulted in his removal as governor. Bienville, wounded that he was not made the permanent governor, wrote to the Comte de Pontchartrain, denouncing all charges of wrongdoing. He asked for a pay raise, a promotion, and a new assignment. A year later he got his reply: "Behave yourself and you will get your reward." But neither man seemed able to comply with this edict. Cadillac wrote to France, accusing Bienville of causing trouble among the inhabitants and working against Crozat's interests in the colony. Bienville responded to his superiors that Cadillac criticized him only because he had refused to marry Cadillac's daughter.

The new governor was not long in Louisiana before he managed to alienate almost everyone. His arrogance toward local Indian tribes caused an uprising among the proud Natchez that Bienville had to smooth over. Nor did Cadillac have any kind words for the Louisiana settlers, whom he described as "the dregs of Canada, or the colony." After several years of such acrimony, both Crozat and the Crown realized that Cadillac was not the right man for the job. So Cadillac was recalled, leaving Bienville as the acting governor.

Bienville, however, was replaced quickly with Jean Michiele, Seigneur de Lepinay et de La Longueville, who arrived in March 1717 with Marc Antoine Hubert, the colony's new commissary. The new governor wasted little time before he, like his predecessor, was at odds with Bienville. Lepinay, however, did not last as long as Cadillac and was recalled after only six months. In a letter to France, Hubert claimed Lepinay surely would have destroyed the colony if he had not been removed from office. Bienville was in charge once again.

At about this time Crozat, never even having seen his colony, decided to divest himself of Louisiana which had cost him over 2 million livres in five years. In his letter to the ministry of marine, the merchant-nobleman reflected on the failure of his Louisiana venture to produce the wealth he had imagined: "My three principal projects: discovery of mines of gold and silver, the establishment and maintenance of workers for plantations of tobacco, [and] com-

merce with Spain were dissipated." Crozat asked the Crown to revoke the charter and release him from its responsibilities. On August 13, 1717, Philippe, Duc d'Orleans, and regent for the young Louis XV (Louis XIV had died two years earlier), relieved Crozat from his obligations.

While Crozat took a financial battering in Louisiana, it was the colony that had been truly victimized. Crippled by the laws and regulations of France, by Crozat's monopoly, and by low prices for furs, Louisiana had continued to be a problem rather than an asset. The French throne did not have to wait long before John Law, an adventurous Scotsman, forwarded a new scheme. Law, after founding the "Banque Generale" of France in 1716, convinced the Duc d'Orleans that Louisiana had potential for great wealth if administered properly. He then formed the Company of the West in 1717, a joint-stock company, and sold shares at 500 livres. Rapidly, the value of the shares climbed

to as much as 8,000 livres. On September 6, 1717, the company was granted an exclusive charter to Louisiana, including the Illinois country—an area that had not been part of Crozat's earlier grant. Under the terms of the charter the company promised to send 6,000 settlers and 3,000 slaves to the colony within 10 years. In 1719 the Company of the West was combined with all other French colonizing companies into the Company of the Indies, which promised even greater things for Louisiana. In addition to Louisiana, the new company received charters and special privileges in Africa, Argentina, St. Domingue (Santo Domingo), China, and the East Indies.

Law's Louisiana venture was, perhaps, the biggest and most successful public-relations scheme ever perpetrated on the European people up to that time. Handbills and posters inundated southern Germany, Switzerland, and France encouraging everyone to emigrate to Louisiana, the land of inestimable oppor-

tunities. (There actually were "inestimable opportunities" for some, namely the company's wealthy investors who were given "concessions" of thousands of acres that later were developed into important plantations up and down the river.) Thousands of Germans and Swiss did grab at the opportunity to leave their poverty behind and to make a fresh start in what had been described as a bountiful land.

The success of Law's campaign is also suggested by the variety of colonists attracted. There were the sons of the lesser nobility in France who came to the colony to seek their fortunes, as well as artisans in all of the trades, and even hard-working German farmers who provided the colony with fresh food. (Many of the Germans who remained settled on the west bank of the Mississippi several miles above New Orleans in an area later called the *Cote des Allemands,* or simply *Des Allemands.* German family names gradually gave way to Gallic

spellings and pronunciations, such as *Zweig* (twig) to *LaBranche* or *Himmel* to *Hymel.* The descendants of these Gallicized Germans still live in the area.) Undesirables were also given the opportunity to go and make a new beginning. For a time, convicts and prostitutes were given their freedom if they would marry and go to Louisiana, but the regent ordered this practice stopped in early 1720. Another group, the "casket girls," so-called because each carried a government-issued chest of clothing and linen, came to marry the men who had arrived before them.

The result of this influx during the first four years of Law's control was that the colony's population grew from about 400 to over 8,000, including African slaves. The use of African slaves as opposed to Indian slaves, who were purchased from warring Indian tribes, had proven more satisfactory to the colonists. Indians — both in Louisiana and those shipped to

Below
Antoine Crozat's heavy financial losses in Louisiana from 1712 to 1717 led to a revocation of his charter and the formation of the Company of the West. (THNOC)

Facing page
Le Page Du Pratz, who arrived in the Louisiana colony the year New Orleans was founded, chronicled the plant and animal life of the region and made observations on life in the colony in general. These illustrations of a wildcat, a wood rat, a skunk, and a tree appeared in a history by Le Page. (THNOC)

Chat Sauvage.

Rat de Bois.

Bête puante

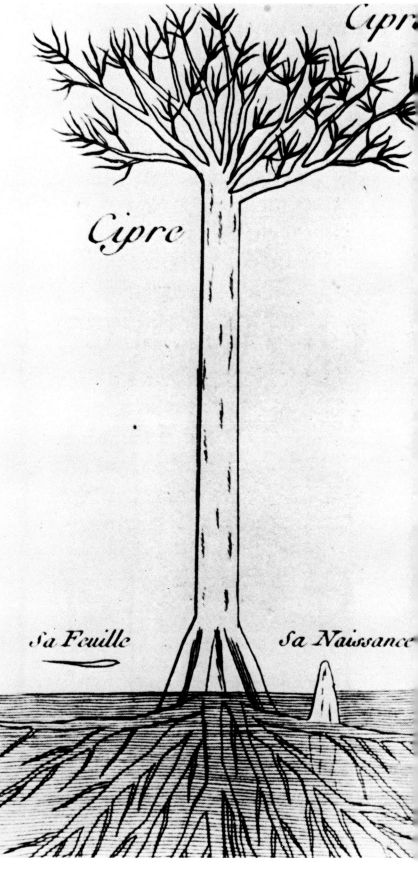

Cipre

Cipre

Sa Feuille

Sa Naissance

West Indian islands — were of little value to their captors. Those kept in Louisiana usually ran away, while those shipped to the islands pined away until they died.

The Negro trade had not been sanctioned officially until Crozat's 1712 charter. The Company of the West, and its successor, the Company of the Indies, reportedly imported more than 2,000 black slaves by 1731. By 1724 the slave and free-black populations had increased to such numbers that the Crown enacted the *Code Noir*, or Black Code, a far-reaching set of laws that was an adaptation of the code being used in Santo Domingo. The *Code Noir* restricted, protected, and defined the activities of slaves and free blacks. It forbade the practice of any religion other than Roman Catholicism, going so far as to order Jews expelled from the colony. The code prohibited marriage or concubinage between whites and blacks. Slaves could not hold property nor could they be a party to civil suits. Striking a master, his family, or even a free Negro could bring the death penalty for a slave. Although the code was spe-

Although it is believed that slaves were brought to Louisiana as early as 1708, the slave trade was not officially sanctioned until 1712. Slaves were counted in the population of Louisiana. (THNOC)

cific in its regulations, officials were lax in enforcing many of its provisions, especially those concerning coupling between the races.

Because of the *Code Noir,* Negro slaves enjoyed considerably more freedom in colonial Louisiana than their counterparts did in the British colonies. In fact the last article of the code is often considered a precursor to portions of the United States Constitution and its amendments:

We grant to manumitted slaves the same rights, privileges, and immunities which are enjoyed by freeborn persons. It is our pleasure that their merit in having acquired their freedom shall produce in their favor, not only with regard to their persons, but also to their property, the same effects which our other subjects derive from the happy circumstances of their having been born free.

One of Law's major goals was building a permanent settlement on the Mississippi both to cement France's claim to the river valley and to provide the company with a major port where French vessels could fill their holds with the expected riches of Louisiana. A site for the town — to be called New Orleans after the Duc d'Orleans — was chosen 30 leagues upriver at an Indian portage shown to Iberville in 1699. Bienville had pushed for this location because of its elevation and its proximity to Lake Pontchartrain through Bayou St. John, along which French settlers had located since 1708.

Land-clearing at the New Orleans site began in the spring of 1718 under the supervision of Bienville. By the end of the year very little land had actually been cleared of its thick, jungle-like growth, and only a few palmetto huts had been constructed. In 1719 a flood wiped out all that stood, causing company officials to consider moving the town upriver, an idea that was discarded. Very little progress was made in developing New Orleans for the next three years.

The "casket girls" (so called because their belongings were held in small, government-issued chests) were said to be wards of the Ursuline nuns in Louisiana until they found suitable marriage partners. (THNOC)

The growing slave population of Louisiana caused Bienville to enact the Code Noir (Black Code), which defined the activities in which both slave and free blacks could participate. The code was adopted from a similar code in use in Santo Domingo. (THNOC)

Bienville had returned to the colony at Mobile where he was preoccupied with internal quarrels. But Father Pierre Francois-Xavier de Charlevoix, visiting the primitive settlement in 1721, described what he believed was New Orleans' special destiny:

I have the best grounded hopes for saying that this wild and deserted place, at present almost entirely covered with canes and trees shall one day . . . become the capital of a large and rich colony. . . . Rome and Paris had not such considerable beginnings, were not built under such happy auspices, and their founders met not with the advantages of the Seine and the Tiber, which we have found the Mississippi, in comparison of which, these two rivers are not more than brooks.

Bienville apparently agreed with the good father on the importance of the Mississippi Valley, for in 1719 he moved the capital of Louisiana from Mobile to Biloxi and finally, in 1722, New Orleans became the capital, remaining so until well into the American era.

In March 1721 chief engineer Pierre Le Blond de La Tour dispatched Adrien de Pauger to supervise construction of New Orleans. Despite uncooperative company officials, snakes, mosquitoes, and heavy rains, Pauger and 10 soldiers had cleared enough land in less than a month to plot three streets facing the river. Nine months later, the town had 470 inhabitants. But nature ravaged the settlement again in September 1722 when a hurricane struck, destroying most of the town's buildings. This was in fact fortunate, since none of the original buildings were aligned with the engineer's plan and would have had to be demolished in any case.

The earliest-known complete plan of New Orleans was signed by La Tour and dated April 23, 1722. This plan comprised the section of New Orleans now known as the *Vieux Carre* (Old Square, or French Quarter) that remained the legal extent of the city until the end of the 19th century. Hugging the east bank of the Mississippi on a large crescent bend, the early town was laid out in a grid pattern surrounding a riverfront parade ground called the Place d'Armes (now Jackson Square). Behind the square was space for the parish church. The Church of St. Louis (later St. Louis Cathedral) was first designed by Pauger in 1724 and construction completed in 1727. (The present-day St. Louis Cathedral is the third edifice to stand on that spot.) Following La Tour's plan this time, soldiers, Canadians, Frenchmen, and Negro slaves built sturdier houses and public buildings. The new structures were built of framed timbers with a *bousillage* of clay and moss stuffed between the timbers; the exteriors were covered with wide clapboards. After the first brick kiln was built on the Indian trail leading from the town to Bayou St. John in 1724, bricks-between-posts would replace the clay and moss. The kiln also manufactured roof tiles for the church, government, and other major buildings. (Although early plans of New Orleans indicated pallisades around the town, little effort was made to fortify it until the Natchez Indian massacre in 1729. But even then only part of a moat was completed. Wooden fortifications were not built around the town until 1760 at the height of the French and Indian War.)

Naming the streets of early New Orleans was a masterpiece of 18th-century diplomacy. Bourbon, Orleans, Burgundy, and Royal streets were named for the royal family of France; while the Conti, Chartres, and Conde families were cousins to the Bourbons and Orleans.

The early dwellings of New Orleans were not very substantial structures and were often destroyed by hurricanes and floods. (THNOC)

(Conde Street used to be that section of Chartres stretching from Jackson Square to Esplanade Avenue before it was changed in 1865.) St. Peter Street was named in honor of one of the ancestors of the Bourbon family. The saint-king Louis IX was not forgotten: hence St. Louis Street. Toulouse and Dumaine streets were named for Louis XIV's royal bastards. Louis XV's father, the Duc de Burgundy, was also remembered. By 1728 the settlement, despite its shaky beginnings, was a village. On April 24, 1728, a young Ursuline nun, who had just arrived in New Orleans, described the colonial capital in a letter to her father in France:

Our city is very pretty, well constructed and regularly built. The people have worked and still work to perfect it. The streets are very wide and are laid out in straight lines. The main street is nearly a league in length. The houses are very well built of "collombage et mortier." They are white washed, paneled and filled with sunlight. The roofs of the houses are covered with tiles [shingles] which are pieces of wood in the shape of slate. . . . It suffices to say that there is a song sung openly here in which the words proclaim that this city is as beautiful as Paris.

While New Orleans was taking shape, Bienville once again was having problems with his detractors, most notably with the engineers La Tour and Pauger. The Company of the Indies sent Sieur Jacques de La Chaise and the Sieur de Sauvoy to the colony in 1723 to investigate. The two envoys arrived at Ship Island in early April, but Sauvoy soon died, leaving La Chaise to conduct the inquiry. La Chaise's initial reports to the company were complimentary to Bienville, but later deteriorated as the two became enemies. La Chaise accused Bienville of showing favoritism to the Canadians over native French settlers. Even more devastating was La Chaise's charge that Bienville intentionally tried to undermine the company's economic efforts in the colony, in the hope that the king would revoke the company's charter and give Bienville freer reign to do as he pleased. The weight of these complaints against Bienville became too much to bear for the directors of the company. At their request, the regent, in the name of Louis XV, ordered Bienville back to France and instructed Pierre Dugue de Boisbriant to travel from the Illinois country and take command at New Orleans.

Bienville and his brother, Chateauguay (who had been with Bienville in Louisiana) arrived in France in August of 1725. Bienville's nephews in Louisiana petitioned the regent to reinstate

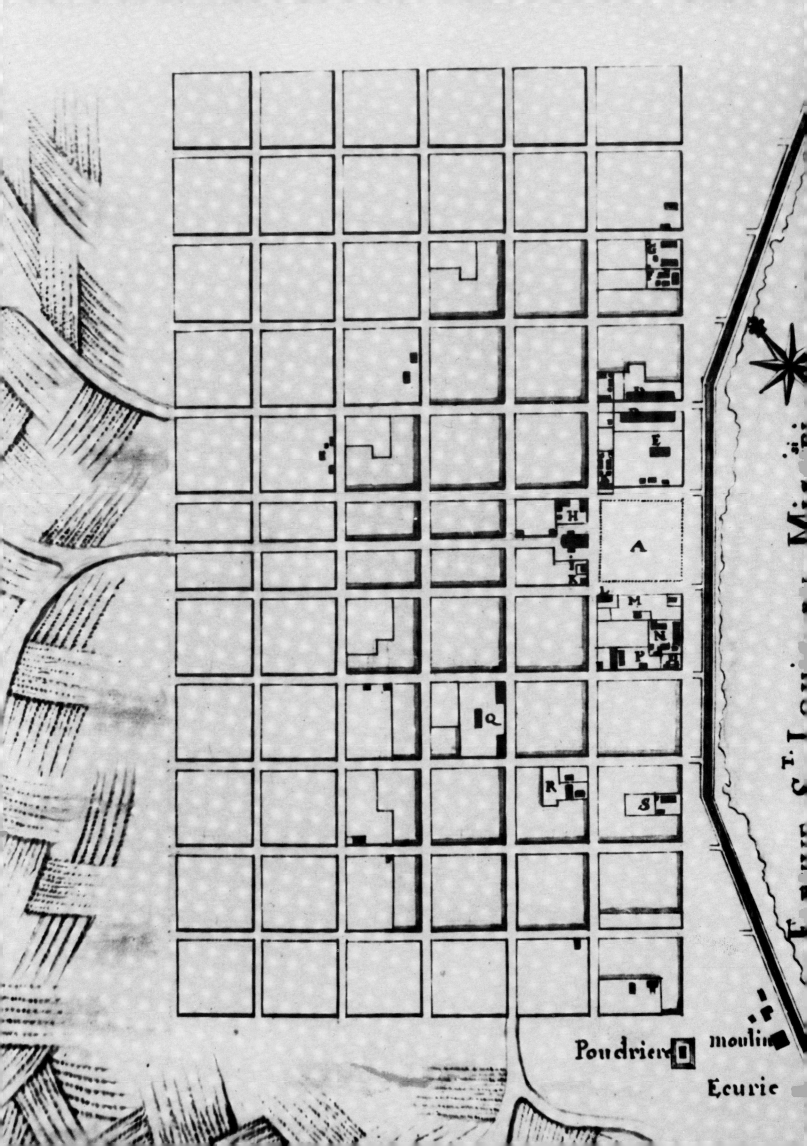

Plan St Louis et Mi:sipi

Poudrier moulin

Ecurie

their uncle, but to no avail. The regent pensioned Bienville and forbade him, along with Chateauguay, to return to Louisiana.

As if the Company of the Indies did not have enough trouble in Louisiana with Bienville and a feud between the Jesuits and Capuchins over jurisdictional rights, the company's financial condition in France was even worse. By early 1720 Law's so-called "Mississippi Bubble" was in deep financial trouble. All reports from the colony reaching the company's stockholders were bad: Colonists who had come dreaming of a new life were suffering and dying, crops failed, and the promised silver and gold mines did not materialize. The company had received little return on the vast sums of money invested, and the expected trade with the Spanish and English failed to develop to any great extent. Investors began withdrawing gold and silver deposits from the bank, leaving France flooded with paper money. The government tried to avert disaster by printing more money, but the country was on the verge of bankruptcy. An order went out — but was ignored — prohibiting anyone from holding more than 300 livres in gold and silver. Thousands of investors lost their fortunes — including Law, who narrowly escaped being stoned to death by angry mobs in the streets of Paris. For a brief period Law received a pension from the French government, but later he traveled to England and then back to the Continent, where he died in obscurity in 1729.

Soon after the collapse of 1720, the Company of the Indies reorganized and, with fresh money, tried to revitalize the Louisiana venture, but still the profits were not forthcoming. After 1723 the company lost interest in Louisiana because other colonies (for example India where the company held a similar financial arrangement with the Crown) were providing greater return. Finally, after word reached Paris that Fort Rosalie (near present-day Natchez) had been wiped out by Natchez Indians in November 1729, and of the ensuing Indian war, the company's directors threw up their hands. They had had enough. In early 1731 the Crown granted the company's request to be relieved of its reponsibilities in Louisiana.

Despite the company's financial failure in Louisiana, it did succeed in firmly planting the colony's roots in the lower Mississippi Valley. It

had founded the city of New Orleans which, because of its position near the mouth of the Mississippi, was destined to become one of the most important ports in North America. In addition, the population of the colony had grown from less than 1,000 in 1717 to over 7,000 by 1731. But most importantly, the company gave the colony an economy — industry, commerce, and trade conducted by company agents and planter-merchants.

The industry and manufacturing in French colonial Louisiana was small-scale. Plantations produced bricks, candles, faience, tiles, lumber, pitch and tar, and barrels, surpluses of which were an important part of Louisiana's export trade. Records indicate that during the colony's early years it had already built up an assortment of artisans and tradesmen, including bakers, armorers, carpenters, locksmiths, harnessmakers, millwrights, barbers, coopers, stonemasons, gold and silversmiths, tanners, tailors, blacksmiths, shipbuilders, cabinetmakers, toolmakers, a wig-maker, and a baker.

Because the usual objects of European colonization — commodities such as gold, silver, and spices — did not materialize, commerce and trade became colonial Louisiana's primary industry. During the first 60 years of the colony's existence, Louisianians maintained a moderately successful import and export trade with France, the Spanish in Florida, the West Indies, the Illinois country, and the British colonies on the Atlantic. Ships carrying commodities to and from these points encountered numerous difficulties, however. Storms, poorly built

After the hurricane of 1722 flattened the settlement at New Orleans, Adrien De Pauger, working with plans from chief engineer Le Blond de La Tour, laid out the streets of New Orleans in a grid-like pattern. (THNOC)

ships, privateers and pirates, and the repeated skirmishes between the colonial powers, not to mention the financial solvency of the colonial entrepreneurs, hampered the young colony's growth. Nonetheless, goods got through. Ships from France brought spices, cloth, cutlery, utensils, wines, food, and other items, including luxury goods. Louisianians sent France tobacco, indigo, lead, sassafras, quinine, naval stores, and lumber. To the West Indies, which became increasingly important to Louisiana's trade after 1720, went lumber, meats, bricks, tiles, corn, beans, naval stores, and tallow. Ships returned with sugar, coffee, rum, rare woods, drugs, cocoa, tanned leather, spices, tortoise shell, syrup, and other "goods," including slaves.

Louisianians at times conducted a small amount of trade with their Spanish neighbors in Florida and the English along the Atlantic Seaboard. Although trade with these colonies was illegal, Louisianians continued to smuggle in British goods even when France and England were at war with each other. British colonials had manufactured goods to sell and the French colonists desperately needed them.

New Orleans and other French Gulf Coast ports were also the exchange points connecting Europe and the West Indies with the wild and rugged back country and upper regions of the Mississippi River. From the Illinois country came lead, furs and hides, flour, corn, beef, pork, tallow, lard, tobacco, leather, lumber, and beeswax. The lower Mississippi and its tributaries also exported tobacco, indigo, cotton, lumber, tallow, and vegetables. Boats, pack trains, and traders returned up the treacherous river loaded with manufactured goods such as liquor, furniture, tools, farming equipment, and items used to trade with the Indians.

After the Company of the Indies withdrew from Louisiana in 1731, the colony was once again under royal control. The governor was Etienne de Perier, who had replaced Boisbriant in 1726. His administration had been plagued by Indian troubles, especially with the Chickasaws and with the Natchez massacre in 1729. In 1732 the Crown asked 52-year-old Bienville to come out of retirement to be governor of Louisiana for the fourth time. Upon his return to the colony, Bienville immediately set about rejuvenating the spirits of the demoralized colony. Soldiers were put to work repairing military equipment and rebuilding barracks. Civilians gathered food and repaired buildings that had been damaged or simply permitted to decay. Then Bienville turned to reestablishing diplomatic relations with the Indians.

Lumbering was just one of the industries in colonial Louisiana. Surplus products from such industries were important sources of export from the colony. (THNOC)

The British had been successful in enticing the Chickasaws and other tribes into their camp and were making headway in alluring the Choctaws. Bienville thought that the best way to teach the Chickasaws a lesson would be to attack their strongholds. With the help of Choctaws, who had been won back by the French, the veteran Canadian launched a coordinated offensive in the summer of 1736. After four years of intermittent bloodshed during which Bienville had been unable to subdue the Chickasaws, he finally signed a peace treaty with them in 1740. Bienville once again was relieved of office in May 1743, but this time at his own request. He sailed for France, never to return to Louisiana.

His replacement was Pierre-Cavagnial de Rigaud, Marquis de Vaudreuil, the brash, arrogant, and flashy son of a former governor of Canada. Vaudreuil's administration in Louisiana has become best known for its colonial-styled Versailles elegance, high society, and corruption. Although popular with the colony's elite, the "Grand Marquis," as Vaudreuil was nicknamed, and his wife were loathed by those outside the inner-circle coterie. Reports reaching France accused the governor of selling military supplies to the highest bidder while issuing inferior goods to the troops; granting monopolies to a favorite few; and forcing merchants to sell goods owned by the governor and his wife at fixed prices.

Vaudreuil inherited Bienville's problems with the Chickasaws with whom peace was fragile at best. When the French were unable to match the quality of British trading goods, the Chickasaws, and a few Choctaws, once again went over to the British. In 1747, and again in 1748, the Indians marched south, raiding and burning white settlements along the Mississippi. Many settlers were killed and others fled to New Orleans for protection. By 1752 Vaudreuil had had enough. He sent a large force against the Indians, burned their villages, and destroyed their crops. The French had little trouble with the Chickasaws thereafter. Military morale and discipline, however, declined to a new low and public morality degenerated to a point that in 1751 Vaudreuil promulgated strict police regulations governing the behavior of the general populace.

Trade and commerce began to languish in the colony during Vaudreuil's administration, while the volume of smuggled British goods increased. But also during this period an addition was made to the Louisiana economy that would have far-reaching importance. Jesuits in Santo Domingo sent sugarcane to their Louisiana colleagues to see how it would grow along the Mississippi. Experiments with the plant had been conducted as early as 1742, but it was not until 1751 that sugarcane plantations began modest production that would grow into such an important industry for the state.

In 1752 Vaudreuil was rewarded for his services with an appointment as governor of Canada. He was succeeded in Louisiana by Louis Billouart, Chevalier de Kerlerec, a capable navy veteran who had the misfortune to be governor of Louisiana during the French and Indian War, when France lost most of its colonial empire. Unlike Vaudreuil, Kerlerec enjoyed considerable success in regaining an alliance with the Choctaws and other Indian tribes of colonial Louisiana. Although Kerlerec lost many of his troops to the war raging in North America, he managed to strengthen the colony's defenses. He built a wall around the city of New Orleans in 1760, and placed a ship at the mouth of the Mississippi to be sunk in case of a British invasion.

But like Bienville, Kerlerec had problems with infighting. Beginning in 1759 a group of officers and officials plotted to have him removed from office. After four years, the conspiracy finally was broken and the conspirators were sent to France, where they were held as guests of the Crown in the Bastille. Kerlerec also had constant problems with his commissary, Vincent-Pierre-Gaspard, Sieur de Rochemore, and Rochemore's successor, Nicolas-Denis Foucault who, like his predecessor, schemed against the governor. Moreover, he inherited the ongoing feud between the Jesuits and Capuchins. The Jesuits eventually were expelled from the colony.

In 1763 Kerlerec, who had served the Crown and the colony well, returned to France, where his enemies were waiting. He was thrown into the Bastille, but his few friends finally secured his release shortly before he died.

When Kerlerec boarded the ship for France, he and other Louisianians had no way of knowing Louisiana was no longer a French possession. Unbeknownst to all but a select few, it had been passed to Spain a year before.

The First Louisianians

Caddos, Tunicas, Natchez, Atakapas, Chitimachas, and Muskhogeans today are strange-sounding words with only a little relevance to present-day Louisianians. But to the Le Moyne brothers — Bienville and Iberville — and the early French settlers in colonial Louisiana, these words had extreme significance as the names of the six Indian family groups in what is now the state of Louisiana. During the early years of French colonization on the Gulf Coast, these tribes — the Bayougoulas (often spelled Bayagoulas), the Mougoulachas, the Chitimachas, Acalopisas, Tunicas, and Natchez Indians — often gave assistance to the French that meant the difference between survival and death. They provided food, knowledge of the terrain, clothing, and, at times, shelter and companionship for the struggling Louisiana colonists.

Some accounts report that almost 13,000 Indians inhabited what is today the state of Louisiana when the French arrived in 1699. Most of them built their villages along the bayous, rivers, and lakes in southern and southeastern Louisiana. Today's metropolitan New Orleans was once the territory of the Muskhogean family, whose scattered tribes occupied areas now known as the Florida and River parishes, from West Feliciana and Point Coupee parishes to the mouth of the Mississippi. From two of these tribes, the Bayougoulas and Mougoulachas, Iberville learned in 1699 the location of the Mississippi River and of an Indian portage on the Mississippi close to Lake Pontchartrain which later became the site of the city of New Orleans.

Until recently, knowledge of these pre-European aborigines was limited to the first-hand accounts of clerics, explorers, military officers, government officials, and settlers. Today professionally trained archaeologists, searching ancient village sites and burial grounds, are unlocking the secrets of these ancient people.

The Canadians and Frenchmen found the culture of the Indian tribes of south Louisiana to be well defined, but still quite primitive. Their somewhat circular villages (which lacked protective palisades) were composed of round huts built of poles and thatched with grass, palmetto leaves, or other vegetation and arranged around a ceremonial lodge and open space. Their possessions generally comprised little more than a few bowls, baskets, jars, bedding, and weapons. The usual sustenance consisted of corn, beans, sweet potatoes, pumpkins, berries, nuts, fish, as well as the wild game they killed with their bows and cane arrows, spears, and reed blowguns. Transportation for the Indians of southeastern Louisiana was limited to walking or riding in a dugout canoe made from a cypress log.

The Indians' clothing, of course, was adapted to the seasons. They wore robes of animal skins during the cold winter months; but during the hot season, which was a considerable portion of the year, men wore only breechclouts. Women usually wore full-length dresses, but on occasion they joined the menfolk with the simple but colorfully decorated breechclout made of bark. Some tribes permitted the men to wear nothing at all during extremely warm weather. By all accounts, the Indians of Louisiana were fond of colorful clothing, and most tribes took great delight in tattooing and painting designs on various parts of their bodies. Some tribes followed the custom of shaping the heads of their children by fastening a flat piece of wood to the forehead and another to the back of the head with leather straps. As the child's head grew, the wood and bindings forced the head to grow flat and oval-shaped.

Louisiana's early Indian tribes had a strong sense of morality and were deeply religious. They resisted the Biblical teachings of the early French missionaries, clinging tenaciously to their own gods and beliefs. Sometimes these beliefs and customs proved to be too much even for the Europeans who were themselves no strangers to death and mutilation in the name of God and the king.

Andre Penigault, a master carpenter who recorded Iberville's expedition to Louisiana, described a scene among the Taensa tribe:

A frightful thunderstorm suddenly arose: lightning struck their temple, burned all their idols, and reduced their temple to ashes. Immediately the savages ran out in front of their temple making horrible shrieks, tearing out their hair, and raising their arms aloft. Facing their temple, they invoked the Great Spirit, like men possessed, to extinguish the fire; then they seized dirt and smeared it on their bodies and their faces. Fathers and mothers brought their children and strangled them and cast them into the fire. . . . In spite of all our efforts they succeeded in throwing seventeen of them into the fire; and had we not hindered them, they would have thrown more than two hundred.

Most of the Indian tribes kept their religious beliefs to themselves. The Yazoos believed in the Great Spirit Minguo-Chitou. The Tunicas had nine gods: heaven, earth, the sun, fire, thunder, and the four points of the compass. The Chitimachas and most other tribes had numerous gods of varying importance with an entire set of ceremonies and beliefs surrounding each. The Caddos had a curious belief in their teachings which followed closely the story of the Great Flood in the Judeo-Christian Bible. According to the Indian legend, there once was a flood which destroyed the people except for a few that the Great Spirit led to a high hill. The people of the world today were descendants of those few survivors.

By the mid-1700s the native Louisiana tribes were no longer a threat to the French. Instead, the French became embroiled with the English in a life and death struggle for colonial domination in North America with two mighty southern Indian nations — the Choctaws and Chickasaws — caught in the middle of the bloody diplomacy.

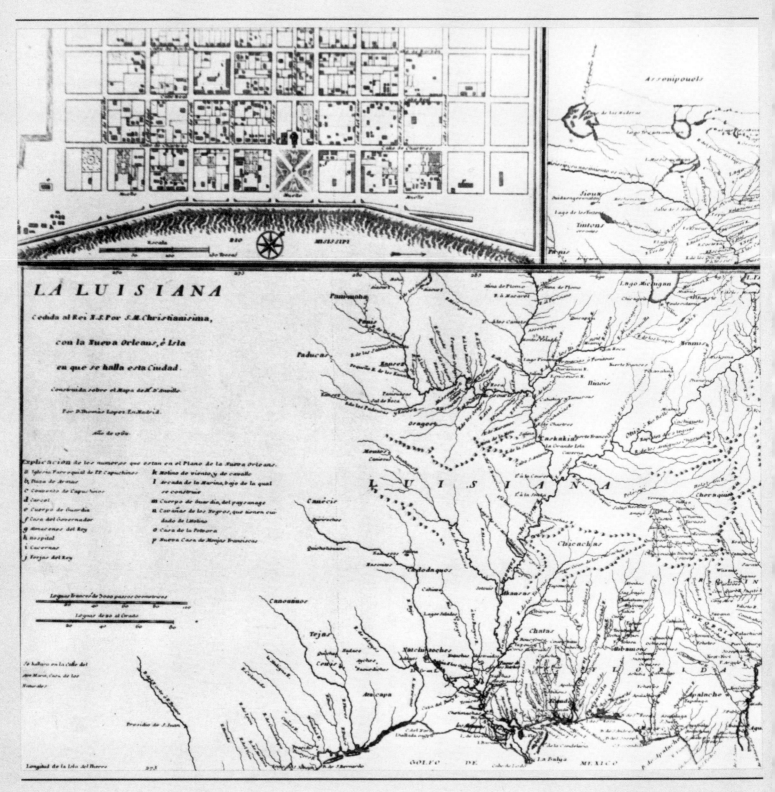

A 1762 Spanish map of La Luisiana. The Spanish were interested in Louisiana mainly because it provided a buffer to westward expansion by English colonies on the Eastern Seaboard. (THNOC)

For almost a century and a half, the three major European colonial powers in North America—France, England, and Spain—had been expanding their borders and claims further into the western wilderness. By the early 1750s both France and England were claiming one area, the Ohio Valley. A military confrontation developed in North America in 1754 and spread to Europe in 1756. Sides were quickly chosen by the European continental powers as the fighting spread to India, the Mediterranean, and the East and West Indies. In 1762 Spain entered the war in an unsuccessful attempt to turn the balance of power in favor of France. The "Seven Years War," as it was known in Europe, or the "French and Indian War," according to the British colonists in America, would realign the colonial structure throughout the world.

The war ended in 1763 with the Treaty of Paris. Defeated France was forced to cede to Great Britain all of its territory in North America, including Canada and Louisiana east of the Mississippi. It kept two small islands in the St. Lawrence River and later regained two of its rich West Indian sugar islands—Guadeloupe and Martinique—as well as some of its holdings in India and Africa. By treaty the British returned to Spain the Philippine Islands and Cuba, which had been captured by the British, in return for both East and West Florida.

Carlos III, king of Spain, was given Louisiana in a secret treaty of 1762. He was a cousin of France's Louis XV. (THNOC)

New Orleans and Louisiana west of the Mississippi were not included in the treaty concessions. Louis XV of France had given western Louisiana and the "Isle of Orleans" the year before to his cousin Carlos III, king of Spain, through a secret treaty signed in 1762 at Fontainebleau, France. France had been able to convince Spain and Britain that New Orleans was on an island, and therefore was not part of the eastern bank of the Mississippi. As proof they pointed to maps showing the city on a narrow finger of land surrounded completely by water. According to the French, and later the Spanish, the "island" was bordered to the south by the Mississippi and to the north by lakes Pontchartrain and Maurepas. The lakes and the Mississippi were connected by Bayou Manchac, which connected with the Amite

River and then emptied into Lake Maurepas. The island's aqueous border to the east was formed by the lakes emptying into Lake Borgne and then into the open Gulf.

Louis XV apparently decided to cede Louisiana for both economic and political reasons. Louisiana had cost the Crown a considerable amount of money with little in return. In addition, the commercial class in France wanted nothing to do with the colony after the burst of the "Mississippi Bubble." Under these circumstances, Louis began to use the colony as a pawn to achieve his purposes in the war over colonial territory. First in 1761 France offered to give Louisiana to Spain if Carlos III would grant France a loan and enter the war against England. The Spanish monarch wanted Louisiana, but he refused France's conditions. In the meantime, Spain offered to act as a mediator for England and France, but the British refused, accusing Spain of openly aiding France. The situation changed drastically when England declared war on Spain on January 2, 1762. During the rest of that year, British troops brought havoc to Spain's colonial possessions. By August France wanted peace with Britain; but peace was impossible while Spain was still fighting them. Again the French monarch offered Louisiana to his Spanish cousin, but this time to end the fighting—not to enter it. A month later the offer was looking better to King Carlos after Havana had fallen to the British. English troops were already in Florida, and if they should reach Louisiana as well, the British would soon walk through the front door to the riches of New Spain. So Spain accepted France's offer of Louisiana, hoping to limit the expansion of the British, whose territory already extended west to the Mississippi River.

With the signing of the Treaty of Fountainebleau and the Treaty of Paris the following year, Louisiana's days as a French colony ended. Louisiana west of the Mississippi and the Isle of Orleans were Spanish, while Louisiana east of the Mississippi belonged to the British.

Although Louisiana and New Orleans officially belonged to Spain as of 1762, Louisian-

Antonio de Ulloa arrived in New Orleans in 1766 as the first Spanish governor of Louisiana. His arrival and ensuing policies brought much displeasure to the strongly loyal French colonists living in the territory. (THNOC)

ians were ignorant of this fact until October 1764. The transfer was announced to the stunned colonists by Jean Jacques-Blaise d'Abbadie, who had succeeded Governor Kerlerec in 1763. The economy of the colony during this period suffered not only as a result of France's continued neglect, but also because West Indies merchants refused to trade with the colony until its position in either the French or Spanish colonial system was clarified. Events over the next four years continued to deteriorate, giving rise to the much-celebrated, and often romanticized Revolution of 1768, which has been described as the first revolt on American soil against a foreign monarch. The news of the transfer prompted a mass meeting in New Orleans to decide upon a course of action. At the suggestion of Attorney General Nicolas Chauvin de Lafreniere, Jean Milhet — the richest man in New Orleans — was chosen to go to the French court in Paris and petition the king to keep Louisiana. In Paris Milhet enlisted the aid of Bienville, now in his eighties. But even with the venerable Bienville at his side, Milhet could not change the mind of Louis XV's minister of state, the Duc de Choiseul, who had been instrumental in convincing the king to give up Louisiana in the first place. Choiseul offered his regrets, but said there was nothing he could do.

All hope vanished when word reached the colony that Don Antonio de Ulloa, a respected Spanish scientist and captain of the royal navy, had been appointed the first Spanish governor of Louisiana. Unfortunately, communications with the colony were sketchy and Louisianians were apprehensive about the changes the Spanish would bring. Perhaps some of their fears would have been quieted had they known Ulloa's initial instructions from Carlos III:

I have decided that in this new acquisition, for the present, no change in the system of government shall be undertaken and consequently, that in no way shall it be subject to the laws and practices observed in my dominion of the Indies, but that it shall be regarded as a separate colony, even with respect to all trade between them.

On July 10, 1765, Ulloa wrote to the Superior Council in Louisiana, stating he expected to arrive in the near future. Eight months passed, however, before the new governor set foot on Louisiana soil, and when he did drop anchor on March 5, 1766, he came utterly ill-prepared for the task. Waiting to greet the new Spanish governor was Captain Charles Philippe Aubry, the highest-ranking official in the colony since the death of d'Abbadie. Ulloa had brought with him only three civil officials and 90 Spanish troops under the mistaken impression that French troops in Louisiana would join his forces. On the advice of Aubry, Ulloa delayed taking formal possession of the colony until extra troops could be sent to man the various garrisons; these troops never arrived. This led to the bizarre situation of Ulloa attempting to govern the colony through Aubry.

The predominantly French population, already angered by the cession of their colony and a worsening economy, bristled at the tactless Ulloa, who found himself with a multitude of problems. He infuriated the colonists by leaving New Orleans and staying for seven months at La Balize near the mouth of the river where he awaited his Peruvian fiancee. Ulloa added to his problems when he married her at La Balize instead of in New Orleans.

From the beginning Ulloa was engaged in a power struggle with the Superior Council. In addition, the Crown had a change of mind and imposed on Louisiana mercantile regulations similar to those being enforced in other dominions. The commercial edict of May 6, 1766, restricted foreign commerce to a few Spanish colonies and Spain, Martinique, Santo Domingo, and France. Smuggling was to be stopped and the governor would fix all import and export prices. Another edict promulgated in March 1768 restricted trade to certain Spanish ports. Under pressure from the Superior Council, Aubry did not enforce the unpopular edicts and Ulloa backed down. (Louisianians from the early days of the colony had enjoyed almost free trade through the neglect of France or an inability to stop it in the case of the Company of the Indies.) Compounding Ulloa's problems was a lack of money and support from Spain. The government, as well as the merchants and planters, slipped deeper into debt because Spain failed to send silver currency to the colony. The value of paper currency declined rapidly and Ulloa implored his superiors to send silver to pay the government's debts.

By the end of 1767 finances in the colony were near chaos. In a letter to his superior — the governor of Havana — Ulloa expressed grievous concern:

Having described to Your Excellency on previous occasions the miserable and critical state in which this colony finds itself through lack of funds, I have nothing more to add, because the longer the delay the more the want and troubles increase.

Six months later, Ulloa sent a stronger letter of warning to Havana. The financial situation had become so desperate in the colony that dangerous clouds of trouble were lurking. He reminded his superior that Louisianians were new subjects of the Crown. "Their fealty has not become deep-rooted nor their confidence been won, [that] distrust cannot fail to be widespread."

By 1768 Lafreniere, along with a dozen or so important business, military, and political leaders in the colony, had had enough of Ulloa. They conspired to rid the colony of him and the Spanish. To do so they needed the masses behind them. Lafreniere was the leader and voice of the revolt. To enlist the aid of the newly arriving Acadians, the conspirators told them that Ulloa had planned to sell them into slavery. John Law's Germans living upriver were told that Ulloa had no intention of paying the money owed them by the Spanish. When Ulloa learned what the rebels were saying, he sent an envoy to pay the Germans; but before the envoy could carry out his assignment, he was arrested by the conspirators.

The night before the guns guarding the entrances to the city had been spiked. On the morning of the 28th, upon learning that Ulloa had rejected the Superior Council's demands, about a thousand armed colonists, including Acadians and Germans residing upriver from New Orleans, marched into the city. Ulloa and his wife took refuge on the Spanish frigate *El Volante* and later transferred to the French ship, *Le Cesar*. On November 1 they set sail for Havana. Ulloa's three civil officials, however, Esteban Gayarre, Martin Narvarro, and Jose de Loyola, were held by the rebels as security for debts owed to the colonists by the Spanish government.

Having forced Ulloa to leave in a bloodless coup, the rebels asked the French monarch to take Louisiana back into his fold. Again they were refused. One rebel, Pierre Marquis, a colonel general of the colonial militia, suggested Louisiana be declared a republic. His idea was given some consideration by the Spanish king and his ministers, but it was dismissed. Most of the petitioners declared their loyalty to France.

Both Ulloa and Aubry urged their superiors to punish the rebels, and especially Lafreniere. In a letter to the governor of Havana, dated December 8, 1768, Ulloa said he could not return to Louisiana under the existing circumstances. Moreover, he wrote, his initial and subsequent instructions from the Crown were not enforceable since the colonists were not loyal to Spain. But the colony's fate was not destined to be left in the hands of the rebels. It had been decided in Spain that however insignificant Louisiana might be in the Spanish empire, the Crown could not allow its prestige to be tarnished by a handful of rebels. Besides, the colony was still of value to the empire as a buffer to the westward-expanding English colonists on the Atlantic Seaboard.

All doubts about Louisiana's immediate fate were removed from the rebel's minds on July 24, 1769, when the Spanish fleet dropped anchor at the mouth of the river. On board was General Alexander (Alejandro) O'Reilly — a native Irishman in the Spanish service — with 2,600 Spanish troops under his command.

O'Reilly, like so many of his countrymen, left Ireland to join the Spanish, French, or any other army with an excuse to fight England. His father, Thomas O'Reilly, had been a lieutenant in "Reilly's Dragoons" in the Spanish army. Alexander distinguished himself during the French and Indian War, first in the Austrian army, then in the French, and later as a lieutenant colonel in the Spanish army. During the war he led a brigade that captured Chares and Pancorro in Portugal, which was allied with England. After the war and several promotions later, O'Reilly reorganized the government and army in Cuba, founded a military academy at Avila in Spain, and became military governor of Madrid, where he saved Carlos III from angry mobs during the Madrid riots of 1765. A grateful king promoted the Irishman to the rank of lieutenant general; and when the king decided to suppress the revolt in his new Loui-

DON ALESSANDRO
O'REILLY

siana colony, O'Reilly was his man for the job.

When word reached New Orleans of O'Reilly's arrival, Lafreniere and two rebel ringleaders asked Aubry for a letter of introduction to O'Reilly so they could explain their actions and profess their obedience to the Spanish Crown. They implored the king's representative not to treat the colony as a conquered land. O'Reilly heard their arguments, treated them cordially, and sent them back to New Orleans confident that all would be well. O'Reilly arrived in New Orleans with full force on August 18. Salutes were fired, down came the flag of France, and up went the Spanish colors. During formal ceremonies in the Place d'Armes, Aubry handed over the keys to the city to Spain.

O'Reilly wasted little time. Three days after his arrival in the city, he ordered the arrest and trial of the 12 leaders of the conspiracy. On October 24 O'Reilly handed down the court's decision: Six, including Lafreniere, were to be executed, and the others were to be imprisoned and have their property confiscated. (One of the rebel leaders sentenced to death already had died in a Spanish prison ship while awaiting trial.) In an act of conciliation, O'Reilly granted a general amnesty to everyone else who had signed the petition expelling Ulloa or who had participated in the revolt. The next day Lafreniere and four of his fellow conspirators were shot to death by a firing squad close to the present-day site of the old U.S. Mint building at the foot of Esplanade Avenue. From one pro-rebel account came Lafreniere's dying words: "To die for our king—to die Frenchmen—is there anything more glorious?" Another account has Lafreniere sounding the call of liberty: "I do not fear death . . . the cry of liberty has been heard, it will conquer later."

With the revolt suppressed and its leaders either dead or imprisoned, "Bloody" O'Reilly, so-called by future generations of Louisianians, went about reorganizing the colony with an almost free hand given to him by the Crown. He improved the colony's fortifications and met with the chiefs of the various Indian tribes. He ordered a census taken which placed the population of New Orleans at 3,190 inhabitants and the entire colony at 13,500. (The population had more than doubled since the early 1740s.) The new settlers included several thousand Acadians who began arriving from Nova Scotia during and shortly after the French and

Indian War. O'Reilly abolished the Superior Council and created the Cabildo, or town council (the building on Jackson Square got its name for the council, or *cabildo,* which met within its walls). He also issued the "Ordinances and Instructions of Don Alexander O'Reilly" or "O'Reilly's Code," as it was called, which was a combination of Spanish laws and regulations used in other Spanish colonies, his own regulations, and a variation of the French *Code Noir* of 1724.

To help economic matters, O'Reilly eased commercial and trade regulations, recommending free trade with Spain and Havana, and temporarily suspended import and export duties. Although smuggling remained illegal, he looked the other way at illegal trade with the British in West Florida when it was beneficial to the economy of the colony. He also abolished the remnants of the Indian slave trade. By mid-February 1770, O'Reilly was satisfied that he had done all that was necessary to fix Louisiana in Spain's colonial orbit. A month later, O'Reilly turned the colony over to his successor, Don Luis de Unzaga y Amezaga, and left for Spain, where he arrived by way of Havana at the end of May. For his service in Louisiana, O'Reilly was promoted to director-general of the Spanish infantry.

Unzaga, who had been colonel of the Reg-

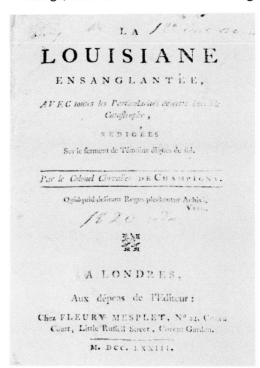

iment of Havana before coming to Louisiana, carried on O'Reilly's goal of making Louisiana a loyal Spanish colony. He endeared himself to French Louisianians by marrying a local girl of the St. Maxent family; ironically, she was a relative of one of the rebels executed by his predecessor. He too overlooked illegal trade with the British in West Florida and along the Gulf Coast. Unzaga, like some of his French predecessors, had problems with religious disputes in the colony, especially squabbles between the Spanish and French Capuchins. It was during his administration that the American Revolution broke out. Although the fighting was in the distant old Northwest and Atlantic Seaboard, Unzaga gave considerable aid and supplies to the Americans. Unzaga, weary from his years in office, wrote repeatedly to his superiors, pleading with them to let him retire and return to Spain. But instead of a most deserved retirement, he was named captain general of Caracas.

On January 1, 1777, Unzaga was succeeded by one of the most colorful, capable, and popular figures in Louisiana's colonial history: 29-year-old Bernardo de Galvez, colonel of the Louisiana Regiment. Galvez was the scion of a distinguished Spanish family. His father, Don Matias de Galvez, served as captain general of Guatemala and viceroy of Mexico. His uncle, Don Jose de Galvez, was Carlos III's secretary of state and president of the Council of the Indies.

Galvez, who had served under O'Reilly in Algiers, was popular among Louisiana colonials because of his amiable nature and his ability to deal with and understand the personality of the predominantly French Creoles. Like his predecessor Unzaga, Galvez married a Louisiana Creole, Felicie de St. Maxent d'Estrehan. (Apparently Unzaga's example was followed by several other high-ranking Spanish officials in the colony. Don Esteban Miro, a military officer and a later governor of Louisiana, married Marie Celeste Elenore de Macarty. Jacinto Panis, another military officer who would be important in future military expeditions against the British in West Florida, wedded the widow of one of the men executed by O'Reilly.)

Soon after Galvez's arrival in the colonies, he began rebuilding the city's defenses and constructing naval craft to take control of the Mississippi in case Spain was drawn into war with Great Britain. In subsequent months he increased the number of men bearing arms from 437 to almost 1,500, adding to the ranks new recruits arriving from Mexico and the Canary Islands. He also secured the loyalty of local Indian tribes. In another move guaranteed to find favor among colonials, Galvez reduced export duties and held meetings with planters to discuss their problems. This young governor also permitted trade with the British in West Florida. But most of all Galvez gained prominence in the annals of Louisiana history for his aid to the Americans rebelling against England and his daring invasions of British West Florida.

After the Treaty of Paris of 1763, the British were quick to settle Florida and Louisiana east of the Mississippi. This included the former French territory stretching from Baton Rouge through what today is the Florida Parishes north of Lake Pontchartrain to the Perdido River east of Mobile. The British divided these colonies into West and East Florida. Today the predominantly Anglo-Saxon look of this area is in marked contrast to the unmistakable Gallic-Hispanic one found south and west of Lake Pontchartrain.

Spanish Louisiana contributed heavily to the cause of the British-American colonists in their revolt against Great Britain. Beginning during the term of Governor Unzaga, and increasing under Galvez, the Spanish sent quantities of supplies and munitions to the American rebels.

The Spanish also permitted an American agent, Oliver Pollock, to conduct the affairs of the rebel government in New Orleans. Oliver Pollock played a prominent role in the American Revolution, but has received little more than a footnote in history. Pollock came to William Penn's colony from his native Ireland in 1760. While still in his early twenties, he became a trader with many business dealings in the Spanish West Indies. During a voyage to Cuba after the French and Indian War, he befriended a Spanish official and fellow Irishman, Alexander O'Reilly. The fortunes of business took Pollock to New Orleans in 1768, where he renewed his friendship with O'Reilly. Not long after his arrival Pollock rescued the colony during a food shortage by selling a shipment of flour to O'Reilly almost at cost. Being on the good side of O'Reilly, and his successor Unzaga, meant special favors for Pollock which certainly were good for business. In less than five years, Pollock had amassed considerable wealth and had trading interests stretching from upper and lower Louisiana to the West Indies. When the American Revolution broke out, the Continental Congress appointed Pollock to be its purchasing agent in New Orleans. With the help of Unzaga, and later Galvez, Pollock was able to send large quantities of supplies to the American forces. Pollock's shipments have been credited with enabling George Rogers Clark's successful campaign against the British in the old Northwest.

Pollock's devotion to the American cause also resulted in his financial ruin. The Continental Congress badly needed the supplies Pollock sent, but it was slow in sending money to pay for them. The American agent used his own money until that ran out and then borrowed heavily from the Spanish Crown and private citizens in the colony. Deep in debt and with no money coming from the American Congress, Pollock might have been thrown into debtor's prison had it not been for Galvez, who personally underwrote Pollock's loans. In desperation Pollock wrote the Congress asking for money to pay his debts, but nothing came. Not until after the Revolution did the United States finally repay part of Pollock's claims.

During the war Galvez warned the British not to molest American ships on the Mississippi River: "Whoever fights on the river will incur the disapproval of my sovereign, and in consideration of my duty, I would have to oppose to the extent of my power." But at the same time Galvez disrupted English commerce and shipping whenever possible as well as permitting Americans to take refuge in New Orleans, even after some had pillaged settlements in British West Florida.

The most notorious of these American raiders was James Willing, the black sheep of a prominent Philadelphia family and the brother of a business partner of Robert Morris (a member of the First Continental Congress and financial wizard of the American Revolution). Before the Revolution, James Willing settled in Natchez, where he failed as a merchant. When the Revolution began, Willing tried unsuccessfully to get residents of the Natchez area to rise in revolt against the British. He pulled up stakes and returned to Philadelphia, where he convinced Congress to support his leading an expedition against West Florida. With Con-gress's blessing, Willing and about 30 men boarded the gunboat *Rattletrap* in January 1778, beginning their infamous invasion of British West Florida.

Willing's expedition did absolutely nothing to further the cause of the Revolution. He plundered Natchez and plantations in the lower Mississippi Valley, capturing the British gunship *Rebecca*. When the expedition reached New Orleans, Galvez extended his hospitality and protection to Willing and his men. But the Revolution was a long way from Willing's mind. He sold his ill-gotten booty in New Orleans and instead of sending the proceeds to the American forces, he and his men spent it all on high living. When the money ran out, Willing and his men launched another raid on the Baton Rouge area, where they were repulsed by armed citizens. Willing and his "rebels" returned to New Orleans, living there off of Pollock's dwindling resources.

Meanwhile, both Pollock and Galvez had had about enough of Willing. Pollock sent repeated messages to Congress asking that Willing be recalled. At one point Pollock threatened Congress with stopping all supplies to the war effort until Willing left. Shortly thereafter, Willing departed for Philadelphia, but along the way he was captured by the British and taken to New York as a prisoner. He escaped and was recaptured, and eventually was traded in a prisoner exchange.

But in Louisiana and West Florida, Willing had done much harm to both the American cause and Galvez's designs on the neighboring British territory. Willing's actions in West Florida drove many of its residents, some of whom were considering joining the American cause, deeper into the Loyalist camp. Moreover, the British strengthened their defenses in the colony, especially along the Mississippi River, the border between Spanish Louisiana and British West Florida. Of course Galvez's motives for helping the Americans were not entirely altruistic. He and Spain welcomed the chance to do whatever they could to help break up the British colonial empire in North America.

In 1779 Galvez, hearing reports of massive troop buildups in Mobile and Pensacola, sent envoy Jacinto Panis to the two British settlements; his ostensible mission was to discuss Louisiana's neutrality rights in Britain's conflict

Spanish governor Bernardo de Galvez (right) was a great friend of the American colonists in the Revolutionary War, sending them supplies and military goods. His engagement of the British at Pensacola (facing page) was one of several campaigns against the British in their Florida territory. From Cirker, Dictionary of American Portraits, Dover, 1967. (THNOC)

with its colonies, but his true purpose was to gather military intelligence information in the two port towns. In July 1779 word reached Galvez that war had been declared between Spain and Great Britain. His British counterparts in West Florida, however, had not received the news. Galvez had learned earlier, through intercepted letters, that the British were concentrating troops in West Florida to attack New Orleans as soon as war came. But Galvez struck first and through a series of brilliant military maneuvers, he and his approximately 650-man army of Spanish regulars, Mexicans, Canary Islanders, free-people-of-color, Anglo-Americans, Acadians, and French Louisianians, captured Fort Bute (located where the Mississippi River meets Bayou Manchac) and Baton Rouge in September 1779; Natchez in October 1779; Mobile in March 1780; and Pensacola in May 1781. With the fall of Pensacola to Galvez, the British surrendered

the entire province of West Florida. Both Floridas passed to Spanish control with the Peace of Paris in 1783 which also ended the American Revolution.

Galvez's success against the British in the Floridas brought him great fame and reward from the king of Spain. He was able to add the words "Yo Solo" — meaning "I alone" — to his coat of arms for his bravery and courage in capturing Pensacola. In 1785 he was named viceroy of New Spain and departed for his new post in Mexico early the following year. Only a few months later, however, he contracted a fever and died in Mexico City.

Besides their role in the American Revolution, Galvez and his second-in-command and later governor, Esteban Rodriguez Miro, are remembered in Louisiana history for the assistance they gave to immigrants. They gave refuge to the increasing number of Acadians searching for homes in Louisiana, many of

whom settled north of New Orleans, or along Bayou Teche and Bayou Lafourche. Anglo-Americans fleeing the war in the British colonies were given land, tools, and a new start. To get more colonists, Galvez — through his influential uncle, Don Jose de Galvez — induced several hundred Canary Islanders, or "Islenos" as they are called today, to come to Louisiana. They settled in *Terre-aux-Boeufs* below New Orleans (now St. Bernard Parish), along Bayou Lafourche northwest of New Orleans and at the northern tip of the Isle of Orleans along Bayou Manchac. Galvez also welcomed approximately 500 Malagans who founded New Iberia on Bayou Teche in about 1779. Like their French and Spanish neighbors, these new settlers provided New Orleans with much-needed foodstuffs, building materials, and products for commerce.

The census of 1785 showed that the colony had doubled in size since 1769. The Isle of Orleans had in excess of 25,000 inhabitants, while New Orleans had grown to almost 5,000. The population of the *Cote des Allemands et Acadiene* was placed at approximately 4,500.

Miro carried on and expanded Galvez's commercial policies and as a result, trade between Louisiana and the Americans in the upper Mississippi and Ohio valleys increased dramatically. Greater numbers of flatboats loaded with agricultural products, timber, and naval stores, arrived in New Orleans from upriver. Some days dozens of American boats could be seen in the harbor, far outnumbering the ships of other nations, including Spain. The two regions increasingly became dependent on each other economically. Although the situation was lucrative to the Spanish in New Orleans, it set into motion events that would end Spain's domination in the colony.

Also during Miro's administration, the most devastating disaster in the city's history up to

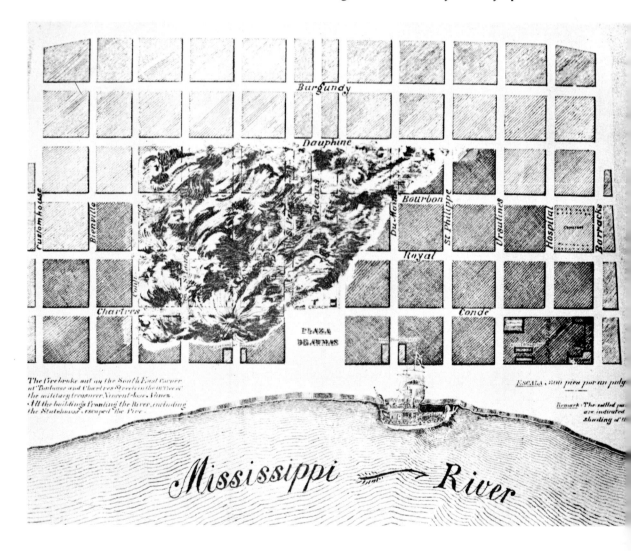

that time began at 1:30 p.m., March 21, 1788 — the Great Fire of 1788. According to legend, a candle ignited a curtain in the home of a Spanish official. The fire spread rapidly, but the clergy would not allow the fire bells to be rung because it was Good Friday. Also, the predominantly French-speaking population could not understand orders being shouted by Spanish-speaking officials. (Mexico City's *Gaceta de Mexico* reported that the fire in New Orleans was further fueled by gunpowder stored in private homes contrary to official orders.)

In less than six hours, almost a thousand buildings and their contents reportedly were destroyed by the fire. Approximately four-fifths of the city was reduced to ruins. One of the few buildings spared by the flames was the Ursuline Convent, which still stands today as the oldest surviving colonial building in the French Quarter. The Parish Church of St. Louis, the Presbytere, O'Reilly's Cabildo, and the building that housed the *corps de garde* and the jail were destroyed.

In a report to his superiors, Miro described the misery he found throughout the city's charred ruins:

. . . night momentarily removed the sight of so many misfortunes, but the dawn the following day brought a worse one, that seeing along the road, crying and sobbing and in most abject misery, so many families who, a few hours before, enjoyed considerable riches and conveniences. Their cries, weeping and pale faces told the ruin of a city which in less than five hours had been transformed into an arid and horrible wilderness; the work of seventy years since its foundation.

After clearing away the ruins, Miro fell quickly into rebuilding New Orleans. With the financial help of Don Andres Almonester y Roxas, public and government buildings were rebuilt including the Church of St. Louis and the Presbytere. Also, a butcher's arcade was built on the levee across from the Place d'Armes — the beginning of today's famous French Market.

The calamity in New Orleans did not go unnoticed by the outside world. Miro's efficiency in handling the aftermath of the disaster gained recognition for him and the city in the *London Chronicle* which described New Orleans as the "most regular, well-governed, small city in the western world."

As a springtime forest fire brings new growth, so the Great Fire of 1788 brought new growth to New Orleans. While the rubble was being cleared away in the city, Madame and Don Beltram (Bertrand) Gravier decided to subdivide their plantation into city blocks and sell them off to people who no longer wanted to live in the crowded Vieux Carre. The Gravier Plantation, located on the upriver side of the city, became New Orleans' first suburb, called Faubourg Ste. Marie (St. Mary), at the site of today's Central Business District.

Royal Surveyor Carlos Trudeau drew up the plans for the subdivision on April 1, 1788, dividing the plantation into squares separated by three cross streets and cross-sectioned by four perpendicular roadways with one oblique street splintering off at an angle. The cross streets today bear such familiar names as Magazine, Camp, and St. Charles streets. The perpendicular ones, running to the river, are called Poydras, Girod, and Julia. The oblique street was named Gravier in honor of the developers. Americans and other immigrants would continue to flock to Faubourg Ste. Marie, which became known as the American Sector because of its predominantly American population and Greek Revival architectural style so common in the Atlantic-Seaboard states.

The heavy weight of war, diplomacy, the fire in 1788, and over 20 years in America had tired Miro. He was ready to go home to Spain and, in 1791, he finally got his wish. He had been a popular and able governor during his tenure in Louisiana. But his successor would prove to be colonial Louisiana's most skilled. He was Don Francisco Luis Hector, Baron de Carondelet, a native of Flanders in the Spanish service.

Carondelet earned his place in Louisiana history for his remarkable achievements in New Orleans. He established the city's first theater in 1792 on St. Peter Street and divided the city into four wards, placing them under the administration of an *Alcalde de Barrio,* similar to a city borough. Also in 1792 he established and edited the city's first newspaper, *Le Moniteur de la Louisiane,* and created the city's first police department in 1796. About a dozen *se-*

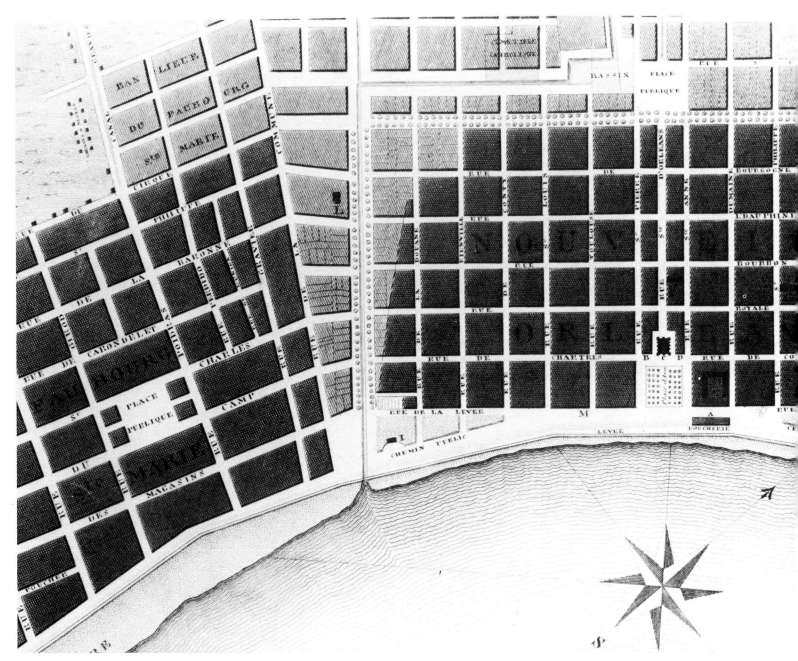

renos patrolled the streets at night to keep order and herald the time. He also ordered the lighting of city streets at night by oil lamps suspended from ropes and tied diagonally across street intersections. He ordered the city's fortifications rebuilt and oversaw the digging of the Carondelet Canal which not only drained the rear sections of the city, but also provided a navigable waterway for commerce from the city's rear gates to Bayou St. John and hence to Lake Pontchartrain.

New Orleans suffered three devastating hurricanes and two more fires during Carondelet's

administration. The fire of 1792 did not inflict heavy damages, but the 1794 fire destroyed over 200 buildings, including once again the jail and the *corps de garde*. After the 1794 fire Almonester y Roxas financed the construction of the new Cabildo from the destroyed *corps de garde*. Carondelet reported that the fire of 1794 had not destroyed as many buildings as the 1788 fire, but the financial losses were far greater. After three hurricanes and three fires, little was left of the original French settlement.

With a good portion of the city reduced to ashes once again, Carondelet, acting on the

After the fire of 1788, the plantation of Marie and Bertrand Gravier was divided into squares. It became the Faubourg Ste. Marie (St. Mary). (THNOC)

petition of attorney general Miguel Fortier, drew up a stringent new building code for the city. All new buildings with more than one story located in the heavily populated sections of the city had to be built of brick or adobe, using either red or yellow tiles for the roof. Wooden roofs were forbidden and houses had to be constructed close to the sidewalks, or *banquettes*. New Orleans began taking on the appearance which has become so well known to generations of residents and visitors. Neat brick and *colombage* structures lined the *banquettes* abutting each other with passageways to scenic and comfortable rear patios. Balconies, with wrought-iron railings from local forges, decorated the facades of many new buildings. Within a few years, wealthy American and other English-speaking merchant-planters would build their Greek Revival homes in the American Sector or among the Spanish styles in the Old Quarter. Eventually a mixture of the styles would produce a new and vernacular architecture to suit the culture and climate of New Orleans.

When Carondelet was not at work making New Orleans a modern and viable city, he was busy with political problems. In 1793 the French Revolution, raging in far-off France, came knocking at the gates of New Orleans. Although the revolution got under way in 1789, New Orleanians paid little attention to it until Louis XVI was beheaded in 1793 and Spain and France declared war on each other shortly after the execution. Many French New Orleanians got caught up in the revolutionary rhetoric and zeal, and finding their own despot to behead seemed to be the popular idea. Although French New Orleanians had little to complain about since Spain had brought them only prosperity, mobs marched through the

Among the improvements made during Carondelet's administration was the installation of oil lamps on the city's streets. The lamps were lit each day by paid workers. (THNOC)

streets calling Carondelet a *cochon de lait* (a suckling pig) and shouting such slogans as the "Liberty, Equality and Fraternity" ones so popular in France at the moment. They sang revolutionary airs. Pamphlets and letters from France and the Jacobin Society in Pennsylvania were sent to New Orleans, urging the colonists to rise in rebellion.

Fearing a bloody uprising in New Orleans and the lower Mississippi Valley, Carondelet acted quickly and sternly. He sent for more troops to keep order and issued a proclamation forbidding writings and meetings in which the French Revolution or the political affairs of France were discussed. Violators of his regulations could be fined heavily or sent to cool their revolutionary heels in a Havana prison. Thus Carondelet was able to maintain order. He later gave refuge to French aristocrats fleeing chaos and bloodshed in France.

The governor also had troubles with restless and westward-expanding Americans, or "Kaintocks" as they were called by the Creoles. Since Miro's time, New Orleans had become essential to the commerce of Americans living in the West. It would not have taken much to

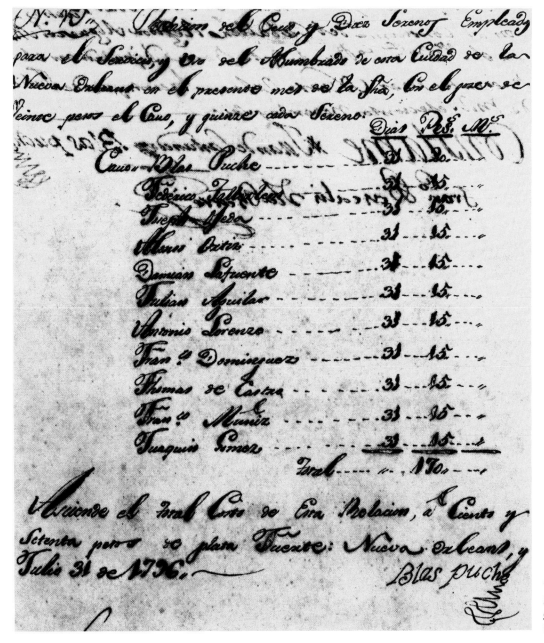

This receipt for payment to lamplighters shows that the government paid for this service. (THNOC)

convince Americans that New Orleans should be annexed to the United States and "Citizen" Edmond Charles Genet, France's ambassador to the young nation, was just the man for the job. Genet, with a full war chest, conspired to raise an army of western Americans — with the famed George Rogers Clark at its head — to march on New Orleans. But before the expedition could be launched, Genet had managed to alienate President George Washington, Secretary of the Treasury Alexander Hamilton, and Secretary of State Thomas Jefferson. Jefferson was about to ask France to recall Genet when word arrived that Genet's revolutionary party in France was out and a more radical element was now in power. The radicals, or Jacobins, also wanted Genet home, but the shrewd diplomat knew what fate awaited him in France. If he returned, he surely would lose his head. He therefore sought, and got, political asylum in the United States, where he settled down in New York and married the governor's daughter.

Genet's aborted invasion did not lessen the tensions between Spanish Louisiana and the United States. During the decades following the American Revolution, the unofficial alliance between the young nation and Spain steadily worsened. Statements made by American leaders during and after their Revolution, assuring Spain that the United States had no designs on Louisiana, were no longer convincing to Spanish officials by the early 1790s. Two major points divided the two nations: navigation of the Mississippi and the northern boundary line between Spanish West Florida and the United

The Treaty of San Lorenzo (also known as the Pinckney Treaty because of its American signer Thomas Pinckney) granted the United States free navigation of the Mississippi River and allowed American merchants to deposit their goods at the port of New Orleans for shipment. The treaty expired in 1802 and was a factor in the negotiations with France that led to the Louisiana Purchase. (THNOC)

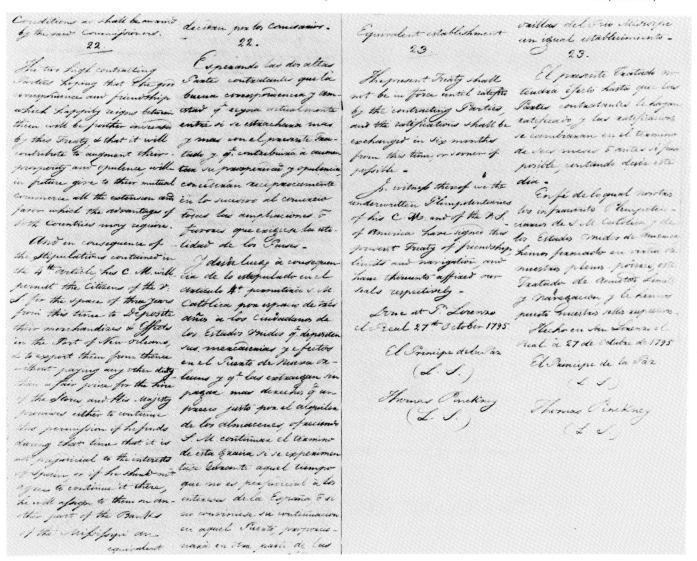

States. According to the 1783 Peace of Paris ending the American Revolution, Great Britain gave the infant nation the right of free navigation of the river, a right Spain claimed England had no right to give since the mouth of the Mississippi clearly was within Spanish territory. As to the West Florida border, the United States contended the 31st parallel (present northern border between the State of Mississippi and the toe of the Louisiana boot) formed its boundary with Spanish West Florida. Spain, however, insisted the border was much further north above Natchez.

Although suspicions and hostilities increased, American commerce on the river continued to grow. Spanish officials occasionally seized American flatboats on the river and the Americans answered with rattling sabres and threats of invasion. Trade with the Americans was officially ordered to stop in 1784, but Governor Miro disregarded those orders because of the colony's need for American commerce. In 1787 a royal decree legalized the trade but put a 25-percent duty on their cargoes, although the duties gradually decreased in following years. The fire of 1788 boosted trade in New Orleans and American flatboats arrived in increasing numbers with loaded decks. By the end of the century, almost three-fourths of the ships and vessels to use the port would belong to Americans.

Governor Carondelet, having problems with the French Revolution and his own citizens in New Orleans, urged his government's cooperation with the United States. By so doing, he hoped to stave off English intervention in the growing separatist sentiments of many Americans living in the trans-Appalachian West. Spanish Louisiana had greater fear of powerful English presence in the region than it did the weaker Americans.

Finally in 1795 Spain and the Americans signed the Treaty of San Lorenzo (also known as the Pinckney Treaty) in which Spain granted the Americans free navigation of the Mississippi with the right of deposit at New Orleans for three years. Moreover, Spain recognized the American's border claim with West Florida. Although the right of deposit legally expired in 1798, the privilege continued until October 1802 when Juan Morales, the Spanish intendant at New Orleans, ordered it stopped.

In the meantime, Carondelet's administration in Louisiana came to an end on August 5, 1797. He was followed by Brigadier General Manuel Luis Gayoso de Lemos, the former governor of the Natchez district. Carondelet was off to his new post as president of the Royal Audience of Quito.

The list of Carondelet's achievements in New Orleans is long, but one of the most important events during his tenure was one with which he had nothing to do. In 1796 Etienne Bore harvested a sugarcane crop on his plantation upriver from New Orleans near present-day Audubon Park. Although earlier Louisianians had planted cane and produced sugar, Bore has been credited with raising sugar production to the level of making it a profitable industry. Bore had believed that sugar produc-

The tiled roofs on some colonial New Orleans houses were flat and served as elevated patios. These took advantage of breezes from the river and also provided a view of the growing city. (THNOC)

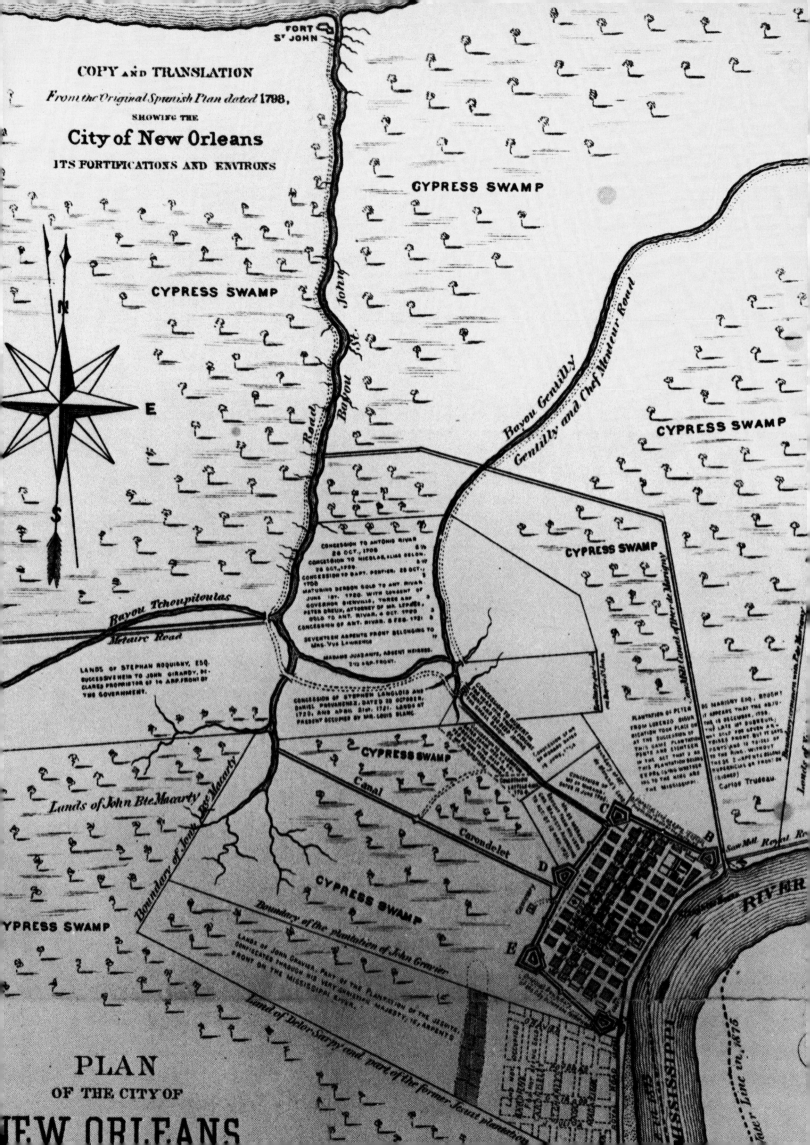

COPY and TRANSLATION
From the Original Spanish Plan dated 1798,
SHOWING THE
City of New Orleans
ITS FORTIFICATIONS AND ENVIRONS

FORT
Sᵗ JOHN

CYPRESS SWAMP

CYPRESS SWAMP

CYPRESS SWAMP

CYPRESS SWAMP

CYPRESS SWAMP

CYPRESS SWAMP

CYPRESS SWAMP

Bayou Tchoupitoulas

Metaire Road

LANDS OF STEPHAN ROQUIGNY, ESQ.
SUCCESSIVE HEIR TO JOHN GIRARDY, DE-
CLARES PROPRIETOR OF 14 ARP. FRONT OF
THE GOVERNMENT.

Lands of John Bte. Macarty

Boundary of John Bte Macarty

Boundary of the Plantation of John Gravier

Canal

Carondelet

Land of Delor Sarpy and part of the former Jesuit Plantation

RIVER

MISSISSIPPI

Levee Line in, 1875

PLAN
OF THE CITY OF
NEW ORLEANS

tion had to be large-scale to be profitable. He planted larger quantities of cane and built a bigger sugar house. With the help of an experienced sugar maker, Bore sold his 1796 crop for a considerable profit, marking the beginning of an important industry for Louisiana.

Gayoso was popular among New Orleanians, but his administration was to be cut short when he died of a fever in July 1799. He became the only colonial governor to be buried beneath the floor of St. Louis Cathedral. During his two years in office, Gayoso served well, spending most of his time dealing with the increasing number of American immigrants. Moreover, Gayoso had the honor of entertaining the only royalty New Orleans had ever seen. Louis Philippe, Duc d'Orleans and later king of France, visited the city with his two brothers, the Duc de Montpensier and the Comte de Beaujolais. All three were great-great-grandsons of New Orleans' namesake, Philippe, the Duc d' Orleans, and were keeping the Atlantic between themselves and the new authorities governing France after the revolution, who would dearly have loved the young men's royal heads. New Orleanians were thrilled by the royal visits and did all they could to make their guests feel at home in the would-be Paris on the Mississippi.

After Gayoso's unexpected death, Francisco Bouligny and Nicholas Maria Vidal took charge until a new governor could be sent to the colony. Officials in Cuba dispatched the Marques de Casa-Calvo to serve as acting governor until a permanent appointee could be sent from Spain. The man finally chosen, brigadier general Don Juan Manuel de Salcedo, had a brief and undistinguished career in Louisiana. Old and perhaps senile, the governor left many government matters to his son, who was more concerned with his own profit than the good of the colony.

Salcedo was Louisiana's last Spanish governor, for in the meantime, the colony had been retroceded to France in 1800 through the secret Treaty of San Ildefonso. Napoleon, who had forced the treaty upon Spain, let the Spanish continue to administer Louisiana until he chose a convenient time to occupy it. Little did New Orleanians realize, but a chapter of their history was about to come to an end. Louisiana soon would be no longer a colonial possession of a European power.

By the end of Spanish rule in 1803, New Orleans had come a long way; from its shaky beginning as a remote outpost in the French empire to a major North American city. The population of New Orleans in 1803 has been placed at anywhere from 8,000 to 11,000 people. One estimate accounted for approximately 10,000 residents — 5,000 whites, 2,000 free-people-of-color, and 3,000 slaves. The city could boast of well-constructed brick and stucco-covered buildings and a good harbor. The busy quays held cargoes of all types and descriptions from the interior of North America, the West Indies, and Europe, while merchants, roustabouts, and draymen went about their work. New Orleans had become an international city where the English-speaking culture clashed head-on with the Creole of Louisiana.

New Orleans by this time already had gained a reputation as a gay and colorful city with Mardi Gras balls dating back to the French era. By the end of the Spanish period the affluent Creoles had taken on all the trappings of their European counterparts, Americans were assuming a leading role in the city's commerce, and a large population of free-people-of-color — increased by refugees from the slave revolts in the West Indies — gained prominence in many walks of life in New Orleans. The *gens de couleur libres,* often labeled mulatto, quadroon, or a host of other designations for their percentage of European to African heritage, had developed a sophisticated society, which to a degree paralleled white society. The fabled beauty of the women has become an important part of the city's legend.

By the end of the colonial period, the elements of New Orleans' future fame were already in place. Visitors to 20th-century New Orleans enjoy the mystique of the colonial survivals — the Cabildo, the Ursuline Convent, and the Gallic street names. The Creole food, with its combined French, Spanish, Indian, and African influences, is known throughout the world. *Gris gris, voodoo,* and *banquette* are words that conjure up thoughts of the city's colonial past. Visitors to the city spend hours and days peering down the long passageways into the damp but serene patios with their thick growths of vegetation, looking for a glimpse or a sound of a long-gone colonial New Orleans, and are not disappointed.

CHAPTER III
THE NOBLE BARGAIN

There is on the Globe one single spot, the possessor of which is our natural and habitual enemy. It is New Orleans, through which the produce of three-eighths of our territory must pass to market. . . . The day France takes possession of New Orleans . . . from that moment we must marry ourselves to the British fleet and nation."

So wrote President Thomas Jefferson in a now-famous letter to Robert Livingston, American minister to France, when he learned in 1802 that Spain had secretly retroceded Louisiana to the French two years earlier. The situation was a serious one, and Jefferson's reaction to it was extreme, for well he knew that joining with England would have allied the United States with the one country it distrusted more than France. But pressures from the emerging territories in the West, which needed the use of the Mississippi Gulf port for trade with the East Coast and Europe, and from Napoleon's imperial wars were requiring a resolution to the disposition of the Louisiana problem. War between France and the United States would be narrowly averted by the Louisiana Purchase of 1803, which doubled the territory of the United States and ensured its future position as a world power.

In an attempt to avoid war with France, Livingston had been instructed to enter into negotiations with Napoleon to buy the Isle of Orleans and

West Florida. He made little headway at first. "There never was a government in which less could be done by negotiation," he wrote to Jefferson, "There is no people, no legislature, no counsellors. One man (Napoleon) is everything. He seldom asks advice, and never hears it unasked."

Napoleon had more immediate concerns than what to do with his backwater frontier land across the ocean. For more than three years after its acquisition in 1800, he had allowed Spain to continue to govern Louisiana. Tensions between the Spanish in New Orleans and the Western Americans increased during this period, especially because of the expansion of United States shipping activity on the Mississippi. By 1802 ships flying the American flag greatly outnumbered the ships of other nations, even Spain and France. American seamen, enjoying the tawdry delights of the city's riverfront saloons and bordellos, were quick to express their resentment toward Spanish officials with a word, gesture, and sometimes a fist fight.

In late 1802 Juan Morales, the acting Spanish intendant at New Orleans, closed the river to American ships. When this news reached Jefferson in January of 1803, he sent his friend James Monroe (who would become the fifth President) to assist Livingston with his negotiations. Jefferson wrote to Livingston in Paris: "Every eye in the United States is now fixed on the affairs of Louisiana. Perhaps nothing since the revolutionary war has produced more uneasy sensations through the body of the nation."

Later that month the President informed the British *charge d'affaires* that the United States would never relinquish its claim to free navigation of the Mississippi River, so essential to the development of the West, and would resort to war if necessary to insure access. In February a Senate resolution that would have authorized Jefferson to occupy portions of the Isle of Orleans failed. But another resolution calling for the outfitting of 80,000 militiamen was passed.

Since war with Great Britain was seemingly imminent, Napoleon made a decision that sur-

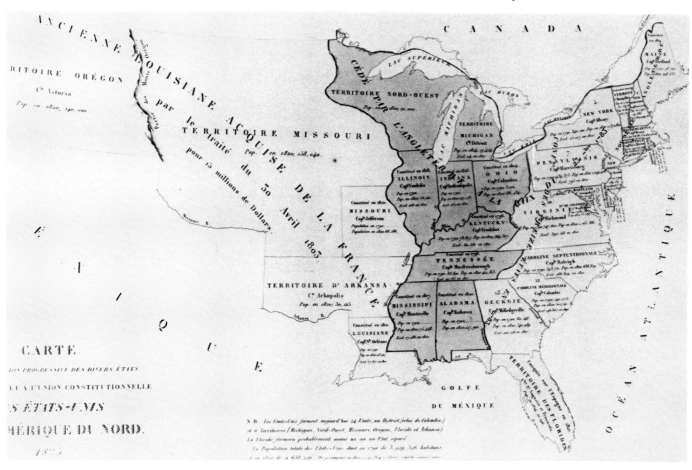

prised the United States. He agreed not only to sell the Americans the land they had requested, but all of Louisiana. This decision probably had less to do with the protracted negotiations than with Napoleon's need for money to continue his imperial wars. He also doubted his ability to hold the territory against a British — or even an American — attack. If France couldn't control the Mississippi, Napoleon would much rather see it in the hands of the United States than his ancient rival England. In issuing the order to sell to his minister of the treasury, Barbe-Marbois, Napoleon wrote:

> They [the British] shall not have the Mississippi which they covet. . . . I renounce Louisiana. It is not only New Orleans that I cede: it is the whole colony without reserve. . . . I renounce it with the greatest regret; to attempt obstinately to retain it would be folly.

On April 12, 1803, during a dinner party given by Livingston to celebrate Monroe's ar-rival in Paris, Barbe-Marbois arrived and shocked the Americans with the announce-ment that Napoleon was willing to sell all of the Louisiana Territory. Negotiations over the price, in which Monroe joined Livingston, lasted for more than two weeks. The United States finally agreed on April 29 to pay $11.25 million for the land, and to assume French debts of $3.75 million incurred to American citizens during the recent wars, bringing the total price of the transaction to $15 million. The treaty was dated April 30, although it was actually signed on May 2. Livingston's remarks at the signing would prove prophetic: "We have lived long, but this is the noblest work of our lives. . . . From this day the United States take their place among the powers of the first rank."

Napoleon's comments after the sale would likewise come true: "This accession of territory affirms forever the power of the United States, and I have just given England a maritime rival that sooner or later will lay low her pride." Had the English been able to foresee the future, they

With Livingston and James Monroe in Paris, and Jefferson in Washington, news of the negotiations and instructions were accomplished by letter. Because of the highly secret nature of the negotiations, this particularly sensitive passage from one of Livingston's let-ters to Jefferson was written in a numerical code. (THNOC)

might have gone forward with their own plans to invade New Orleans, which were to be carried out with the resumption of the war between France and Great Britain. Livingston learned of the invasion plan a week after the signing of the treaty, and he quickly informed London of the Louisiana Purchase.

When the time came to actually pay France the approximately $15 million for Louisiana, however, the United States found itself embarrassed: the fledgling country simply did not have that much money in its treasury. But arrangements were made to sell bonds to the banking houses of Baring in London and Hope in Amsterdam to pay Napoleon. The total cost of the Louisiana Purchase, including interest and claims against the government, eventually came to $23,527,872.

Acquiring sufficient funds was not the only problem that Louisiana presented its American purchasers. The extent and exact boundaries of the vast territory had never been clearly delineated. When Livingston asked the French foreign minister Talleyrand for information, he replied, "I can give you no direction; you have made a noble bargain for yourselves and I suppose you will make the most of it."

Not all Americans were happy with the Louisiana Purchase. Jefferson's opponents in Congress argued that the Constitution had made no provisions for acquiring land in such a way or for administering it. New Englanders complained that a large sum was being paid for land that would only benefit Americans living in the West. They were also reluctant to have a rival in New Orleans for their own port cities.

The reaction to the purchase in New Orleans itself was, for the most part, positive. Pierre Clement Laussat, the envoy sent by Napoleon to officiate the return of the colony from France to Spain, however, could not believe the rumors he had heard about the purchase. He wrote to his superiors describing the "incredible falsehoods." The Americans in the city were wild with joy over the news, he wrote, while the Spanish residents expressed pleasure that New Orleans would not be returned to the French. Many of the French Creoles, who were looking forward to a reunion with France, were now in despair, he continued, and were considering selling their possessions and moving away. Laussat soon received word that the rumors were indeed true and he was ordered to receive the colony from Spain and hold it for the United States.

At the time of the Louisiana Purchase, New Orleans was still in a way a frontier city, but yet unlike any other frontier city in the nation. The population in 1803 had risen to more than 10,000 with another 3,000 residents living below the city. The population consisted primarily of Creoles, Anglo-Americans, free-people-of-color and Negro slaves, and a few Indians.

The city's West-Indian flavor, contrasted, for example, with its Roman Catholic religious ceremonies, must have been a strange sight from the more conservative Eastern-Seaboard Protestants moving into the city to open commercial establishments or plantations along the Mississippi River and connecting waterways. During the early years of the American period, New Orleans became well-known for its dens of vice along Tchoupitoulas Street and in the infamous Swamp, a collection of brothels, saloons, and gambling halls where life was not worth a *picayune* (about 6 cents) — the price of a drink. The Swamp, a favorite place for the Kaintock flatboat men of Mike Fink fame and the dregs of the *demi-monde,* was located behind the American Sector of the city at the end of Girod Street near Liberty Street and the Protestant Cemetery, or in the general area of today's Louisiana Superdome. There was perhaps no other city in the Union where a spectator could watch a religious procession wind through the streets, visit a colorful Mardi Gras ball in one of the many white ballrooms, or the famous biracial Quadroon Ballroom, or per-

The French minister of the treasury, Barbe-Marbois, was ordered by Napoleon to negotiate the sale of the Louisiana Territory with the Americans. (THNOC)

haps wander over to Congo Square in the rear of the old city to watch the French-speaking slaves enjoy a day off, singing, beating the drums, rattling the bones, or dancing the Calinda, Bamboula, or the Counjaille (or Counjai), many of which were later made famous in music by New Orleans composer Leon Gottschalk.

New Orleans already had begun to grow beyond its original boundaries with the construction of Faubourg Ste. Marie. Later other Faubourgs would be added, such as Marigny and Treme. By 1810 New Orleans was the largest city in the South, boasting a population of over 24,000 residents, and it was the fifth-largest city by population in the nation. Between 1804 and 1810 the population of the city increased dramatically as French Creoles, free blacks, and slaves fled to the city, escaping revolutions in the French West Indies. In 1809 alone over 5,700 emigrants sought refuge in New Orleans. The mass influx of white and black West Indians caused serious housing, economic, and racial problems for the young American government.

New Orleans could boast of an active opera and theater and many fine homes in the Old Quarter and suburbs, as well as some of the fine plantation houses above and below the city. But according to some visitors, New Orleans was dirty, unhealthy, and decayed, even though it had practically been rebuilt after the fires of 1788 and 1794.

This painting depicts the signing of the Louisiana Purchase treaty on May 2, 1803. (THNOC)

UNDER MY WINGS EVERY THING PROSPERS

Visiting the city shortly before the purchase, Perrin du Lac, a visiting Frenchman, noted his findings in the Crescent City:

> *Nothing equals the filthiness of New Orleans. . . . The city, the filth of which cannot be drained off, is not paved and probably never will be in the hands of the Spaniards. Its markets which are unventilated are reeking with rottenness. Its quay is adorned with fish that rot there for want of purchasers. Its squares are covered with the filth of animals which no one takes the trouble to remove.*

Another Frenchman, C. C. Robin, had much of the same to say about conditions in the city. The streets of the city, he said, were, in some places, impassable even to carriages:

> *There were chasms where carriages would be broken to pieces if they attempted it. The pedestrians could take refuge on the sidewalks or banquettes, built along the houses. . . . In many places they are broken and covered with mud, so that one must be an expert in the art of equilibrium in order to follow these pieces of wood without slipping.*

Robin, however, was very optimistic about Louisiana's future: "In the New World there are as yet very few of those useless families that permit themselves the time of doing nothing. The universal desire to acquire wealth insures that no profession is despised as long as it makes money."

The Louisiana Territory was vast but sparsely settled with approximately 50,000 inhabitants, excluding Indians. Most of the residents lived in the present-day state of Louisiana, primarily in and around New Orleans. The huge acquisition would later be divided and subdivided to form 15 other states, or parts of states, in the nation.

Shortly after the purchase, the federal government started reorganizing the territory. On March 26, 1804, Congress divided the purchase into the Territory of Orleans (present state of Louisiana minus the Florida Parishes, which were annexed in 1810, and an area near the Sabine River) and the Louisiana Territory which comprised the rest of the acquisition. John Quincy Adams and other New Englanders objected, stating that the Constitution made no provision for determining how the people of a purchased territory would govern themselves. When the time came for Jefferson to name a governor to the Territory of Orleans, he first considered two men: the popular Marquis de Lafayette and James Monroe. Jefferson finally named William Charles Cole Claiborne to the post after both Monroe and Lafayette declined. One of Claiborne's first official duties came on December 20, 1803, during ceremonies in New Orleans when he and General

James Wilkinson took possession of Louisiana — just 20 days after disappointed French Commissioner Pierre Clement Laussat had received the colony from Spain.

Claiborne, Virginia-born and two years away from his 30th birthday, had been the governor of the neighboring Mississippi Territory when Jefferson sent him to New Orleans to accept Louisiana from the French. The new governor, a Protestant who could not speak a word of French, faced a difficult task in making Louisianians Americans. The people felt they were being slighted because the territory was not made a state immediately. The American legal system was confusing to them; they resented the ban on importing slaves, a practice that they had enjoyed since Galvez's days, and rumors persisted that Louisiana would soon be returned to either France or Spain. Claiborne also wrote to Jefferson praising the people of Louisiana, but warning him that certain Americans, namely Edward Livingston, a scion of the plutocratic New York family, Irish-born Daniel Clark, and others were trying to turn the local population against him.

In March 1805 Congress created the first legislature for the Territory of Orleans. A year later Claiborne was writing to Jefferson again complaining of his problems with that assembly: "I always thought that an early extension of the Representative system in this Territory was a hazardous experiment; and of this I am now convinced."

New Orleans city government retained Laussat's mayor and municipal council system in varying degrees until the territorial legislature incorporated the city on February 17, 1805. Laussat's mayoral appointment, Etienne Bore, had continued in office until he was replaced in 1804 by James Pitot. The city charter of 1805 called for the election of a 14-member board of aldermen, presided over by a recorder and mayor, both of whom were appointed by the governor. The board of aldermen elected the city treasurer and the mayor appointed most other city officials. The board of aldermen, which was based on American municipal concepts, among its many functions, fixed prices and passed ordinances. The mayor, as the city's chief magistrate, presided over the council and headed the city's police and fire departments.

Under the new 1805 charter, Claiborne appointed John Watkins mayor, and later James Mather. In 1811 the city charter was amended to provide for the election of the mayor by property-owning white males. Nicholas Girod, a French-speaking Creole, became the city's first elected mayor in 1812. (Girod would gain fame in Louisiana for his offer of sanctuary to Napoleon, who was brooding away in exile on the island of St. Helena. In 1821 Girod and his supporters collected money to buy the schooner *Seraphine* which was to sail to Napoleon's rescue; but before the ship could depart New Orleans, word reached the city that Napoleon had died.)

The city government created by the 1805

Right
Thomas Jefferson appointed William Charles Cole Claiborne, a Virginian by birth, civil governor of the newly purchased Louisiana Territory. (THNOC)

Below
The Territory of Orleans, established in 1804, comprised most of the present-day state of Louisiana. Lafon's map of 1806 also shows West Florida, part of which became Louisiana's Florida Parishes. (THNOC)

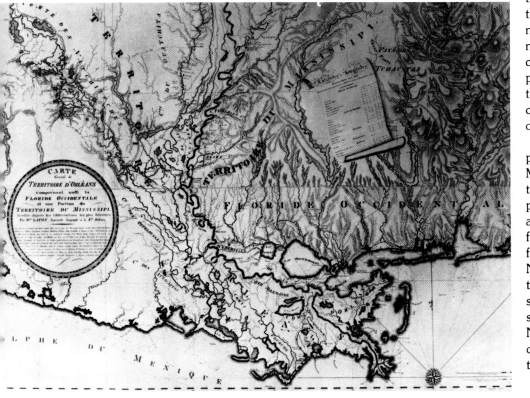

charter also set out to clean up New Orleans. Cockfights were outlawed and the military was ordered to stop using the levees as latrines. The police force was reorganized, newly arrived ships were inspected for diseases, and additional streetlights were installed. Roads and bridges were repaired and a new meat market was built. More firefighting equipment was purchased and a building code was enacted. (The council passed an ordinance requiring each household to keep two buckets on hand in case of fire.) In 1808 the city council enacted an ordinance compelling theater owners to submit all plays to the mayor's office for review before performing them for the public. This law was passed at the request of Mayor Mather because of a "lewd" play he attended at the St. Philip Street Theatre.

The first decade or so of the American era in New Orleans was a period historian John Clark described as one of "excitement, uproar, flux, boom and bust, disasters, disappointments, and achievements." Thousands of people died in the yellow-fever epidemics of 1804, 1807, 1808, 1811, and 1813. American and foreign sailors frequently slugged it out on the levees and in taverns, while Creoles lavished their contempt on Anglo-Americans. Collector of Customs William Brown absconded in 1809 with $150,000 in customs receipts and a year later a slave insurrection just above the city in St. John the Baptist Parish was suppressed. The heads of many of the leaders of the revolt were mounted on poles along the levee for

Left
Although appointed by Laussat, Etienne Bore remained mayor of New Orleans until 1804, when he was replaced by James Pitot. (THNOC)

Below
Among the early improvements made in the city of New Orleans was the construction of a new butcher's market on the levee. (THNOC)

other slaves to see and take heed.

Aside from the purchase itself, the events that left the most significant impressions on the collective imagination in those years were the Aaron Burr conspiracy of 1805–1807; Jefferson's Embargo Act of 1807; statehood in 1811–1812; and the British invasion of 1814–1815.

Former Vice-President Aaron Burr, whose political career ended when he killed Alexander Hamilton in a duel in 1804, allegedly conspired with General James Wilkinson and others to wrest Louisiana and Western states away from the United States or a part of Mexico from Spain to set up his own country. In the summer of 1805 Burr was in New Orleans to meet with Edward Livingston, Daniel Clark, and members of the Mexican Association, a group of traders

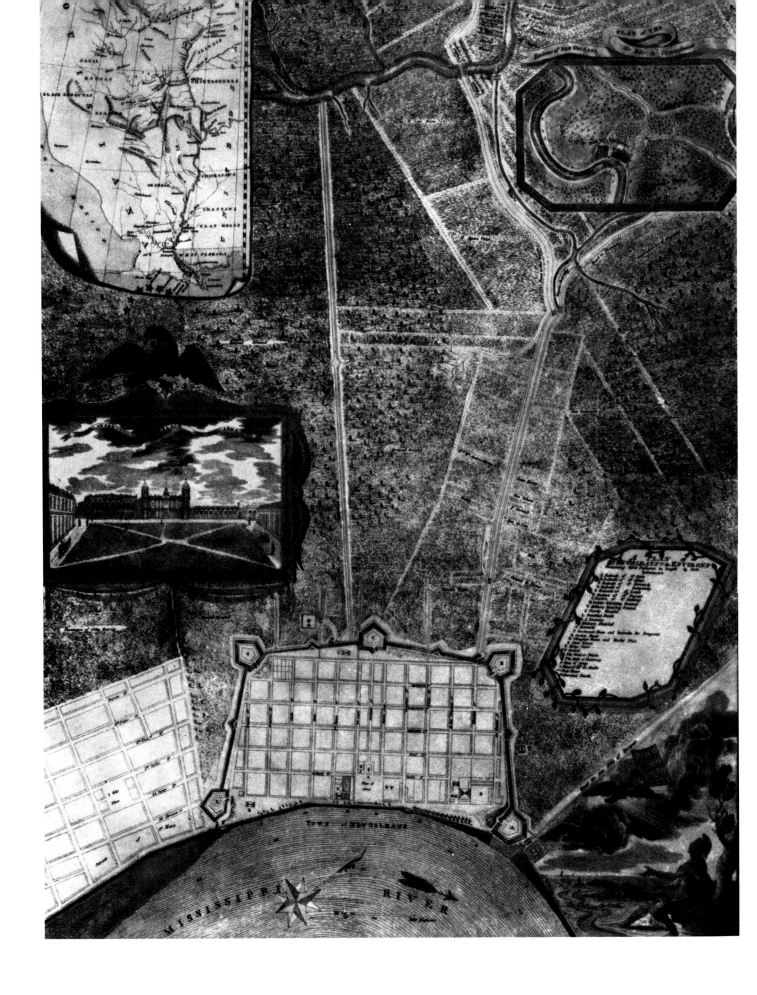

and adventurers that wanted to invade Mexico. To New Orleans Burr carried a letter of introduction from Wilkinson (then governor of the Louisiana Territory, not including the Territory of Orleans, but formerly a spy in the service of the Spanish). What Burr was really up to may never be fully known: Burr had previously told British, French, and Spanish ministers in Washington of his plans to separate the Western Territory and states from the Union; and told others he was going to settle property he owned along the Ouachita River area in the Territory of Orleans; to still others he told of his intention to invade Mexico.

In 1806 and 1807 New Orleans was alive with rumors of Burr's advancing army and every new arrival from upriver, especially Kentucky and Tennessee, was suspected. Many New Orleanians believed that the Spanish in neighboring West Florida were working with Burr to regain Louisiana. Governor Claiborne interviewed all newcomers in the city from upriver to satisfy himself that they were not vanguards of Burr's army. The cabal never fully materialized, however, and Burr was later arrested, tried, and acquitted.

While fears of the Burr invasion subsided in 1807 war was blazing on the Atlantic between Great Britain and France. Although the United States professed neutrality in the conflicts, hundreds of its ships were seized at sea by both

England and France. Repeated appeals by President Jefferson were ignored, so the President and Congress reacted by passing the Embargo Act of 1807, prohibiting all exportation of American goods to either of the warring powers.

This act had devastating effects on the American economy — particularly on port cities such as New Orleans. Smuggling became commonplace and American exports fell from $108 million in 1807 to $22 million the following year. In the same period imports dropped from $138 million to less than $57 million. Jefferson stuck by the act and his course of action, hoping to force the French and British to respect America's rights on the seas. In New Orleans, mercantile companies foundered and young men who came to the city with dreams of making their fortune became destitute. Such was the case of young Nathaniel Cox, who came to New Orleans in 1806 from Kentucky. Writing to his business associate back home on May 2, 1808, he described the effect of the Embargo Act on their business prospects:

*. . . This infernal Embargo has so effectively
stopped our Commercial career that the
prospects once so flattering have become
extremely gloomy — and the profits arising
from the business we are now doing will not
justify the step.*

Lamenting his inability to build a home and settle down, Cox wrote on September 15, 1809:

*If there had been no failures in New
Orleans, no frays with the Chesapeake — no
Embargo — no non-intercourse — no Burr — no
Wilkinson, no proclamations — and in short, if
the usual commertial [sic] arrangements had
continued between the United States and
Europe my calculations might in some
measure [have] been realized.*

By 1812 the depredations committed by the British upon the American nation, coupled with expansionist ideas, led the young nation into a war which up to that point had been a European affair.

While the attention of the rest of the nation

was directed to the growing menace of war with Great Britain during 1811 and well into the next year, New Orleanians were pressuring Congress for statehood. The 1810 census showed the population of the Territory of Orleans had risen to over 76,500 residents — 60,000 was the number required for statehood. In January 1811 the territory's delegate to Congress, Julien Poydras, proposed statehood in the House of Representatives and numerous petitions were sent from New Orleans to Congress in support of the move. The following month Congress authorized the territory to draw up a constitution. Delegates met in New Orleans at Tremoulet's Coffee House, and after long debates even on a name for the state (the name "Jefferson" was discussed and summarily dismissed), Congress ratified the document on April 8, 1812. At first the Florida Parishes, which had been annexed to the territory after the West Florida rebellion of 1810, were not included in the constitution. A few days later, however, they were added to the state by an amendment. Louisiana became the nation's 18th state on April 30, 1812. During the subsequent gubernatorial election, Claiborne — appointed governor six times by Jefferson — defeated Jacques Villere, a prominent Creole.

Many observers, including Jefferson and Claiborne, believed that many years would pass before New Orleanians would be ready to participate as full citizens in the Union. After all, the reasoning went, they had never known the democratic process and had always lived under one monarchy or another. But perhaps the population was better suited for its new status than most critics realized. In addition to the many Anglo-Americans already living in New Orleans before and shortly after the purchase, there were subtle differences between the French and Spanish Creoles and their counterparts in Europe. Louisianians during the colonial era did not receive hereditary titles as did the Europeans or even those in other colonies. Many were titled before coming or after returning to their homelands. The Louisiana colony also lacked the strict class delineation found in the mother countries. People — from all strata of society — most often came to Louisiana in quest of opportunity. To make their fortunes, which many did, they worked side by side. Such was the case of Louis Brasillier, called "Touranjeau," who came to Louisiana in 1717 as an illiterate valet to a military officer, and Captain Renault D'Hauterive, a member of the French gentry, who arrived in the colony in

Below left
As a territorial delegate to the U. S. House of Representatives, Julien Poydras proposed statehood for the Territory of Orleans in 1811. Congress made Louisiana a state in 1812. (THNOC)

Below
Creole Jacques Villere was defeated by William C. C. Claiborne in the gubernatorial election that followed statehood. Villere later became a governor of Louisiana. (THNOC)

1720. After three decades, Brasillier was a prosperous plantation owner on nearby Bayou St. John. The Brasilliers by the next generation owned a successful shipping concern. By this time D'Hauterive's son was signing his name Dauterive in the more egalitarian fashion. Both the Brasilliers and "Dauterives" married into the same New Orleans families.

Another major event in New Orleans—one that would shortly revolutionize commerce on the Mississippi and its thousands of miles of tributaries—took place the same year, although not everyone paid it the attention it deserved: On January 10, Nicholas Roosevelt arrived on the *New Orleans,* the first steamboat on the Western territorial waters.

Only slightly more than a month had passed since Louisiana gained statehood when Congress declared war against Great Britain. Since the end of the American Revolution, the young nation had endured repeated insults to its national sovereignty at the hands of the British. American ships were stopped at sea and their seamen impressed. British ships blockaded American ports. In violation of the treaty ending the Revolution, Great Britain maintained forts on American territory near the Great Lakes from which they encouraged Indians to attack westward-moving settlers. British harassment was not the only incitement for the War of 1812: "War Hawks" in Congress and Westerners believed that in the event of war, Canada and Spanish Florida would fall easily to the United States. Some Westerners also believed that war would solve their agricultural problems and enable them to ship their cotton, tobacco, and wheat to markets for higher prices. Despite opposition in the New England states, war came and the United States was hardly prepared to fight.

The steamboat New Orleans, *whose reconstructed plan is shown here, was the first steamboat to ply the western territorial waters of the Mississippi River. (THNOC)*

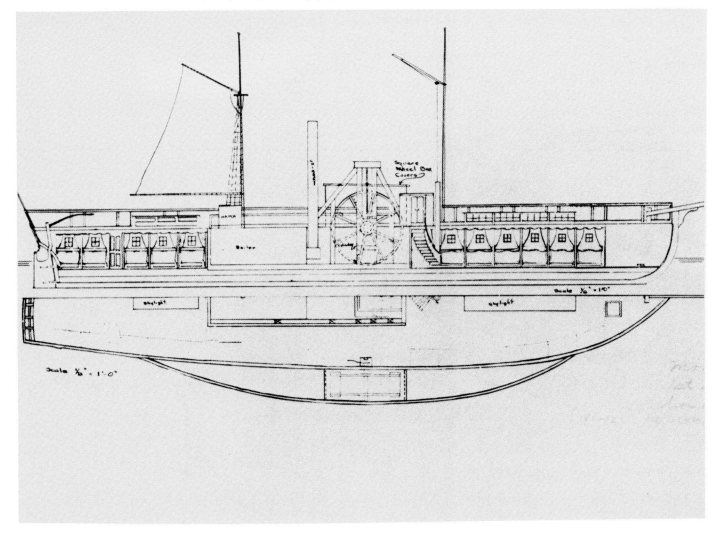

The Americans enjoyed some success early in the war, especially Oliver Hazard Perry's victory in the Battle of Lake Erie. The British successes, however, were more impressive. They defeated the Americans at Fort Dearborn (Chicago) and Detroit. They captured and burned Washington, D.C., and effectively blockaded American ports. America's dreams of capturing Canada vanished when several invasion forces were soundly defeated and turned back.

In Louisiana, Governor Claiborne was busy preparing for a defensive war while two British blockade ships sat at the mouth of the Mississippi. Not all Louisianians were enthusiastic in their support of the American war effort. Some French Creoles asked the French consul in New Orleans for protection, claiming they were French, not American, citizens. Other New Orleanians were ready to fight the British, while still others were suspected of supplying the enemy with important intelligence. In early 1814 General Andrew Jackson marched south from Tennessee to suppress the Creek Indians who, at the instigation of the British, had massacred white settlers along the Alabama River.

Meanwhile, Claiborne met with Caddo Indian chiefs at Natchitoches to make sure they did not follow the lead of the Creeks.

By the spring of 1814 word began reaching Louisiana that the British were planning an attack against New Orleans and the Gulf Coast area. Claiborne ran helter-skelter trying to prepare the city's defenses against a possible British attack. On August 24, Claiborne wrote to Jackson and complained about the lack of cooperation: "I have a difficult people to manage; native Americans, native Louisianians, Frenchmen, Spanish, with some English."

In September 1814 the British brig *Sophia* dropped anchor near Grande Terre, the stronghold of the celebrated pirate Jean Lafitte (also Laffite). Captain Nicholas Lockyer presented Lafitte with a letter from British Lieutenant Colonel Edward Nicholls, who had occupied Pensacola with an expeditionary force in July. Nicholls offered Lafitte the rank of captain in the British forces, and land and money in return for his help against the Americans. While Lafitte was passing this information along to state officials, Claiborne and the Committee of Defense sent a force of regular United States

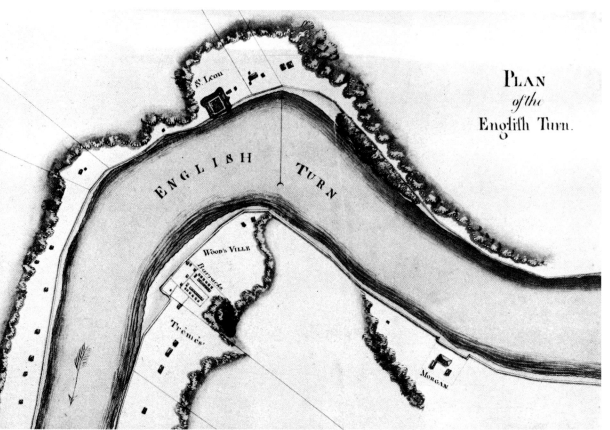

B. Lafon drew this plan of English Turn. Fort St. Leon on the Mississippi River below New Orleans was one of several forts, both active and abandoned, which defended the city and its approaches. Lafon was commissioned to make a survey of existing and projected military fortifications in the Gulf South. (THNOC)

soldiers and navy out to capture Lafitte and to break up his sanctuary. Although most of the Baratarians escaped, including the Lafitte brothers, others were taken as prisoners.

Nicholls soon left no doubt in the minds of Louisianians what the British intentions were when a proclamation began appearing all over the city:

Natives of Louisiana! On you the first call is made to assist in liberating from a faithless, imbecile government, your paternal soil: Spaniards, Frenchmen, Italians, and British . . . you also I call to aid me in this just cause. The American usurpation of this country must be abolished, and the lawful owners of the soil put in possession.

In response, Jackson issued his own proclamation, which read in part:

Louisianians! The proud Briton, the natural and sworn enemies of all Frenchmen, has called upon you, by proclamation, to aid him in his tyranny, and to prostrate the holy temple of our liberty. Can Louisianians, can Frenchmen, can Americans, ever stoop to be the slaver or allies of Britain?

Word also circulated throughout the city and state that the British planned to arm slaves and give them their freedom if they would rise up against their owners.

In September British forays against Mobile were driven off by Jackson and later the next month, Jackson moved successfully against Pensacola, sending Nicholls and his troops back to their ships. Claiborne flooded Jackson with dispatches describing the problems—both real and imagined—the governor was facing in preparing Louisiana to defend itself. Not enough troops, not enough money, spies, and trouble with the state legislature filled the governor's letters to the general. Jackson often lost his temper with Claiborne's seeming inability to take hold of the situation.

Meanwhile, reports continued to arrive in Washington describing the massive buildup of British troops and supplies in Jamaica in preparation for the invasion of Louisiana. With this information in hand, Jackson set out from Mobile to New Orleans on November 22, only days before the British set sail on their Gulf Coast expedition. Jackson arrived in the Crescent City on December 2.

Eight days later the British fleet of 50 ships dropped anchor off North Chandeleur Island near Lake Borgne. Aboard was an army of over 10,000 troops commanded by General Sir Edward Pakenham, the Duke of Wellington's brother-in-law. The fleet itself was under the command of Admiral Sir Alexander Cochrane. So confident were the British of victory that aboard their ships they brought civil officials to take over the Louisiana government as well as their wives and those of the military officers. Also aboard was a government printing press to promulgate the new government's policies and proclamations.

Lord Castlereagh, British foreign secretary, was so confident that the New Orleans campaign would be successful, that he wrote on his way to the Congress of Vienna in December 1815: "I expect at this moment that most of the large seaport towns of America are laid in ashes, that we are in possession of New Orleans, and have command of all the rivers of the Mississippi Valley and the lakes, and that the Americans are now little better than prisoners in their own country."

Upon his arrival in New Orleans, Jackson began immediately to prepare the city for war. He ordered Major Arsene Lacarriere Latour, an engineer sent to Louisiana by Napoleon in 1802, to rehabilitate and strengthen the city's

General Andrew Jackson was the commander of the American forces at the Battle of New Orleans. (THNOC)

defense lines. With the help of Mayor Nicholas Girod, every available person — both white and black, free and slave — worked furiously. Batteries and earthworks were thrown up at the Rigolets, Chef Menteur Road, and the two forts below the city on opposite banks of the river.

Jackson's dilemma was determining where the British would attack first. Would they come over land from Mobile and attack the city from the east or northeast or would they sail up the river in a head-on attack? Perhaps they would sail into Lake Borgne and attack by land from the south. Jackson had to prepare for all possibilities. He ordered troops standing by in Baton Rouge, Mobile, Natchez, and in other sections to march to New Orleans as soon as possible. He also sent Captain Henry Miller Shreve, and his steamboat *Enterprise,* who had just arrived downriver from Pittsburgh, back upriver to pick up supplies. Everyone who could carry a weapon was needed. Jackson took a bold step for the times — despite considerable local opposition — and accepted the help of free black military units of Louisiana which had distinguished themselves during the French and Spanish colonial periods. Earlier Jackson had sent a letter to Claiborne making known his wish to use the free blacks:

Above
The Battle of New Orleans was truly a group effort on the part of the American forces. In addition to regular troops, free blacks and the band of "pirates" led by Jean Lafitte also fought. (THNOC)

The free men of color in your city are inured to the southern climate and would make excellent soldiers. They will not remain quiet spectators of the contest. They must be either for or against us. Distrust them and you make them your enemies. Place confidence in them, and you engage them by every dear and honorable tie to the interest of the country by extending to them equal rights and privileges with white men.

These free-people-of-color again distinguished themselves on the battlefield as they had done under Galvez against the British almost four decades earlier.

Jackson made another bold move, again against Claiborne's advice, by inviting Lafitte and his Baratarians to fight the British. Lafitte and his men were given full pardons in return for their service. Lafitte offered Jackson badly needed flints, muskets, and other armaments along with his own skilled artillerists.

New Orleans was alive with activity as Latour so graphically noted:

Below left
Captain Henry Miller Shreve's innovations in steamboating made routes on the water to Northern Louisiana navigable. His accomplishments were instrumental in breaking the steamboat monopoly on territorial waters. (THNOC)

The citizens were preparing for battle as cheerfully as if it had been a party of pleasure, each in his vernacular tongue singing songs of victory. The streets resounded with 'Yankee Doodle,' the 'Marseillaise,' the 'chant du Depart,' and other martial airs, while those who had been long unaccustomed to military duty were furbishing their arms and accoutrements.

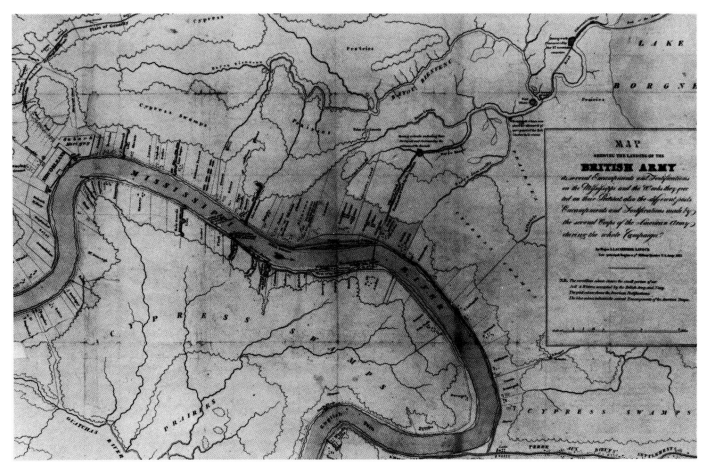

Jackson did not have to wait long to learn the direction of the British attack. On December 14 Admiral Cochrane sent troops from the south in oared barges to destroy the small American naval force in Lake Borgne which was under the command of Lieutenant Thomas ap Catesby Jones. The British concentrated their forces on Pea Island at the mouth of the Pearl River. On December 22 British forces began moving across Lake Borgne to Bayou Bienvenue and set up camp on the Villere Plantation on the banks of the Mississippi River. In a brilliant strategic move, Jackson decided to attack the British on the night of December 23. The weary British army was taken completely by surprise when they saw the American ship *Carolina* drifting on the river toward their position. They were even more surprised when the *Carolina* opened fire, inflicting havoc and carnage in their camp. Then Pierre Denis de la Ronde and John Coffee at the head of 600 mounted Tennessee volunteers, Hind's Dragoons, and John Beale's Rifles attacked the British right flank. Jackson led the advance

against the left flank with the 7th and 44th Regulars, Plauche's Orleans Volunteers, Daquin's Battalion of Free Colored, and Jugeat's Choctaws. When the smoke had cleared and the utter confusion abated, 24 Americans were dead, 115 wounded, and 74 missing. The British suffered 46 killed, 167 wounded, and 64 missing.

For the rest of December the British continued to land troops and supplies and Jackson dug in along the Rodriguez Canal above the Chalmette Plantation. Behind hastily built fortifications of dirt mounds, cotton bales, and cypress logs, Jackson waited. On December 28 the British attacked the American line to determine its strength but retreated. The British right actually turned Jackson's left flank in the cypress swamp. They possibly could have driven the American main force from their lines had not Pakenham lost control of his reconnaissance. He sounded recall when victory was within his reach. The retreat severely wounded the morale of the proud British regiments, as was recounted by one of their officers:

The map showing the plan of attack at the Battle of New Orleans was drawn by Major Arsene Lacarriere Latour. Much of the territory traversed by the British on their way to attack the city was swampy, and this fact of geography hampered their efforts. The Americans were diligent in their attempts to defend all possible approaches to the city. (THNOC)

When the fog lifted on the morning of New Year's Day 1815, the British artillery brought in from the ships opened a barrage on the American line. The American artillery responded, and after almost five hours of bombardment in both camps, a considerable proportion of the British cannon had been silenced. A British soldier later wrote: "It was a sad day for men who, a year before, had marched through France from the Pyrenees to the sea."

During the following days, 2,000 Kentuckians and other militia units arrived to reinforce Jackson's army. He dispatched many of them above New Orleans to prevent a surprise attack from the north and sent over 800 troops along with General David Morgan to guard the west bank of the river. Jackson is estimated to have had about 3,000 troops at Chalmette with another 1,000 in reserve. Pakenham had between 5,000 and 6,000 men with which to attack Jackson with 1,200 in reserve. He sent another 1,200 across the river to attack Morgan. The Americans also had eight batteries of cannon fixed on the open stretch of field separating the two opposing armies.

As the day of the main attack neared, Pakenham expressed grave reservations against a frontal attack across such a wide open space. Sarcastically, Admiral Cochrane told Pakenham that the navy would take on the task if the army believed it too difficult: "The soldiers can then bring up the baggage," he said.

On January 7 the armies prepared behind their lines for what both sides knew would be the decisive battle. Shortly before daybreak, on January 8, two signal rockets were fired into the sky from the British lines. The battle and drama were about to unfold. When the low-lying fog lifted, the Americans, crouched behind their defenses, could see coming toward them three columns of brightly uniformed British soldiers. With drummers beating cadence and bagpipes wailing ancient regimental airs, the 93rd Highlanders dressed in their kilts and tartans, the 95th Rifles, the 44th Regiment, the Duchess of York's Light Dragoons, the King's

A cease-fire at New Orleans was called shortly after the death of General Sir Edward Pakenham (pictured here). It was a serious blow to the British troops. (THNOC)

Own, the 21st Royals, the West India regiments, and others marched forward with weapons and ladders to scale the breastworks. Cannon fire savagely ripped through their lines, but still they marched on. American riflemen joined in with the artillery to mow broad swaths through the British ranks. The few attackers who managed to reach the American line were soon felled by sharpshooters. Finally, the carnage was too much even for the disciplined British troops to endure. Their ranks broke and ran to the rear, discarding weapons along the way. Pakenham himself was killed when he rode forward to rally his troops. "Shame! Shame! Remember you're British! Forward, Gentlemen, Forward!" the general shouted before the fatal bullet struck.

A cease-fire was called to allow both sides to tend to their dead and wounded. A British officer later described the horrors he had witnessed in the British camp:

The scene now presented at de la Ronde's plantation was one I shall never forget; almost every room was crowded with the wounded and dying. . . . I was the unwilling spectator of numerous amputations; and on all sides, nothing was heard but the piteous cries of my poor countrymen, undergoing various operations . . . and I cannot describe the strange and ghastly feelings created by seeing a basket nearly full of legs.

Shallow graves were made for many of the fallen British troops on "the field of slaughter" and after a light rainfall, parts of bodies could be seen, making the field resemble a gruesome garden. Wounded British prisoners were taken to New Orleans for medical care. When space could not be found for them in the barracks and hospitals, New Orleanians opened their homes to them and nursed their wounds.

British forces lingered in the area for several more weeks before rejoining the fleet on January 27. The fleet had just returned from an unsuccessful attempt to bombard Fort St. Philip into submission. The British then moved on to Mobile Bay where they were met by fresh reinforcements from England. The battle for New Orleans had only begun. Fort Bowyer at the entrance of Mobile Bay fell to the British as they planned a new overland attack against New Orleans.

Jackson had returned to New Orleans in triumph. January 23 was declared an official day of celebration. the *Te Deum* was sung in the Cathedral and an arch of triumph was erected in the Place d'Armes (later renamed Jackson Square in the general's honor). Public opinion soon turned against Jackson for he was determined to maintain martial law as long as the British fleet remained near New Orleans. Reports had reached the city that the United States and Great Britain had signed a peace treaty at Ghent, Belgium, on December 24, two weeks before the battle of January 8. Jackson maintained that he would continue martial law and keep the local milita in service until he received official word of the treaty from Washington. One of the more interesting events occurring from the martial law edict was the arrest of New Orleans' Judge Dominic Hall and United States District Attorney John Dick. Jackson ordered Louis Louaillier arrested for publishing uncomplimentary statements about the general and Hall ordered Louaillier's release on a writ of habeas corpus. Jackson in turn had Hall and Dick arrested. Hall later fined the general $1,000, which he paid. Twenty-nine years later, Congress reimbursed Jackson the amount of the fine plus interest.

On March 13 Jackson received word from Washington that the treaty had been signed. The Battle of New Orleans was over. Martial law was suspended and the following month, Jackson returned to Nashville with his wife Rachel and adopted son. The British troops replenished their supplies and joined their countrymen in defeating Napoleon at Waterloo.

Reports differ slightly on the number of casualties suffered on both sides that fateful day in early January. One participant on the American side placed fatalities at 13, 39 wounded, and 19 missing. The British reported 858 dead, 2,468 wounded, and many others missing. The gargantuan accomplishment of American military arms in the British campaign against New Orleans has been recalled for generations. The Battle of New Orleans dispelled any fears held by other Americans that New Orleanians might not make good Americans. This people of diverse and unique ethnic background fought side by side courageously against a common enemy — an enemy of the United States.

This view entitled New Orleans from the Lower Cotton Press *looks upriver toward the Vieux Carre. By the mid-19th century New Orleans was a large, growing city extending both upriver and down from the original settlement. (THNOC)*

The nearly five decades preceding the Civil War are referred to as the golden years of New Orleans. New Orleans became synonymous with prosperity. It was a boom town, pulsating with energy — the energy of commerce, business, change, and expansion.

The city's Caribbean-flavor marketplaces teamed with the sights and smells of prosperity: produce, wild game, and seafood; spices, European wines, and hundreds of other commodities that eventually found their way into New Orleans' homes. People of every size, hue, and shape mingled among the stalls, either hawking their wares or purchasing food for their tables, candles to light their homes, or cloth for their garments.

The city and surrounding areas experienced commercial and population explosions. By 1840 the population of the state had reached 350,-000, almost half of whom were either slaves or free-people-of-color. New Orleans had become the fourth-largest city in the nation and vied with New York for the title of the country's leading port.

The great changes in New Orleans during those years were hastened by the arrival of the steamboat *New Orleans* in 1812. Behind the *New Orleans* venture were Robert Livingston, the American negotiator for the Louisiana Purchase, and steamboat pioneer Robert Fulton. Livingston and Fulton believed the economic future of the Western lands would be carried on the decks of steamboats. To ensure their own fortunes, the entrepreneur and the inventor secured from the territorial legislature a complete monopoly for steamboat commerce on territorial waters in the West.

All went well for a couple of years, until Captain Henry Miller Shreve arrived in New Orleans in December 1814 aboard his own steamer, the *Enterprise*. Acting in behalf of the Mississippi Steamboat Navigation Company, Edward Livingston, a kinsman of Robert Livingston, tried to seize the boat with a court order. General Jackson saved Shreve's day by sending him and the *Enterprise* upriver for needed supplies to fight the approaching British. After a series of legal maneuvers and counter-maneuvers, a New Orleans court broke up the Livingston-Fulton monopoly in April 1817. Shreve went on to improve steamboat construction, invent the "snag boat" and open the Red River to commerce by de-snagging the Red River Raft. The city of Shreveport bears his name today.

The Mississippi and Ohio rivers and their hundreds, even thousands of miles of tributaries, became highways for steamboats ladened with cotton, sugar, and other agricultural and manufactured goods en route to their point of export in New Orleans. The rivers also became the return highways for imported goods from Europe and South and Central America passing through Bienville's port city.

A traveler visiting the New Orleans docks in the early 1830s noted the vitality and vibrance

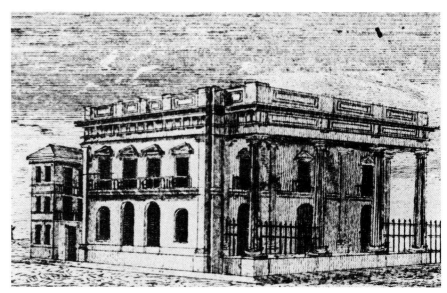

of the city's port:

> *With what astonishment did I, for the first time, view the magnificent levee, from one point or horn of the beauteous crescent to the other, covered with active human beings of all nations and colors, and boxes, bales, bags, hogsheads, pipes, barrels, kegs of goods, wares, and merchandise from all ends of the earth! Thousands of bales of cotton, tierces of sugar, molasses; quantities of flour, pork, lard, grain and other provisions; leads [and] furs . . . from the rich and extensive rivers above; and the wharves lined for miles with ships, steamers, flatboats, arks, and four deep! The business appearance of this city is not surpassed by any other in the wide world; it might be likened to a huge bee-hive, where no drones could find a resting place. I stepped on shore, and my first exclamation was, "This is the place for a business man!"*

With the burgeoning commercial activity in the port came the cotton and sugar factories, importers and exporters, and banking houses and insurance companies. The first bank estab-

lished in New Orleans after the Louisiana Purchase was the Louisiana Bank in 1804. In 1811 the Bank of Orleans and the Louisiana Planters Bank appeared on the scene. The Louisiana Bank, located on Royal Street in the building currently occupied by the famous Brennen's Restaurant, closed in 1818, but reopened in 1824 as the state-supported Bank of Louisiana. By 1827 five banks were operating in New Orleans, including a branch of the United States Bank, and the Consolidated Association of Planters Bank.

Banks in New Orleans were mostly financed by banking institutions from the Northeast, and especially from England. Banking in antebellum New Orleans was based primarily on the returns of immediate profits rather than long-term meaningful investments. Banks took mortgages on land, slaves, and houses and sold bonds on these mortgages to foreign speculators. The money obtained from the sale of bonds was then passed on to borrowers, who in turn put up their future crops as collateral.

New Orleans grew and prospered despite severe economic depressions in 1820, 1837, and 1839, which were caused in part by shaky banking practices; the adverse financial impact

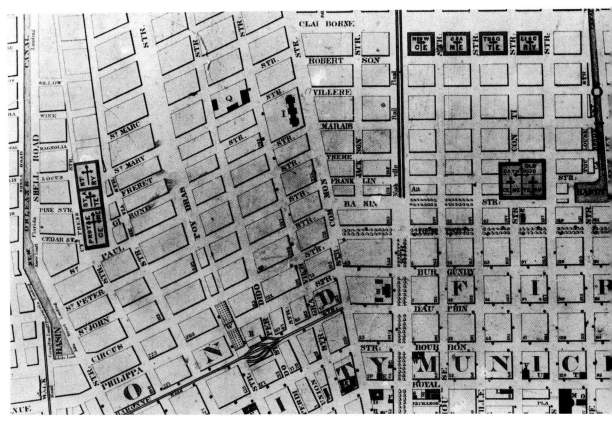

of the new canal system in the Northeast; and the constant fear of yellow-fever epidemics in the port city. As a result, increasing quantities of Western products were transported directly to Eastern ports along the new canals, including the Erie Canal, and along the emerging railroads.

The importance of canals and railroads to commerce was not lost on New Orleanians. In 1830–1831 local investors built the Pontchartrain Railroad from the lower end of the market out through Elysian Fields to Milneburg. They had hoped to develop a port on the lake that would benefit the development in Faubourg Marigny. Other investors above Canal Street, however, especially entrepreneur Samuel J. Peters, were not to be outdone. They formed the New Orleans Canal and Banking Company and, with a charter from the state legislature, built the New Basin Canal from the American Sector to Lake Pontchartrain. Although scores of immigrants lost their lives digging the canal

through the mosquito-infested terrain, the new waterway had a significant impact on the economy of the American Sector. In 1832 another group of investors planned to build a canal to link the city directly to Lake Borgne, but the project failed. Three years later, the Carrollton Railroad began service, connecting the village of Carrollton with New Orleans. The Carrollton Railroad contributed significantly to the development of the suburbs and communities above the city. Today, fashionable residential neighborhoods, universities, and parks line the trackbed of the old railroad, which is still in existence as the St. Charles Avenue Streetcar.

The decades before and after the depressions of 1837 and 1839 were a bustle of activity in New Orleans. Faubourg Ste. Marie above Canal Street was slowly transformed into neat and classically designed "Yankee-styled" red-brick row buildings. Americans and newly arriving immigrants moved upriver to the fashionable Coliseum Square area or to other communities along the river, like the town of Lafayette and the "Garden District," which were annexed by the city in 1852. In the Old Quarter Esplanade Avenue developed its opulence as wealthy Creoles strove to maintain their identity in a changing culture.

Competition was the spirit of the times from the 1830s through the 1850s. Rivalry thrived not only among commission merchants and others seeking their fortunes, but also between cultures.

Architect Benjamin Henry B. Latrobe, writing in his journal in late January 1819, reflected on the changes and cultural clashes taking place in New Orleans during this period:

The state of society at any time here is puzzling. There are in fact three societies here: 1. the French; 2. the American; and 3. the mixed. The French society is not exactly what it was at the change of government, and the American is not strictly what it is in the Atlantic cities. The opportunities of growing rich by more active, extensive and intelligent modes of agriculture and commerce diminished the hospitality, destroyed the leisure, and added more selfishness to the character of the Creoles. The Americans, coming hither to make money. . . . are in an eternal bustle. Their limbs, their heads, and

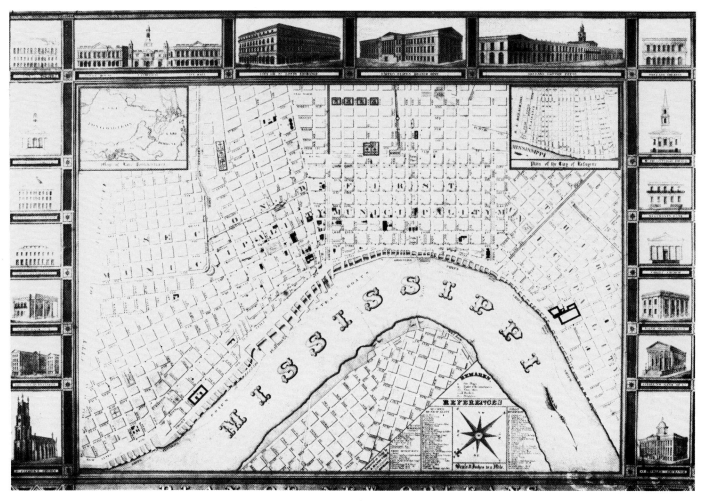

their hearts, move to that sole object, cotton and tobacco, buying and selling, and all the rest of the occupations of a money-making community.

In the early 1830s there existed three well-defined sections in the city: the American Sector above Canal Street, or the Faubourg Ste. Marie; the Vieux Carre; and Faubourg Marigny below Esplanade Avenue. As mentioned earlier, Faubourg Marigny was laid out by the colorful, if not prudent, Bernard Marigny, who gave the streets such interesting names as Desire, Frenchmen, Good Children, and Love.

The competition commercially, politically, and culturally had become so intense by 1836 that the state general assembly gave the city a new charter which divided the city into three separate municipalities. The First Municipality consisted of the Vieux Carre and its predominantly Creole population. The Second Municipality was the American Sector and the Third

Municipality was comprised of the remainder of the city below Esplanade Avenue, including the Faubourg Marigny. Although the three were united theoretically under a mayor and general council, each municipality had its own recorder and council. With minor exceptions, all actions taken by the general council had to be approved by the three individual councils before they could be put into effect. This system lasted until 1852 when the city again was given a new charter. This charter signaled the new political dominance of the American Sector in that the seat of government was moved from the Cabildo at the Place d'Armes to Gallier Hall facing Lafayette Square. This shift in political power away from the conservative sugar planters and French population to the burgeoning American faction was ultimately symbolized by the removal of the state capital from New Orleans to Donaldsville in 1830–1831, then back to New Orleans until 1849 when it was moved to Baton Rouge.

This 1840 Plan of New Orleans was drawn by L. Hirt. New Orleans was divided into distinct sections, each with its own character. The three municipalities were superseded by municipal districts. The Vieux Carre (Old First Municipality) became part of the Second Municipal District, and the American Sector (formerly called the Second Municipality) became part of the First Municipal District. (THNOC)

The emergence of political parties in the 1830s, matched with the cultural differences in the city, made politics a violent business in New Orleans. During the 1840s and 1850s many elections were marred by armed confrontations between Whigs and Democrats and later Native American Party "Know-Nothings" and Democrats. The most serious incidence of political violence was during the election of June 1858. The city became a battlefield between Know-Nothings and the Vigilance Committee which had vowed to "maintain the rights unviolable of every peaceful and law-abiding citizen, restore public order, abate crime, and expel or punish, as the law may determine, such notorious robbers and assassins as the arm of the law has, either from the infidelity of its public servants, or the inefficiency of the laws themselves, left unshipped of justice." The committee decreed that it was assuming police powers and pleaded with the people to join its cause. It seized the state arsenal, the courts, and the jail, and set up an armed camp in Jackson Square. Supported by confiscated artillery, the vigilantes held off Know-Nothing attackers. The group finally dispersed after the elections. The New Orleans *Bee* described politics during those years as "the despotism of faction."

Prosperity and the competitive spirit between sections of the city dramatically changed the landscape of New Orleans. Americans, wanting to emulate other prosperous cities on the East Coast, and Creoles, with their eyes to Europe and to their own architectural heritage, built antebellum New Orleans. Above Canal Street stood such splendors as the St. Charles Hotel, City Hall (Gallier Hall) on Lafayette Square, the University of Louisiana on Common Street, blocks of three-storied red-brick row houses, and the new Customs House at the foot of Canal Street. Below Canal, Creoles and residents of that area boasted of the splendors of the U.S. Mint at Esplanade Avenue and the levee, the newly rebuilt St. Louis Cathedral, and the magnificent Pontalba Buildings facing the Place d'Armes. The construction of these buildings, and the renovation of the Place d'Armes (not yet named Jackson Square) were directed and financed by the Baroness de Pontalba, who had fled to New Orleans with her family after the 1848 revolution in France. She was no stranger to the city, however, for she was the daughter of Don Andres Almonester y Roxas, who contributed considerable sums of money to build a hospital, the Cabildo, St. Louis Cathedral, and other public buildings in

Left
The Second Municipality Hall, as this building was originally named, became the seat of city government in 1852. The building is now known as both Old City Hall and Gallier Hall, after architect James Gallier. (THNOC)

Facing page, bottom
The First Presbyterian Church, Gallier Hall, the St. Charles Hotel (middle distance), and the low dome of the St. Louis Hotel may be seen in this city view looking toward the Vieux Carre. (THNOC)

colonial New Orleans after the fires of 1788 and 1794.

Landscape architect and diarist Frederick Law Olmsted, traveling through the Southern states in 1855–1856, had little good to say about the South except for New Orleans whose uniqueness intrigued him. But he disliked most of the public buildings he encountered in the South, and the city's antebellum St. Charles Hotel was no exception: "I was landed before the great Grecian portico of the stupendous, tasteless, ill-contrived and inconvenient St. Charles Hotel." Not all visitors to the city agreed with Olmsted's opinion of the St. Charles. L. Webb, a young North Carolinian, apparently was awed by the hotel. He noted in his diary on January 24, 1853:

. . . stopping some time to take a look at that most magnificent of hotels, the St. Charles, which was reopened today — two years and one week since it was burned down. It is by far the most elegant hotel I ever saw. The exterior appearance of the building is beautiful in style and architecture with the most perfect and harmonious proportions I ever beheld.

Below
Construction of the Customs House on Canal Street began in 1848. The structure, made of granite, was massive. It took nearly 30 years to complete. Its Marble Hall is reputed to be one of the finest Greek Revival interiors in the U.S. (THNOC)

This second St. Charles Hotel burned to the ground years later and was replaced with a third hotel bearing the same name. But unfortunately, in recent years this New Orleans landmark fell victim to the wrecker's ball and an ill-conceived business venture. The site is now a parking lot.

Ironically, many of the urban reforms made in New Orleans during the early-19th century were initiated not by industrious Yankees but by French-born Joseph Roffignac, who served as the city's mayor from 1820 to 1828. During his administration, the city acquired its first waterworks, which was built by Benjamin Latrobe. Curbs and gutters of the city's main thoroughfares were paved with stone. In 1822 the city sold bonds to pave major streets in the French Quarter and American Sector with cobblestones covered with a layer of fine gravel. Actually, the street-paving began in 1817 with the cobblestoning of a block of Gravier Street between Magazine and Tchoupitoulas streets, but the project proceeded no further. Despite Roffignac's efforts, most of the city's streets went unpaved for several more decades. Roffignac could boast of many more accomplishments during his term in office. Thousands of trees were planted along streets, the levee, and in public squares, many sidewalks — or *banquettes* — were paved with bricks, new drainage canals were dug, two new markets were opened, gutters were flushed with river water, and a clock was placed in the tower of the cathedral.

The St. Charles Hotel, located two blocks from Canal Street, was one of the dominating landmarks in the American Sector of the city. (THNOC)

Built and operated by businessman James Caldwell, the American Theatre (left) and the St. Charles Theater (below left) were located in the American Sector of the city. (THNOC)

One of the most noteworthy events of the Roffignac years was the Marquis de Lafayette's visit to the city in 1825. His visit had a special meaning to New Orleans. Not only was he a famous Frenchman, which endeared him to Creoles, but he was a Revolutionary War hero and a personal friend to both George Washington and Thomas Jefferson. Lafayette arrived in the city on April 10, 1825, aboard the steamboat *Natchez* that had been dispatched to meet him in Mobile. He stepped ashore to a tumultuous fanfare complete with speeches and an arch of triumph erected in the Place d'Armes in his honor. The legislature appropriated $15,000 to prepare an apartment in the Cabildo for his use while visiting the city. From the gallery of the Cabildo, Lafayette overlooked the militia as they passed in review. Special receptions also were held in Caldwell's American Theatre and the Theatre d'Orleans. On April 15 he boarded the *Natchez* and departed for Baton Rouge and other points. Although his visit lasted only four days, it was an event talked about for many years.

Amusement and the arts were always important elements in New Orleans. In the antebellum period town folk and visiting planters with their families frequently enjoyed the many entertainments the city had to offer. The American Theater and others provided plays and concerts by traveling troupes or visiting impresarios. P. T. Barnum and Jenny Lind, the "Swedish Nightingale," were smashing hits in 1851, as was Adelina Patti, the 18-year-old soprano opera singer, a few years later.

Prosperity brought the artists and their studios flourished. Many of the works of both native and visiting artists, such as Adrien Persac, Jules Lion, Vaudechamp, G.P.A. Healy, and John Wesley Jarvis have survived to this day.

Then there was the opera, where blacks and whites, rich and poor — sitting in separate sections, of course — could hear a Bellini, a Meyerbeer, or a Donizetti opera at one of the several opera houses in the city. There was the St. Charles Theater in the American Sector and the Theatre d'Orleans in the French Quarter, and later the new French Opera House on fashionable Bourbon Street.

A gentleman could take fencing lessons from one of the several fencing masters in the Quarter on Exchange Alley; or perhaps an evening could be spent at one of the several gentlemen's clubs, be it the Boston Club on Canal Street, named for the then-popular card game, the Pelican Club, the Pickwick Club, or even Odd Fellows Hall on Camp Street. It was not uncommon for some gentlemen to keep concubines, including mulattoes, quadroons, and octoroons of legendary beauty. Men of less means but of equal infidelity enjoyed the many brothels and "dance halls" for which the city was famous. During certain seasons, a gentleman and his lady could enjoy a cotillion at the St. Charles or equally popular St. Louis Hotel

in the Vieux Carre. Idle time could also be spent at gambling, for which the Creoles were noted, or one of the many sporting events popular during the era, including horse racing, sailing on the lake, rowing in the Mississippi, and boxing.

For a family outing, there was the city library or art gallery, or an afternoon in a public square watching children play a game of cricket. Evenings often were passed listening to a visiting lecturer speaking at one of the many public halls or taking in the sights of a traveling circus stopping over for a few weeks. A fine meal could be had at the St. Charles or St. Louis hotels or one of the many fine restaurants, such as Antoine's, Victor's, or Moreau's.

New Orleans also became famous during these years for its international intrigues. The city abounded with young men looking for adventure, as well as merchants and other financiers ready to stake a filibustering expedition against some small Latin American country with its promise of riches and profits in return. Perhaps the most famous of these New Orleans-based intrigues were the Texas Revolution in 1835; General Narcisco Lopez's abortive invasion of Cuba in 1851; and William Walker's unsuccessful campaign against Nicaragua in 1855. And without question, the city's most famous den of intrigue was the three-story Banks Arcade, on Magazine near Gravier Street, which was built by Thomas Banks in 1833. New Orleanians also thoroughly enjoyed General Zachary Taylor's de-

During antebellum times the St. Louis Exchange Hotel was an elegant place to stay or dine in the French Quarter. It was located at the corner of St. Louis and Royal Streets. The hotel, demolished in the early 20th century, was replaced by the Royal Orleans (THNOC)

parture for the Mexican War in 1845 and were beside themselves with excitement upon his victorious return in 1847.

Without question, however, the most famous of New Orleans' pastimes came once a year — Mardi Gras. Mardi Gras balls in New Orleans were as old as the city itself. But not until the late 1820s did Mardi Gras celebrations begin to take the form for which they have become so widely known.

The Mardi Gras parade reportedly began as early as the 1820s and continued for three dec-

ades as an unwieldly and diverse band of masquers winding through the streets throwing confetti and flour upon onlookers. The practice of throwing flour eventually was stopped when some mischievous masquers threw quick-lime into the faces of spectators. The first parade utilizing vehicles was in 1839 when an odd assortment of wagons and carriages paraded from the Orleans Theater on Orleans Street, up Royal Street to St. Charles, down Julia to Camp Street, Chartres, Conde, Esplanade, and back up Royal to the Orleans Theater. That

night a ball was held at the theater for the more affluent participants. This type of procession continued off and on for the next five or six years. Ironically, the first carnival organization in New Orleans was not formed by the Creoles of the city, but by the Anglo-American community. Taking their lead from the Cowbellions of Mobile, who held their first parade on New Year's Eve 1831, 12 prominent Americans founded the Mistick Krewe of Comus and the

Pickwick Club in 1857. Comus held its first parade that year with Milton's *Paradise Lost* as its theme. Mardi Gras, which at one time had been almost exclusively a Creole event, was by the end of the era celebrated by all segments of the community — whites, blacks, Americans, Creoles, newly arriving immigrants, Catholics, and Protestants.

Not everyone, however, was enamored by the annual festivities, including the young

North Carolinian Webb, who described a Mardi Gras parade in 1853:

The street was full of men, women and children of the lower classes on foot and the higher in carriages —
As I walked down the street, I was met by a crowd of boys and men fantastically dressed and masked running with a crowd at their heels who were hollering and yelling and filling the air with flour, eggs, and mud which they were throwing at the maskers who in turn filled the eyes of all with whom they came in contact with flour — I got out of the way, least they should give me some of their favors in the liberal distribution.
These had hardly passed when I heard not far distant the yelling of the boys which betokened another crowd of maskers coming — I went towards them and saw coming down the street a large cart filled with men in masks and fantastic dresses. Just as I approached, they stopped the cart and sprang out with horrid rath and accused someone in the crowd of spectators of throwing stones at them. They were all armed with short heavy clubs and soon got into a row in which several of the maskers and spectators got bloody noses — One great ruffanly [sic] fellow pounced upon a small boy and beat him badly — arousing my indignation and contempt which I could have given him positive proof of had I been able. . . . After several fights in which neither party gained anything, they mounted their cart and proceeded on followed by a crowd of yelling boys.
There were maskers on horseback and on foot — male and female followed by crowds. The whole street was alive with spectators and the scene to me was certainly strange and as a hideous or foolish looking masker would pass me and the horrid oaths and noises fell upon my ears, I could not help exclaim — Is this festival recognized by the Church of Rome. Can any Christian Church countenance much less allow such a profanation of its ceremonies.

New Orleans was indeed a place in which one could make his fortune or enjoy the many pleasures of life. But there was also poverty, squalor, and disease. The almost annual visitation of yellow fever took thousands of lives and sent wealthier residents fleeing to summer cottages in Mandeville, north of Lake Pontchartrain, or to the Mississippi Gulf Coast to avoid the misery. Cholera, typhus, and other plagues took their tolls as well. New Orleans, famed for its port, also gained recognition as being one of the unhealthiest cities in the world.

In 1856 the Louisiana Board of Health attributed 2,760 deaths in a one-year period to yellow fever, 1,029 deaths to cholera, and 652 deaths to tuberculosis. By far the most serious yellow-fever epidemic hit the city in the summer of 1853. Not knowing the cause of the dreaded disease, city officials tried a multitude of tactics to stop the disease from spreading: cannons were fired into the air in the belief that yellow fever lingered in the clouds, ships entering the port were quarantined, and a day of prayer was offered; mass graves were dug for the dead victims of the pestilence. New Orleanians died in such staggering numbers that open wagons made the rounds through the city to pick up heat-swollen, rotting bodies. In stacks of 50 or more they were carted to the cemetery where they were buried in shallow graves. A reporter for the New Orleans *Crescent* described one mass grave as nothing more than a ditch 14-inches deep. The coffins, he wrote, were placed side by side in the trench with their tops clearly above the ground level. About a foot of dirt was placed over the tops of the coffins. After a rainstorm, the caskets and their grotesque occupants clearly could be seen.

New Orleans businessman Zac Robertson, writing in 1853 to his business associate in Massachusetts, described some of the horrors he saw almost daily in the city:

DIED.

November 1st, 1871, of yellow fever, in Iberville parish, La., **EDWARD TURNER,** son of LEMUEL P. and FANNIE E. CONNER, aged 11 years 7 months and 29 days.

The scourge of yellow fever hit New Orleans and the southern part of Louisiana nearly every summer for many years. Epidemics varied in severity and continued until the early 20th century when improved drainage helped eliminate mosquito breeding grounds. (THNOC)

Despite the heroic work of the city's physicians, nurses, and the benevolent Howard Association, over 8,000 men, women, and children lost their lives that summer. Hardest struck among the city's population were the immigrants arriving in America with hope for a new life. Writing in his diary on June 11, 1853, just before the worst of the epidemic was to strike, Webb reflected on a shipload of German immigrants entering the port:

The Battle of New Orleans, yellow fever, commerce, and steamboats were all major factors in shaping the history of antebellum New Orleans, but perhaps the most interesting aspect of that era was the people themselves. As the visiting Frederick Olmsted graphically described:

This is how New Orleans looked to the thousands of European immigrants who arrived in the city during the two decades before the Civil War. (THNOC)

During the two decades preceding the Civil War, immigrants from Europe arrived in the city by the thousands. Most shipped from the ports of Liverpool, Havre, Bremen, and Hamburg for voyages lasting up to six weeks. Packed into steerage many did not survive the crossing. By far the two largest groups of immigrants were the Irish and Germans, who left the problems of their homelands for the promise of the New World. By 1860 almost 25,000 Irish resided in the city. Many of the Germans who arrived in New Orleans did not remain but moved in farther upriver. Prospects of cheaper land elsewhere, yellow-fever epidemics in the city, and competing slave labor discouraged most immigrants from remaining in New Orleans. Those who did stay became merchants, tradesmen, and laborers. They generally settled along with the Irish below Esplanade Avenue, or in Lafayette, or along the New Basin Canal. Some also settled on small farms in the village of Carrollton above the city. Many Irish and Germans crowded into tenement houses in the "Irish Channel" between Magazine Street and the river.

Two segments of the New Orleans population unique to pre-Civil War America were the Creoles and the free-people-of-color. Historians as well as travelers to the city in the antebellum era often differed widely in their views and descriptions of the Creoles. Even the word Creole, itself, and as it applies to New Orleans, has never been defined adequately. In colonial times, it generally meant native born, but of European ancestry including Irish, German, English, French, and Spanish. To early-19th century Americans, the word was usually used to differentiate the descendants of old colonial families of Louisiana from the new arrivals. During both periods, French-speaking blacks and free-people-of-color also were called Creoles to distinguish them from their English-speaking counterparts from other parts of the nation.

Creoles, as did their American counterparts, occupied all levels of society from laborer, shopkeeper, and merchant to the local aristocracy. By the 1850s the upper classes of all three sections of the city's population—Creole, Anglo-American, and immigrant—were intermarrying, forming not only familial bonds but economic ones. The sons of the wealthier classes of Creoles often enjoyed a Paris education while their daughters were sent to the nuns at the Ursuline Convent for training.

The physical beauty of Creole women is legendary and has been retold by generations. Describing female society in New Orleans in 1819, Benjamin Latrobe wrote:

This French drawing is entitled La Creole. The charms of Creole women in New Orleans have been a topic of conversation—and disagreement—from earliest times. (THNOC)

The Duke of Saxe-Weimar, visiting the city in
the 1820s, praised the Creoles, but Karl Anton
Postl, of Germany, noted that Creole women
were poorly educated and unable to carry on
an intelligent literary conversation. A comparable view came from L. Webb who wrote in
April 1853:

Much has been written about blacks and
slavery in the antebellum South. The horrors of
the system in the "land of the free" have been
condemned and rationalized by generations of
historians and polemics. By 1860 there were
approximately 25,000 blacks living in the city
of which almost 11,000 were slaves owned either by local whites and free blacks or just arriving in the city and awaiting sale on the auction
block. New Orleans, one of the major slave
markets in the South, had a number of auction
places in the city, including the Cabildo; the St.
Charles, and St. Louis hotels; and Maspero's
on Chartres Street.

*As suggested by this drawing
entitled* A Slave Pen at New
Orleans-Before the Auction, *New Orleans was a major
center of slave trade in the
South. (THNOC)*

Although slaves in the border and northernmost slave states shuddered at the thought of being sent "downriver," some historians apparently believe that slaves in New Orleans may have had a better lot than those in other areas. University of North Carolina historian Loren Schweniger wrote that:

. . . many blacks, slave and free, considered the slave trading capital of the south . . . as a place of enjoyment, excitement, and delectation, even, ironically, as a refuge from the brutalities of the South's 'peculiar institution.' They rejoiced at the city's heterogeneous mixture of peoples, its thriving river front, its delightful shops, cafes, restaurants, and hotels, its numerous theatres, amusements and sporting events.

Slaves in the city were generally used in domestic work or were leased out to local shops, companies, the city, and on the docks. The majority of slave owners in New Orleans owned less than three slaves; few owned more than that number, including the approximately 700 free blacks who owned slaves.

A slave could gain his freedom through one of several ways. Freedom could be purchased, which was not an uncommon event, or the slave owner could simply free his slave through legal action or in a will. The legislature could manumit a slave or slaves for some particular service. Almost 300 slaves in the city gained their freedom through the local office of the American Colonization Society. One of the society's founders was New Orleans philanthropist, John McDonogh.

As the abolitionist rhetoric increased in the South in the late 1850s, freedom for a slave

New Orleans community were the free-people-of-color. Free blacks occupied all levels of enterprise in the city from draymen to journalists: there were shopkeepers, cabinetmakers, barbers, plantation owners, artists, writers, publishers, and investors. There were some very wealthy free-people-of-color who owned millions of dollars in real estate in the city. Free blacks also manned the sea-going ships and steamers constantly moving in and out of the port. The life-styles of the free blacks paralleled their counterparts, and often relatives, in the white community.

The *gens de couleur libres,* free-people-of-color, community produced many gifted artists, composers, and writers, many of whom were educated in European universities. Unfortunately, social conditions in New Orleans at the time drove many of these talented people to take refuge in Southern European cities where race was not a barrier to creative expression.

Despite the artificial handicaps of race in New Orleans, the talented *gens de couleur libres* produced. Their contributions in the arts and letters ranged from pedestrian to excellent. The list of writers and poets is a long one and includes Armand Lanusse (1812–1867), editor of *Les Cenelles* (1845), the first anthology of poetry by free-men-of-color in America; Camille Thierry (1814–1875); Pierre Dalcour; and, Victor Sejour. Sejour enjoyed considerable literary success in Paris, including work with the Comedie-Francaise.

Free-people-of-color excelled in the visual arts, and in some cases, gained international reputations. Jules Lion was one of the city's earliest lithographers and daguerreotypists. Without question two of the city's most talented sculptors during this era were the Warburg brothers, Eugene and Joseph Daniel. They were the sons of Daniel Warburg, a member of the important Jewish family of Hamburg, Germany, and his slave-mistress, Marie-Rose, a native of Santiago, Cuba. Warburg freed her and she bore him five children. Eugene moved to Paris where he gained considerable fame while his brother, Joseph Daniel, remained in New Orleans practicing his art. Perhaps Eugene's most famous work is the bust of United States Minister to France, John Young Mason, which was executed in 1855. Joseph Daniel's son, Daniel, carried on the art.

became almost impossible to secure. City and state officials, fearful of outside agitators stirring up trouble among the slaves and free blacks, passed strict regulations governing the personal liberties of both free blacks and slaves.

Perhaps the most fascinating segment of the

The best example of the younger "Daniel" Warburg's work is the carved column of the Holcome-Aiken monument in Metairie Cemetery.

Like their free-black counterparts, many gifted white New Orleanians also traveled to Europe to find success. Such was the case of Paul Morphy, the international chess champion, Louis Moreau Gottschalk, and Ernest Guiraud. Gottschalk was born in New Orleans in 1829 and at the age of 13 traveled to Paris to study music. Before his death while on tour in Rio de Janeiro in 1869, Gottschalk had gained considerable fame and acclaim in Europe and America for his musical compositions, many of which were based on the music and dances he had heard and seen slaves perform in Congo Square. His best-known composition was *La Bamboula,* based on a popular dance among the city's early French-speaking slaves. Guiraud, born in the city in 1837, also went to Paris to study music. During his career in Europe, which spanned several decades, Guiraud gained distinction for his operatic compositions, won the Prix de Rome, and became a teacher at the Paris Conservatory. Perhaps Guiraud's most long-lasting accomplishments were the music he wrote for portions of the famed opera, *Carmen,* after the death of its composer, Georges Bizet, and completion of the unfinished *Tales of Hoffmann,* when Jacques Offenbach died.

The people, architecture, climate, and its history indeed made New Orleans a unique city in antebellum America. Despite highs and lows in its economy, the Crescent City was riding high on a wave of economic prosperity by the end of the 1850s, the golden era of the antebellum years. The banks were strong and the cotton crops were setting new records. European textile mills were buying all the cotton they could get. Sugar prices were kept high by protective tariffs and the city's port was in constant activity. A considerable amount of the commerce of the Midwest passed across the city's wharves each day.

The nation, however, was racing toward civil war. New Orleans joined the political struggle with as much fervor as it did the acquisition of commercial wealth. The city's adherence to the Southern cause was understandable yet confusing. The city had prospered under the economic protection of the United States, and its commercial and familial connections with the North and Midwest were greater than any other Southern city. The Civil War would bring economic ruin and stagnation to a city that had looked ahead only to prosperity.

William Mure, the British consul in New Orleans caught the despair and ruinous impact of secession agitation in the city just after the election of Abraham Lincoln. In a letter to Foreign Secretary Lord John Russell in December 1860 Mure wrote:

Your Lordship is aware that this city, from its geographical position, is the great entrepot of the agricultural produce of the Valley of the Mississippi, and of the great Western States, the value of which received during the last year, reached the enormous sum of 185 millions of dollars. It did not seem probable, therefore, that such vast interests would be imperiled without due and deliberate consideration. And yet, within three weeks after the (Presidential) election, and before any overt act of hostility could be committed by the President-elect, the agitation of the question of dissolution of the Union has been so widespread as entirely to destroy confidence — obstruct the usual channels of trade and depreciate the value of property of all kinds to a runious state.

Before a shot was fired and even before secession and the formation of the Confederacy, New Orleans was feeling the effects of the coming storm.

WASHINGTON ARTILLERY

OF
NEW ORLEANS.

RECRUITS WANTED.

Officers of this Battalion are now in the South to enlist such Young Men, citizens of Louisiana, as are within conscript ages, who may come forward and offer themselves for service.

By special authority of the Secretary of War, any person liable to conscription may be enlisted, and conscripts enrolled may be assigned to fill up this organization.

A bounty of FIFTY DOLLARS will be paid to all liable to conscription, who come properly recommended.

The recruiting stations will be Mobile, Ala.; Jackson, Miss; and other points on the N. O. J. & G. N. R. Road, nearer New Orleans.

Captain M. B. MILLER, 3d Company, will be stationed at Mobile, as Recruiting Officer; and Captain SQUIRES, 1st Company; Captain RICHARDSON, 2d Company, and Lieut. NORCOM, 4th Company, at Jackson, and vicinity, to whom or to the undersigned, at Mobile, applications may be addressed.

J. B. WALTON,

Col. Com'g and Chief of Artillery, 1st Army Corps, Dep. Nor. Va.

I have established my Recruiting Office at Room No. 82, Bowman House, Jackson, Miss.

C. W. SQUIRES,

Captain and Recruiting Officer, Battalion Washington Artillery.

CHAPTER V
"THE UNION MUST AND SHALL BE PRESERVED"

On January 26, 1861, Louisiana somewhat reluctantly seceded from the Union, a decision that would result in death, destruction, financial chaos, and social upheaval. The years of debate on the constitutionality of secession were soon followed by years of war, occupation, Reconstruction, and economic stagnation.

Not all New Orleanians favored breaking off from the Union, although most agreed in principle that a state had the right to secede. Ties to the North, both economic and social, were especially strong in New Orleans. According to historian Charles Roland, "Much of the population of the Deep South's chief metropolis, New Orleans," was against secession. This was especially true among the "merchants and bankers because of their economic ties with the North, and the European immigrants because of their newly kindled American patriotism . . . and their opposition to slavery." The European immigrants, who comprised some 40 percent of New Orleans' white population, also had lingering class resentment they had brought with them from Europe. Even among the sugar planters, who would seem to have had a vested interest in preserving slavery, "there was an important element with exceptionally firm ties to the Union."

Some observers realized that New Orleans and the rest of the South lacked the resources to win a protracted war with the industrially more advanced Northern states. In an 1858 speech to a commercial convention in Montgomery, Alabama, Louisiana newspaper editor J.D.B. DeBow wryly emphasized the South's dependency on Northern industry by describing his journey to Montgomery:

They will start in some stage or railroad coach made in the North; and an engine of Northern manufacture will take their train or boat along; at every meal they will sit down in Yankee chairs, to a Yankee table, spread with a Yankee cloth. With a Yankee spoon they will take from Yankee dishes sugar, salt, and coffee which have paid tribute to Yankee trade, and with Yankee knives and forks they will put into their mouths the only thing Southern they will get on the trip.

After Lincoln's election the voices for moderation gave way to those of the firebrands and the demands in the city press for secession. On December 14 the New Orleans *Bee* claimed: "The North and South are heterogeneous and better apart. . . . We are doomed if we proclaim not our political Independence." Louisiana's representatives in the U.S. Senate, Judah P. Benjamin and John Slidell (a native New Yorker), joined forces to declare: "We must be blind indeed if we entertain the re-

motest hope that widespread ruin, degradation and dishonor will not inevitably result from tame submission to the rule which our enemies propose to inaugurate." Their prediction came true, of course, but directly as a result of the course they steered.

Public reaction to secession was generally enthusiastic. The New Orleans *Picayune* proclaimed: "The deed has been done. We breathe deeper and freer for it. The Union is dead. . . . No government ever rose as she did — none has ever so perished." But some Louisiana residents were deeply sorrowed by the growing schism in the nation. Superintendent William Tecumseh Sherman of the State Seminary of Learning in Alexandria (forerunner of Loui-

Overleaf
One of the oldest military units in Louisiana, the Washington Artillery recruited many volunteers for the Confederate army. Broadsides such as this one helped spread the word throughout the Southern states. (THNOC)

Left
Adolph Rinck painted this portrait of Judah P. Benjamin. Benjamin was a United States Senator from Louisiana, as was John Slidell, when the war broke out. Benjamin also held the post of Secretary of War in the Confederacy. (THNOC)

Below left
This picture entitled Cotton Pressing in Louisiana *illustrates that the economy of the South was primarily a plantation economy, based on agriculture. Slavery made this type of system profitable but produced a heavy reliance on the Northern states and Europe for manufactured goods. (THNOC)*

siana State University) resigned his post. He wrote to Governor Thomas O. Moore, stating that, "if Louisiana withdraws from the Federal Union, I prefer to maintain my allegiance to the Constitution as long as a fragment of it survives."

Louisiana was an independent nation between January 26, the date of secession, and March 21, when it joined the Confederacy. The governor served as president, the legislature as a congress. At first the state flag was used as the national emblem, but in February the convention adopted a new flag, consisting of 13 stripes—six white, four blue, and three red—and a yellow star on a field of red in the upper left corner. The stripes represented the original 13 American colonies; the three colors, the tricolor French flag; and the yellow star, the state's Spanish heritage. The "new nation" began immediately to mobilize for war. Governor Moore appointed a military board to coordinate the establishment of training camps and the issuing of arms to volunteers. Moore also ordered the seizure of U.S. government installations in Louisiana, including armories, barracks, and the U.S. Mint.

The extraordinarily diverse strains of Louisiana's ethnic makeup were brought together in the initial enthusiasm surrounding the anticipation of war. Nowhere was the strange, colorful mixture of national uniforms and weaponry more apparent than in New Orleans. Foreign papers sent correspondents to the city to report on the activities of their former nationals. An English reporter wrote that the streets of New Orleans "were full of Turcos, Zouaves, Chasseurs . . . there are Pickwick rifles, LaFayette rifles, Beauregard guards, Macmahon guards, and Irish, German, Italian, Spanish, and native volunteers." Gangs of Irishmen reportedly roamed the streets, exhorting the city's Spanish residents to join them in the war effort, saying: "For the love of the Virgin and your own soul's sake, Fernandy, get up and cum along wid us to fight the Yankees."

Their chance to "fight the Yankees" would soon come. On April 12, 1861, (less than a month after Louisiana formally joined the Confederacy), Southern troops under Louisiana General Pierre Gustave Toutant Beauregard opened fire on Fort Sumter in Charleston Harbor and the war was on. Louisiana, during the next year of fighting, supplied men and mate-

Left
General P.G.T. Beauregard was one of the South's military leaders during the Civil War. After the war he remained active in public affairs in New Orleans. (THNOC)

Below
This Panorama of the Seat of War *by John Bachmann was published in 1861. In addition to showing the geographic relationships of key cities and forts, it shows how dependent the South was on maritime commerce, and consequently, how much it was affected by the Union blockade. (THNOC)*

rials to the Confederate forces in Virginia, while also preparing in case the clouds of war should descend within its own boundaries. By the spring of 1862, it had become increasingly clear that those clouds would first descend on New Orleans. Possession of the city and the lower Mississippi River was strategically essential to either side's control of the West. But, despite pleas from Major General Mansfield Lovell—Confederate commander of the city and son of former U.S. Surgeon General Dr. Joseph Lovell—the Confederate government which

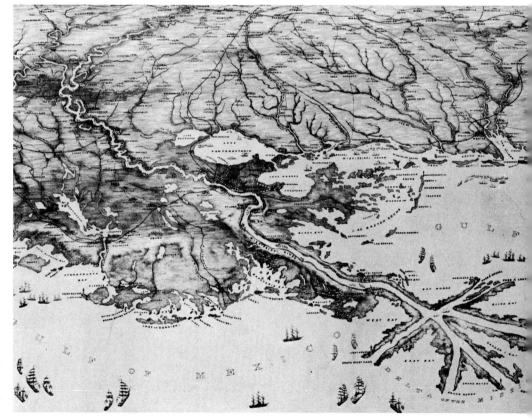

considered the war in the East more important, ignored New Orleans and the rest of the state. Troops and materiel essential to the defense of the Crescent City were sent elsewhere. Lovell was ordered to send most of his trained soldiers to Corinth, Mississippi, to join General Albert Sidney Johnston and General Beauregard. This left the defense of New Orleans to "ninety-day" troops, most of whom were untrained and undisciplined. Moreover, the economy of the port city had been in chaos since the Federal blockade of the Mississippi began on May 26, 1861. Prices soared as imported goods, medicines, manufactured products, and other essential items became scarce. The city opened a free market to feed and clothe hundreds of poor families. The cost of a 40-pound box of soap rose from $5 to $19 and flour brought up to $20 a barrel when available. New Orleanians learned to do without or to rely on their own ingenuity. When coffee, a long-time favorite beverage, became in short supply, newspapers suggested such additives as milled okra, rye seeds, or toasted and ground sweet potatoes. When paper grew scarce, newspapers put out smaller editions or used wallpaper or anything else they could get.

By the end of February 1862, a U.S. Naval fleet, under the command of Flag Officer David G. Farragut, had begun to concentrate near Ship Island off the Mississippi Gulf Coast. On Ship Island was Major General Benjamin F. Butler with a large force of Federal troops.

Union Captain David G. Farragut, who had moved to New Orleans from Tennessee as a child, captured the city on April 24, 1862. Three months later he was promoted to rear admiral. From Cirker, Dictionary of American Portraits, Dover, 1967.

On April 18 Federal gunboats began to bombard Fort Jackson and Fort St. Philip, which protected the lower river and the approach to New Orleans. For the next six days skirmishes continued between the U.S. Navy and the Confederate batteries. Then, in the pre-dawn of April 24, the Federal fleet piped all hands to deck and made a bold run by the forts, which had been considered impassable since the days of the Battle of New Orleans in 1815. Spectators reported that the battle was furious and magnificent.

Confederate Captain William B. Robertson, viewing the action from the batteries of Fort Jackson, described the splendor of the pyrotechnics:

The mortar-shells shot upward from the mortar boats, rushed to the apexes of their flight, flashing the lights of their fuses as they revolved, paused an instant, and then descended upon our works like hundreds of meteors, or burst in mid-air, hurling their jagged fragments in every direction. The guns on both sides kept up a continual roar for nearly an hour, without a moment's intermission, and produced a shimmering illumination, which, though beautiful and grand was illusive in its effect upon the eye, and made it impossible to judge accurately the distance of the moving vessels from us.

A Union army officer, observing the battle from a distance, wrote that one could "combine all that you have heard of thunder, add to it all that you have ever seen of lightning, and you have, perhaps a conception of the scene." From aboard the Union flag ship *Hartford*, an officer likened the battle scene to "the breaking up of the universe with the moon and all the stars bursting in our midst." The grandeur of the spectacle was not lost on Farragut himself, who later said "it was as if the artillery of heaven were playing upon the earth."

Despite over four hours of almost constant fire from both the Union and Confederate forces, the casualties were surprisingly low. On the Union side, 37 were killed and 147 wounded. Fort Jackson had 9 killed and 33 wounded, while Fort St. Philip had two killed and four wounded. Fifty-seven Confederates were killed aboard the vessel the *Governor*

This depiction of the bombardment of forts Jackson and St. Philip appeared in a French newspaper of the time. These forts, located on the Mississippi River some miles below New Orleans, were virtually the only barriers between Farragut's fleet and New Orleans. (THNOC)

A ferocious battle took place between the Union fleet and the forces manning the forts below the city. (THNOC)

Moore and 16 more fatalities were recorded aboard other Confederate naval craft. Union Commander David Porter later denounced Commander Mitchell of the Confederate ironclad *Louisiana* in his journal: "Had her commander possessed the soul of a flea, he could have driven us all out of the river."

After the Federal ships passed the forts, 250 mutineers manning Fort Jackson rose in revolt, spiked the cannons, and ran away. Many of them were later picked up by Federal patrol boats. In desperation, Lovell considered attacking the Federal fleet, boarding the ships and driving the invaders off in hand-to-hand combat: but he later gave up the idea when he could not find enough volunteers.

Defeated, Lovell reported the reasons for the city's loss to his superiors. In addition to untrained troops and insufficient weaponry the "unprecedented" high water in the river had washed away shipping obstructions, contractors had failed to complete the construction of the ironclads *Louisiana* and *Mississippi* on schedule, and two naval officers had disobeyed orders by not placing the *Louisiana* in a battery position near the forts and by not dispatching the fire rafts downriver against the Federal fleet.

"The river-defense fleet," he wrote, "proved a failure . . . unable to govern themselves, and unwilling to be governed by others, their almost total want of system, vigilance and discipline

DIMENSIONS:
4000 Tons,
4 Engines,
2 Wheels,
2 Propellers.

rendered them nearly useless and helpless when the enemy finally dashed upon them suddenly on a dark night."

Panic seized New Orleans residents when word reached the city that Farragut had passed the forts. People began destroying their Confederate money and officials ordered the destruction of anything that could be used by the Yankees. Warehouses of cotton, sugar, molasses, tobacco, and lumber were put to the torch. Ships lying idle along the wharves were sunk. Amid the blaze, smoke, and confusion, the Confederate army withdrew from the city, making its way to the Florida Parishes across Lake Pontchartrain. Angry mobs roamed the streets, looting stores, and hanging a man because he looked like a stranger.

Mayor John T. Monroe, however, refused to surrender the city and for the next week there was a standoff between the mayor and Farragut. Farragut, at one point, threatened to bombard the defenseless city unless it surrendered. Monroe wrote defiantly to the admiral, stating: "We will stand your bombardment, unarmed and undefended as we are. The civilized world will consign to indelible infamy the heart that will conceive the deed and the band that will dare to consummate it." Foreign consuls residing in the city met with Farragut to dissuade him from such a course and the captain

of a French warship in port reportedly told Farragut that he would have to account to the French nation if he bombarded the city.

On April 29 word reached the city that the two forts below the city had surrendered. Farragut ordered Mayor Monroe to lower all Louisiana and Confederate flags in the city. He sent a naval squad ashore to remove the Louisiana state flag from atop the City Hall. Monroe was permitted to remain in office until the Union Army arrived. New Orleans was now an occupied city.

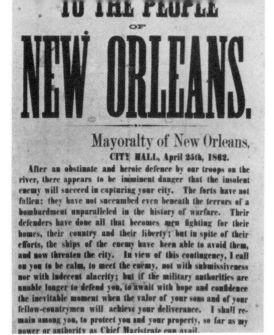

Although fighting continued in the rest of the state until well into 1865 — even after Lee's surrender at Appomattox — the loss of New Orleans had grave consequences for the Confederacy's war effort. According to historian Charles Dufour, the city's occupation gave the Federal forces a base of operations that would eventually allow them to divide the Confederacy in half at the Mississippi River. The flow of supplies from Rebels in Texas to the Southeast would be severely hampered, and the South had lost New Orleans' essential machine shops and foundries. Lost, too, were the ironclads *Louisiana* and *Mississippi* that the Confederacy had hoped to use to break the Union blockade of Southern ports. Beyond these practical considerations, the capture of New Orleans dealt a severe blow to Southern morale.

On May 1, 1862, Major General Butler, a Massachusetts politician turned warrior, arrived in New Orleans and took formal possession of it. He ordered Mayor Monroe and former U.S. Senator Pierre Soule arrested. In Monroe's place, Butler named General George F. Sheply as the military commandant of the city. He established a military provost court to try civil and criminal cases. A month after entering the city, Butler ordered the hanging of William Mumford from the flagpole of the U.S. Mint, where he had cut down the American flag in protest of the occupation of the city. He monitored local newspapers carefully to make sure they did not instigate defiance among the populace against the Federal troops and government. He even admonished several Episcopal clergymen for not offering prayers for President Lincoln.

Five months after taking possession of the city, Butler implemented the Federal Confiscation Act, which the government had enacted on July 17 and which called for the seizure of the private property of all "unreconstructed" Rebels in the Southern states who would not swear allegiance to the United States. By the end of October, almost 70,000 New Orleanians had taken the oath. Because of its early capture, New Orleans would have the dubious distinction of enduring Reconstruction, a term yet to be coined, for a longer period than any other city of the South — nearly 15 years, from May 1, 1862, to April 24, 1877.

Butler's administration has been viewed by

generations of New Orleanians as thoroughly corrupt. His subordinate officers, including his brother, Andrew Jackson Butler, reportedly made fortunes by acquiring confiscated goods at public auction, purchasing items, in many cases for 10 percent of their value. General Butler, whether or not he personally profited from this practice, acquired the nicknames "Silver Spoon" (sometimes just "Spoons") and "Beast Butler." The verb to "Butlerize" became synonymous with "to steal."

But the general's most notorious act was the issuance of General Order No. 28, which was denounced in Europe and even in some quarters in the North. Order No. 28 was designed to counteract "insults" directed against Federal officers and their soldiers, which were often the only way New Orleanians dissatisfied with occupation could fight back. The city's women were reputed to be especially insulting, so Butler devised the following solution:

As the officers and soldiers of the United States have been subject to repeated insults from the women (calling themselves ladies) of New Orleans in return for the most scrupulous noninterference and courtesy on our part, it is ordered that hereafter when any female shall, by word, gesture, or movement, insult or show contempt for any officer of the United States, she shall be regarded and held liable to be treated as a woman of the town plying her avocation.

Modern historians, removed in time from Butler's occasionally outrageous behavior, have been kinder in evaluating his administration. Credit has been given Butler for the improvements and reforms he made in the city. Upon capturing New Orleans, he had quickly restored order to a city he described as "seven miles long by two to four wide, of a hundred and fifty thousand inhabitants, all hostile, bitter, defiant, explosive." He kept his troops under tight discipline, hanging four of them for plundering homes. He fixed prices to prevent unscrupulous profit-taking. Butler instituted special taxes to feed the poor and support orphanages; at one point, 10,000 families were reported to be receiving support. The public school system was reorganized under Butler, and it remained, at least in concept, little changed into modern times. He enforced fumigation laws and quarantine regulations, and put to work thousands of unemployed

Above
Of all the orders issued during Butler's administration, General Order No. 28 is probably the most remembered. This Harper's Weekly *"before and after"* drawing illustrates the effects of this edict from the Northern viewpoint. (THNOC)

Left
Sale of Confiscated Blood-Horses at New Orleans *illustrates how property of those not loyal to the Union was confiscated and sold. Corruption on the part of some officials allowed large fortunes to be amassed from the sale of such goods.* (THNOC)

whites and blacks—almost 10,000 of whom flocked to the city from nearby plantations—cleaning streets, enlarging drainage canals, and rebuilding wharves and levees. Blacks not working on city improvements joined the army or were sent back to the plantations to work the fields as wage earners. Unfortunately, many of them fell victim to unscrupulous Federal bureaucrats who stole their wages. After 1865 the Freedman's Bureau was created by Congress to care for the former slaves and to find land for them among the abandoned and confiscated plantations, an effort which was ultimately unsuccessful. To restore the economy of the city, Butler lifted the Federal blockade into the interior of the state, but Confederates embargoed all goods to New Orleans. The items which managed to get through Confederate lines found a ready market in the city.

On December 12, 1862, Butler was replaced by General Nathaniel P. Banks, a former governor of Massachusetts and speaker of the U.S. House of Representatives. Butler left New Orleans quietly and without fanfare, but not forgotten. Banks perhaps is best known in Louisiana history for his military exploits rather than his reorganization of the "Free State" of Louisiana, which meant that portion of the state occupied by Federal troops.

Banks' troops were long remembered for their expeditions into the Bayou Lafourche and Bayou Teche areas, where they confiscated plantations, cattle, sugar, cotton, and household furnishings, and destroyed salt and sulphur mines so vital to the Confederate cause. Between May and July 1863, Banks with about 50,000 Federal troops, including former slaves and free blacks from New Orleans, defeated the Confederates at the river town of Port Hudson north of Baton Rouge after weeks of siege, bombardment, and bloody skirmishes. Port Hudson, the Confederate's last stronghold on the Mississippi, fell on July 9, five days after the surrender of Vicksburg. It was a battle in which white Confederate New Orleanians fought, killed, and were killed by black New Orleanians wearing the Union blue. Many of their ancestors on both sides had fought together in the 1815 Battle of New Orleans, with Galvez, and even earlier with Bienville against the Chickasaws. When the war first broke out, many free-men-of-color formed their own units, like the Louisiana Regiment of Native Guards, and asked the Louisiana state government to let them fight for the state and the Confederacy. But they were not trusted and therefore not used until the Union came. It must have been a pathetic scene to see the funeral processions for both sides winding through the streets of New Orleans to bury their dead. Where Banks had succeeded at Port Hudson, he failed the following year to defeat Louisiana's Major General Richard Taylor in the Red River Campaign. Taylor—who was President Zachary Taylor's son, as well as Jeff Davis' brother-in-law—performed brilliantly as commander of the District of Western Louisiana. In fast-moving strikes against Union forces, Taylor was able to drive Federal soldiers temporarily from portions of south Louisiana. He even made feints against New Orleans though he never carried through with an attack on the city. The war in Louisiana was one of attrition, that is, to deny supplies to the Confederates and to slowly envelop them. By the end of the war Confederate lines had drawn close to the Confederate state capital in Shreveport.

Banks had his hands full in reorganizing the "Free State" government and trying to make New Orleanians loyal Unionists. When Banks took over the job from Butler, he tried to relax many of Butler's tough restrictions, but doing

so only caused him problems. Incidents like the "Battle of the Handkerchiefs" in 1863 made the general's job even more difficult. On an early morning in February, thousands of women gathered at the levee in front of the city, waving handkerchiefs to cheer Confederate prisoners being shipped out for a prisoner exchange. The women, caught up in the passion of the moment, shouted insults at Union soldiers. Fearing an attack by the parasol-waving Southern belles, the Union commander called for reinforcements.

After that incident Banks began tightening up on New Orleanians. On May 1, 1863, he ordered all registered enemies of the United States out of the city within two weeks. He clamped down on all anti-Union public demonstrations. In 1864 provost judge and future governor of Louisiana Henry Clay Warmoth ordered two "respectable" women to spend 60 days in jail for cheering Jefferson Davis.

In December of 1863 President Lincoln announced his formal plans for "reconstructing" the South. Lincoln and Radical Republican members of Congress disagreed vehemently on Reconstruction. Lincoln argued that the South had never really left the Union and that the President, not Congress, was to administer Reconstruction. Lincoln tried to make it as easy as possible for the 11 Confederate states to resume their positions in the Union. Southerners, with certain exceptions, had to swear an oath of allegiance. The President could recognize a state government once 10 percent of its 1860 electorate had taken the oath and slavery in that state was abolished. These steps were taken by Louisiana and Arkansas in 1864, but Congress refused to seat their representatives. The Radical arm of Congress wanted to treat Rebels as traitors and the South as a conquered territory.

In January of 1864, in accordance with the President's plan, General Banks called for an election to be held the following month to choose a civilian governor, lieutenant governor, secretary of state, treasurer, and other officials. After a heated campaign of "Negro baiting" by all factions, Bavarian-born and long-time New Orleans resident Michael Hahn was elected governor of the "Free State" of Louisiana. The Confederate portion of the state, of course, had its own civil government. On another call from General Banks, a constitutional convention con-

Right
The First Vote *was drawn by artist A.R. Waud. The 1864 constitutional convention, which convened in New Orleans, provided the opportunity of education for all and granted suffrage to black citizens. (THNOC)*

Far right
Henry Clay Warmoth was elected to the United States Congress in the first election in which blacks were allowed to vote. Three years later, in 1868, he was elected governor of Louisiana. (THNOC)

vened in New Orleans to write a new state constitution. Slavery was abolished and a free public school system was set up for all children regardless of race. This was the first time in Louisiana that a constitution provided for the education of blacks.

The real battle of rhetoric came with the debates on whether to grant suffrage to blacks. Many delegates at the convention vowed not to give blacks the vote, but they later changed their minds at the urging of Hahn and Banks. Initially Banks ignored politically the former free-people-of-color. In January 1864 they formed the Union Radical Association and sent a delegate to meet with Lincoln. The meeting was successful. Before the constitutional convention opened, Lincoln wrote to Hahn, asking that the franchise be given to some blacks, especially those who were literate, owned taxable property, and, most importantly, had fought with the Union army against the Confederacy. The black political leaders in New Orleans during Reconstruction were mostly French-speaking and had been free-people-of-color before the war.

Voters living in the occupied section of the state ratified the constitution by a vote of 6,836 to 1,566. The first meeting of the "Free State" legislature ratified the 13th amendment, abolishing slavery, but refused to act on the Negro suffrage issue.

Governor Hahn, who resigned his office in February 1865 to go to the U.S. Senate, where he was refused a seat, was succeeded by Louisiana-born Lieutenant Governor James Madison Wells, who had opposed secession. Wells, who was governor at the time of Lincoln's as-

sassination, was at first popular among Democrats for his open-armed welcome to returning Confederate veterans. But because of this, he gained the displeasure of Radical Republicans.

The Radicals would not recognize Wells's administration nor the state's Congressional delegation. Instead they held their own convention and later elected 23-year-old Illinois native, Henry Clay Warmoth, to Congress. This was the first election in the state in which blacks voted. Warmoth, who would become governor in 1868 and one of the most colorful characters during the state's Reconstruction era, shared the same fate as the state's other Congressional delegation — Congress refused to seat him.

After the inception of the 1864 constitution, blacks became an important force in Louisiana politics. Increasingly, Negro suffrage became a rallying cry for Radical Republicans who needed them as a balance of power against Democrats and Independents. Later, when they got the vote, blacks would be courted by the Democrats as well.

The growing conflict between Republicans and Democrats over the role of blacks in politics caused the bloody Mechanic's Institute riot on Canal Street in July 1866. Radical Republicans convened in the Institute on that date for the purpose of rewriting the 1864 constitution to enfranchise all blacks. Acting on the advice of his Democratic advisers, Mayor John T. Monroe, who was returned to office by voters in 1865, declared the meeting illegal and prepared to use the police force to disband it. However, General Absalom Baird (temporarily in command of Federal forces in General Philip Sheridan's absence) told Monroe "the convention, meeting peaceably, could not be interfered with by the officers of the law." Baird promised to send troops to keep order, but he thought the convention opened at 6 p.m. instead of at noon. By the time his troops got there, the bloody riot was over.

On the day of the convention, Monroe had issued a proclamation asking people to stay home and not to gather near the convention hall. Despite this request crowds of both blacks and whites crowded on Canal Street and around the Institute. A brief disturbance broke out when blacks marched from Burgundy Street down Canal Street to the Institute. The chief of police, hearing about the disturbance, dispatched a detachment to Canal Street and sent word to outlying stations to send reinforcements. Shots rang out on Canal and some of the side streets. Blacks retreated to the entrance of the Mechanic's Institute where they fired on the mob of whites and police. Police reinforcements were sent in and returned fire on the building. The white mob joined the police in the shooting. Both were prepared to rush the entrances when a white flag appeared in an upper window. Thinking this was a flag of surrender, the police advanced only to be met by volleys of fire. The police again returned the fire and the fighting intensified. Blacks trying to escape the building were shot or stoned as they dropped from the windows. Many of the prisoners taken were either shot or beaten to death

by the angry mob.

Monroe reported to President Johnson that 42 policemen and several citizens were either killed or wounded. A U.S. Army officer investigating the riot estimated that 38 people were killed and 146 wounded on both sides. Thirty-four blacks and two whites were killed in the Institute. On July 31 Baird appointed an investigative committee to delve into the cause of the riot. The commission concluded the attack was a result of hostility against the renewal of the constitutional convention.

Above
W. L. Sheppard made this sketch of Electioneering in the South in 1868. After ratification of the 1864 constitution, blacks became a political force to be reckoned with in Louisiana politics. Their votes were eagerly sought by all major political parties. (THNOC)

Left
A meeting of the Radical Republicans in the Mechanic's Institute was held in July of 1866 with the purpose of rewriting the 1864 constitution. Rioting, which began in the street, had its bloody finish in the chambers of the Institute. (THNOC)

General Sheridan returned to New Orleans on August 1 and also made an investigation. In a telegram to General Grant, Sheridan characterized the promoters of the reconvened convention as "political agitators and revolutionary men." He threatened to arrest the leaders if they tried to meet again. Sheridan's letter to Grant accused Mayor Monroe of suppressing "the convention by the use of police force" so brutally that Sheridan considered it murder. "It was an absolute massacre by police. ... A murder which the mayor and the chief of police perpetrated without the shadow of necessity," the letter stated. On August 2 Sheridan recommended that Monroe, "this bad man," be removed from office. Monroe, however, continued as mayor under the watchful eye of General A.V. Kautz, commander of the city. Kautz did not interfere in civil matters and martial law was ended on August 2.

In December a Congressional committee investigating the riot placed all blame on Monroe and the "rebels." A minority report, however, blamed the riot on "the incendiary speeches, revolutionary acts and threatened violence of the conventionists." The incident in New Orleans gave impetus to the Radical Republicans' Reconstruction bill which was passed over President Johnson's veto in early 1867.

The Reconstruction Acts of 1867 grouped Louisiana with Texas into the Fifth Military District under the command of the U.S. Army. The act enabled General Sheridan to suspend

municipal elections in New Orleans, remove Monroe from office, appoint Edward Heath as mayor, and remove the attorney general, the judge of the First District Court, and other officials from office.

At the end of August 1867, President Johnson relieved Sheridan of his duties in the Fifth Military District, naming him commander of the Department of Missouri. The new commander of the district, General W.S. Hancock, pursued a more conciliatory policy toward Louisianians.

The Louisiana constitutional convention of 1867–1868 called for new city elections. After a tense campaign and election, John R. Conway, a Democrat, defeated Republican Seth W. Lewis. Mayor Heath, refusing to recognize the results of the election, had to be forcibly removed from the mayor's office in city hall by the military and city police.

Military control of New Orleans came to an end during Conway's administration, when Congress readmitted Louisiana into the Union in June 1868. At first glance an observer might think Home Rule had been returned to Louisiana, but the opposite was true. Fresh from the victory of obtaining the liberal state constitution of 1868, which guaranteed civil rights, including suffrage, to blacks, Republicans sought to reinforce their strength by more direct means. One such means was the creation of the predominantly black Metropolitan Police Force—considered by many, including historians, to be Governor Henry Clay Warmoth's most despotic action. The Metropolitans were formed because the army refused to use troops in Louisiana to serve Republican ends. In effect the governor had a small army at his call.

Warmoth, realizing that white Republicans were few in number and freed slaves had little chance of protecting themselves, sought to have Congress repeal its law prohibiting the former Confederate states from forming a militia. While Congress eventually cooperated with Warmoth, the governor sought a different solution to obtain a military force in Louisiana that would be even more loyal to him than a statewide militia. In September 1868 the legislature combined Orleans, Jefferson, and St. Bernard parishes into the Metropolitan Police District. Using the remnants of the old New Orleans Police Department as a core, Warmoth built his Metropolitan Police as a military extension of the Radical Republican regime in Louisiana.

Well-armed but poorly trained, the Metropolitan Police force served as the triparish law enforcement agency from 1869 until the end of Reconstruction in 1877.

The force was administered by a board of five commissioners, three of whom were black, appointed by the governor. The board had authority to levy taxes upon the people of the triparish area to pay for the force. In addition the statute stripped the New Orleans city government, including the mayor, of all police powers. In retaliation the city council and Mayor Conway created a city police force and placed it under the control of the city administration and not the governor.

Despite the popular belief, which persists to the present day, the state-operated metropolitan police force was not a new idea or even a creation of Governor Warmoth. It had been around a long time, going back to Sir Robert Peel's Police Act of London, which created a Metropolitan Police District in 1829. In the United States it was considered to be one of the major progressive reform ideas in the last half of the 19th century. Many major cities in the nation already had such a force or were urging its adoption, including New York (1857); Baltimore (1860); St. Louis, Kansas City, and Chicago (1861); and Detroit (1865). The idea persisted to the end of the century as Cleveland and San Francisco adopted it in 1877; Indianapolis (1883); Boston (1885); Omaha (1887); and Charleston, South Carolina (1896).

Aside from its policing function in the state, the Metropolitans were used extensively to ensure Republican victories at polling places by preventing Democrats from gaining control of the ballot boxes, either physically or through

voter intimidation with the help of their secret organizations like the Knights of the White Camelia and the Ku Klux Klan.

Warmoth effectively used the Metropolitans in January and February of 1872, to thwart his opponents' attempts to gain control of the legislature. One of the more amusing results of this tense political struggle was a duel with rifles between George Carter, leader of the anti-Warmoth legislators, and General A.S. Badger of the Metropolitans. Neither man, however, was injured.

Warmoth's administration and the legislature were riddled with controversy and corruption. One New Orleans newspaper declared: "If we were to sum up in one accusation the crimes of which Governor Warmoth has been guilty, we would say that it consists in his having stabbed public virtue to the heart and trampled it under his feet." The state's printing cost rose from a high of $60,000 in the pre-Warmoth days to over $1.5 million in a three-year period. Practically every bill initiated during the 1870 legislature had a bit of corruption tacked on to it. During the Warmoth era the state debt rose from $17.5 million to over $25 million by the end of 1872. One of the primary instruments of corruption was the Louisiana Lottery Company. The company was chartered by the state legislature in 1868 and given a monopoly for the entire state. It reaped millions of dollars in profits each year, out of which it gave the state $40,000 a year for the support of charitable institutions. Bribes (which were not illegal at the time), theft of school funds, land swindles, sale of commissions, and graft in state-backed projects were but just a sampling of the corruption of Louisiana politicians and entrepreneurs during the era. Corruption, however, was not unique to Reconstruction politics in Louisiana and it was as rampant among Republicans as it was among Democrats. Corruption existed before, during, and after Reconstruction. Warmoth was most perceptive in describing these conditions:

These much abused members of the Louisiana legislature are at all events as good as the people they represent. Why, damn it, everybody is demoralized down here. Corruption is the fashion.

Although Warmoth was hated by reformers, Democrats, Liberals, and Republicans alike during his term in office, they flocked to the Warmoth Republicans during the 1872 elections to stop the Custom House Gang and Radical Republicans from getting their candidates for governor and lieutenant governor elected. The Warmoth fusion supported Democrat John McEnery for governor and named D.B. Penn, a member of the Liberal Republicans, as McEnery's running mate for lieutenant governor. The Radical Republicans dubbed William Pitt Kellogg their gubernatorial candidate; for lieutenant governor, they chose C.C. Antoine, a prominent black Louisianian.

When the voting returns came in, both McEnery and Kellogg claimed victory. Supporters on both sides were guilty of massive voting frauds. Warmoth's Returning Board declared

Left
When Governor Henry Clay Warmoth was impeached in 1872, the House of Representatives named the black president of the Senate, P.B.S. Pinchback, to serve the remainder of Warmoth's term. The appointment was approved by President Ulysses S. Grant. (THNOC)

Below
Acting on orders of "Governor" McEnery, Brigadier General Fred Ogden and his troops attacked the Metropolitan Police placed in the Cabildo on Jackson Square. Federal troops eventually dispersed Ogden's forces. (THNOC)

McEnery the winner and the rival Radical Returning Board decided in favor of its candidate, Kellogg. Governor Warmoth called a special session of the legislature to meet on December 9, 1872, to settle the matter. But on December 5 Federal Judge E.H. Durell ordered the U. S. Marshal Samuel Packard to seize the Mechanic's Institute, where the legislature was to meet, and to issue a call for Federal troops if necessary. The next day Packard occupied the "State House" and refused entry to Warmoth legislators.

The House of Representatives impeached Warmoth and named P.B.S. Pinchback, a black and the president of the state senate to serve out the remaining month of Warmoth's term. Despite pleas from Warmoth and McEnery for a fair hearing, President Grant approved the Pinchback appointment. With the power of Presidential recognition, Federal troops, and the Radical state government behind him, Kellogg was inaugurated on January 13.

McEnery, refusing to step aside, was also sworn in the same day in Lafayette Square, then convened his own state legislature in Odd Fellows Hall in Camp Street. Encouraged by the support of the Democratic press, and perhaps a majority of the state's white population, "Governor" McEnery issued a proclamation in February forbidding all citizens to pay taxes to the Kellogg government. Moreover he called for all able-bodied young men to join his state militia under the command of McEnery-appointed Brigadier General Fred N. Ogden.

On March 5 McEnery ordered Ogden and the militia to attack and seize the police stations in the city. The first attack was on the Metropolitan station in Jefferson City, then a suburb of New Orleans. McEnery's troops were successful at first, but were later driven away by Federal troops. The McEnery militia then launched an assault against the Metropolitans stationed in the Cabildo on Jackson Square. An intense battle took place and the Metropolitans, fleeing bullets, took refuge around the walls of St. Louis Cathedral. Approximately an hour

In the disputed governor's election of 1872, Federal troops intervened to oust members of the losing faction. (THNOC)

Facing page
Left
James Longstreet, who attended West Point with Sherman and Grant, led the Metropolitans in the occupation of Odd Fellows Hall, which took place one day after the "Battle of the Cabildo." From Cirker, Dictionary of American Portraits, Dover, 1967.

after the battle began, Metropolitan reinforcements arrived and drove Ogden's militia back to St. Peter Street. With the arrival of Federal troops a short time later, Ogden's force dispersed. After the smoke cleared, three men were dead and eight wounded.

"The Battle of the Cabildo," as the engagement was later called, was a major defeat for McEnery. The next day Metropolitans, under the command of former Confederate General James Longstreet, occupied Odd Fellows Hall and jailed members of the McEnery legislature. The confrontation between followers of McEnery and Kellogg erupted in bloody riots and battles in other parts of the state, such as the bloody race riot in Colfax, in Grant Parish, on Easter Sunday, April 13, 1873.

The gubernatorial election of 1872 eventually ended up in a Congressional investigation. The majority report declared that McEnery ought to have been named governor or new elections should have been held. Congress, however, doubted whether it had the Constitutional authority to set aside state elections. President Grant finally made the decision in a proclamation issued on May 22, 1873. He recognized Kellogg as the legal governor of the state and ordered all citizens to submit to Kellogg and the state government.

The war, Reconstruction, and the political corruption and squabbling had a devastating impact on the economy and cost of government. The state debt escalated to previously unheard-of heights and New Orleans property owners were paying almost 50 mills in state and city taxes, or about $5 on each $100 of assessed property value. Commerce and business, the life blood of New Orleans, had become so stagnated by 1873 that a small group of community business leaders, both black and white and led by the popular P.G.T. Beauregard, tried unsuccessfully to end the strife through what historians now call the Unification Movement of 1873.

Prominent white New Orleanians drew up a far-sighted proclamation calling for the unifica-

General Philip Henry Sheridan and Congressional Committee member W.W. Phelps discuss the situation of the Louisiana governorship. A congressional investigation into the 1872 governor's election was eventually ordered. The majority decision was to either recognize McEnery as governor, or hold an election. President Grant decided to recognize W.P. Kellogg as legal governor. (THNOC)

The attack on Metropolitan troops by the White League resulted in a total of 32 killed on both sides. General James Longstreet led the Metropolitans while the Leaguers were commanded by General Fred N. Ogden. (THNOC)

tion of "our people," which it defined as "all men, of whatever race, color or religion who are citizens of Louisiana, who are willing to work for her prosperity." It advocated recognition of the 14th and 15th amendments of the United States Constitution. In addition, it recognized the civil and political rights of every citizen — whether black or white — under the Constitution. Its resolutions called for the integration of public schools and all public places and conveyances. "We shall maintain and advocate the right of every citizen of Louisiana and of every citizen of the United States," the proclamation further stated, "to frequent at will all places of public resort, and to travel at will on all vehicles of public conveyance, upon terms of perfect equality with any and every other citizen." This was a remarkable document, drawn up by Southerners almost a century before the

Civil Rights Act of 1964. The movement enjoyed considerable support in New Orleans, but it was vehemently denounced by white conservatives in the rural parishes of the state and by white and black Radical Republicans, who decried it as an attempt by white Democrats to subvert the Republican Party.

But subversion was hardly necessary; the Republicans were doomed. Resistance to Kellogg's administration continued through his term. Despite his successes and the ill-fated attempts at political, economic, and social reforms, Kellogg was loathed by conservative whites because he represented the party that blocked their return to power. "Kellogg was far more hated than Warmoth had ever been," wrote historian Joe Gray Taylor. Midway through Kellogg's term, the city erupted into open rebellion. The "Battle of September 14,

1874," also known as the Battle of Liberty Place, between Metropolitans and Democrats, sent ominous shockwaves through the nation's political power structure.

In June 1874 Democrats and their allies formed the White League in New Orleans as a military organization to drive the Republicans from office. The League, under the command of Fred N. Ogden, formed regiments, battalions, and companies, including a cavalry unit. Kellogg, aware that the Leaguers were secretly training, ordered the Metropolitans to be on the lookout for arms shipments. The Metropolitans also began to stockpile weapons, including two Napoleon guns and Gatling guns.

On the morning of September 14, word reached the city that the Metropolitans would attempt to prevent the landing of the steamer *Mississippi,* which had an arms shipment aboard destined for the League. Democratic leaders called for a mass meeting at the Clay Statue (then in the center of the Canal Street neutral ground, with Royal Street on one side and St. Charles on the other) to demand Kellogg's resignation. While speeches were being made to a crowd of over 5,000 spectators, Ogden and his commanders planned the at-

tack. President Grant, however, had gotten wind of the expected events and dispatched Federal troops to the city from their quarters in Brookhaven, Mississippi, but they got there too late.

General Longstreet prepared his defenses to stop the Leaguers from unloading the *Mississippi.* His force consisted of about 600 Metropolitans, including approximately 30 mounted policemen called "Uhlans," and about 3,000 black militiamen. The League had more than 8,000 armed men. Longstreet's defense line extended from Jackson Square to Canal Street, and from the Custom House to the river.

In the afternoon Ogden's force advanced toward Canal Street from Poydras and, amidst rebel yells, artillery fire, and rifle volleys, attacked the Metropolitans, sending them into chaotic retreat. Kellogg's militia fell back on Jackson Square. After the brief but fierce fighting, 11 of the Metropolitans were killed — five black and six white, including a former Confederate officer — and 60 were wounded. Twenty-one White Leaguers were killed and nineteen were wounded.

The Leaguers replaced city and state offi-

The White League was made up of Democrats and their allies for the purpose of forcefully removing the Republicans from state offices. On September 14, 1874, the White League clashed with the Metropolitans in what was termed the Battle of Liberty Place. The White League succeeded in loosening the Republican hold in state politics. From Frank Leslie's Illustrated Newspaper. (THNOC)

cials with those elected with McEnery in 1872. Penn was sworn in as lieutenant governor and McEnery was summoned back to Louisiana to become governor. Leaguers, reveling in their victory, roamed the streets while Kellogg's government fell apart throughout the state. President Grant, however, came to the rescue of his fellow Republicans once again. He demanded that the Leaguers submit to Kellogg's government. To make sure they did, he sent in additional Federal troops and three warships.

But by the end of 1874 Radical Republicans, who for years had been propped up by the army and a Republican administration in Washington, began losing control. On January 4, 1875, Democrats tried to topple the Kellogg legislature. The next day General Philip Sheridan, who had been sent by Grant to study conditions in the South, wrote to Secretary of War W.W. Belknap (who was later forced from office himself for questionable business deals in

the Indian Territory), describing the Democrats as "terrorists" and urging the President to declare them to be "banditti." He said they should be arrested, tried, and punished.

In 1876, while the nation was celebrating its centennial, two elections took place which would set into motion the end of Reconstruction in Louisiana. The first was the gubernatorial race between Maine-born Radical Republican Stephen B. Packard and Liberal Democrat Francis T. Nicholls. On the national scene was the hard-fought Presidential campaign between Republican Rutherford B. Hayes and Democrat Samuel J. Tilden.

When the popular votes were counted in the Presidential election, Tilden clearly defeated Hayes. The Republicans, however, refused to concede defeat and charged that the returns from Louisiana, Florida, South Carolina, and Oregon were fraudulent. The election was eventually thrown into a specially created Elec-

A group of commissioners met with New Orleans residents on November 16, 1876, at the St. Charles Hotel to discuss the Presidential election that had just taken place. The election was fraught with intrigue and corruption. Eventually, the commission selected Rutherford B. Hayes as President. To win support from Southern states, many concessions were made. This dealing eventually led to the end of Reconstruction in Louisiana. (THNOC)

toral Commission, which through complex machinations finally selected Hayes as President. To silence and win support from Southern Democrats, Hayes and the more conservative national Republicans made them several attractive promises, including a pledge to withdraw support from Radical Republican governments still controlling "Reconstruction" states in the South, such as Louisiana. The South was promised a railroad to connect east Texas to the Pacific and Federal appropriations for internal improvements. In addition, at least one Southerner would receive a Cabinet appointment and, most importantly, Federal troops would be withdrawn from the South.

Meanwhile Louisianians back home were participating in their own fraud-ridden gubernatorial election. When the votes were tallied, Nicholls emerged with a majority. The Republican Returning Board, which had been appointed by Kellogg, threw out several thousand Nicholls votes and declared Packard the winner. At least one board member — former Governor James Madison Wells — reportedly sold his vote to the highest bidder. When the Democrats could not meet his price, Wells voted for Packard.

President Grant, remembering the Republican Party's promises, declared that all appointments to state offices had to be approved by both Nicholls and Packard until the legitimacy of one or the other could be established. Packard, unsure of his party's support, permitted Nicholls to gain the upper hand by making appointments. Nicholls appointed Ogden's troops as the state militia, who moved quickly to seize the state arsenal, police stations, and the courts. Grant and then Hayes, after his inauguration in March, took no action against Nicholls in support of fellow Republicans. On March 24, 1877, Nicholls declared his government to be complete and in control. A month later, on April 24, Hayes kept another promise — Federal troops were withdrawn from New Orleans and the South. More than 15 years of violent, bloody, corrupt, and financially devastating Reconstruction in Louisiana was over and Home Rule and Redemption were about to begin.

Horror stories about Reconstruction have been handed down by New Orleanians from generation to generation. Historians delving into diaries and the personal papers of those who lived in the city during those years, however, have found quite another story. For the most part and after the initial shock of the war and occupation, the daily lives of New Orleanians changed but little from the prewar days. Despite the political upheavals during the era, most people, white and black, were more concerned with the activities of their daily lives.

A gray pall did not hang over the city during the Reconstruction years. Canal Street and Esplanade Avenue at times were alive with the gay color of promenaders. The French Opera House and the St. Charles Theater played to large audiences, while the schedule of parties, balls, and picnics at all levels of society kept even the shiest lass busy. The St. Charles and St. Louis hotels, both of which enjoyed national reputations even before the war, had full guest registers. For the more pedestrian tastes, gam-

The inauguration of Governor Francis T. Nicholls took place on the balcony of St. Patrick's Hall. (THNOC)

by 1869 and enjoyed by both blacks and whites. New Orleans boasted of several ball teams with such names as Southerns and Robert E. Lees. Baton Rouge had the Red Sticks. Boxing had also become popular by that same year. New Orleanians always enjoyed a good race, especially a horse race. The city enjoyed several good tracks, but lost the popular Metairie course when its owners converted it into the Metairie Cemetery in 1872. When viewed from the air, the oblong design of the original race track is still visible. Also popular among racing fans and the population in general were the steamboat races that have become legend. The most notable of these was, of course, the famous July 1870 race between the *Natchez* and the *Robert E. Lee* from New Orleans to St. Louis. The *Robert E. Lee* was declared the winner when it arrived in St. Louis 3 days, 18 hours, and 14 minutes after departing the Crescent City. The 1870s was the beginning of the great era of steamboats, many of which became floating palaces and their staterooms, so-called because they bore the names of the states in the Union, boasted the finest trappings.

Reconstruction, however, did bring changes. The war and occupation brought a large influx of Northerners to the city. The migration of Northerners to New Orleans was commonplace before the war, but the attitudes toward the newer arrivals changed during Reconstruction. Many unscrupulous Northerners followed the army into the city, and the South in general, to profit from the chaos. They were referred to as "carpetbaggers." But then there were those Northerners, who like their antecedents before the war, simply came because there were good and honest business opportunities to be had for the industrious. There was another class of opportunists during this time whose name sent shivers through die-hard Southerners — the "scalawags." These were Southerners who collaborated with and took part in the Reconstruction government. These so-called scalawags saw themselves as realists, trying to adapt to a new order and a new South.

Perhaps the greatest changes were for black New Orleanians and the thousands of former slaves who flocked to the city during and after the war. They came from plantations and contraband camps from upriver and neighboring

Francis T. Nicholls (above) initially shared the office of governor with Stephen Packard due to the disputed 1876 election. He was able to make certain key appointments however. By appointing Ogden state militia commander, he was able to seize the state arsenal, police stations, and the courts (facing page). When President Hayes took no action against him, Nicholls declared that the state government was under his control. (THNOC)

bling halls and saloons abounded, while temperance societies continued their prewar struggle against demon rum. Mardi Gras' annual visitation provided its usual merriment, as did the many circus troupes visiting the city. A popular Sunday outing for many New Orleanians was an excursion to Lake Pontchartrain on the Pontchartrain Railroad, or perhaps an overnighter to Mandeville on the north shore of the lake or to the Mississippi Gulf Coast by steamboat. By the end of 1864, the Mississippi River was open to traffic to all points north and ships arrived regularly from the East Coast.

During Reconstruction new sources of entertainment were added to the list of pastime activities. Baseball was on the New Orleans scene

Mississippi. Coming in search of a new life, they met only hostility from whites and many blacks. They glutted the labor market thereby depriving many whites and local blacks of their much-needed jobs. Violence was often the result. Despite various civil rights legislation, the constitution of 1868 and the Federal Civil Rights Act of 1875, the age-old practices of segregation continued. Except for a few Radical Republicans, few whites advocated social equality between whites and blacks.

Blacks in New Orleans, however, did benefit from Reconstruction, especially in educational opportunities. Before the war, state law prohibited the education of slaves, except in areas absolutely necessary to the economy of their white owners. During Reconstruction and under Federal orders, the New Orleans public schools were integrated. Moreover, three institutions of higher learning were established in the city for blacks during the postwar era. In 1869 Union Normal in New Orleans was opened to provide training for black teachers. That same year the Congregationalist American Missionary Association founded Straight University and two years later the American Baptist Home Missionary Society (Northern) opened the doors to Leland University. Whites also attended Straight University's law school to prepare for the state bar. In later years Straight and Union Normal were merged to form Dillard University, which is in operation to the present day.

With the withdrawal of Federal troops in April 1877, one of the most romanticized periods in the city's history was over. Generations of New Orleanians and moviegoers have seen and heard tales about the horrors of Reconstruction and the unequaled political corruption it brought to the city. Corruption did exist, but it was not exclusive to this era. Corruption existed on a large scale during the colonial period and during the magnolia-scented antebellum years, of which much has been written. It continued through Reconstruction — and not just among "carpetbagger" Republicans — and on into the years of Home Rule. Reconstruction was an era when the American principle asserting the equal protection of all citizen's human rights was reinforced and then callously abandoned. But, most of all, it was an era like nearly all eras, where most people went about facing the problems of everyday living.

In the Gilded Age New Orleanians recaptured some of the gaiety they had lived without during Reconstruction. This carnival picture was drawn shortly before the practice of holding daytime Mardi Gras parades was initiated. (THNOC)

CHAPTER VI
NEW ORLEANS IN THE GILDED AGE

New Orleans nearing the turn of the century was still the South's largest city, boasting a population of more than 216,000 inhabitants. In transition from the antebellum and strife-ridden Reconstruction periods to the 20th century, New Orleans benefited from a resurgent economy and a conscious air of boosterism. Palatial mansions began springing up along the major avenues, while the old American Sector began taking the form of the new modern American city.

For the well-to-do there were Sunday excursions to the popular Spanish Fort on Lake Pontchartrain, or the enjoyments of the new sporting rage — bicycling out to West End, Milneburg, Audubon Park, or the Gentilly Road. It was also during this period that Mardi Gras began to take the form we know today, with daytime parades led by Rex — a practice instituted by a fraternal organization founded in 1872 to honor the visit of Grand Duke Alexis of Russia — followed by the Independent Order of the Moon and Phunny Phorty Phellows. Nighttime parades and balls were offered by Comus, Momus, and Proteus. During the next two decades, new carnival organizations came and went each year.

But the 20-year period between 1880 and 1900 was also an era of severe economic depressions, racial retrenchment, corruption and reform, and labor unrest. Violent riots and scandals came with almost as much frequency as the summer's heat and mosquitoes. It was an era during which personal honor still compelled newspaper editors, politicians, and businessmen to take to the streets and alleys to solve their differences, with pistols or by flailing their walking sticks. But these years, most of all, served as an economic, social, and psychological bridge to the new century.

The 1880s in New Orleans were extraordinarily busy, even hectic years. During this decade, the South began to regain some of the momentum and energy — economic, political, and cultural — that the Civil War and Reconstruction had depleted. The South, and New Orleans, joined in full force the industrial revolution that had already begun the transformation of the North. The decade was ushered in on an ironic note, when former President Ulysses S. Grant, nemesis of the city's Democrats, visited New Orleans in 1880. Four years later

this irony was balanced somewhat with the erection of a statue of Confederate General Robert E. Lee that was dedicated at Lee's Circle. In 1884, too, the University of Louisiana became more clearly the city's own when it was renamed Tulane University after Paul Tulane, a New Orleans merchant and benefactor of the university.

But the highlight of public events in New Orleans during the 1880s was the World's Industrial and Cotton Centennial Exposition of 1884–1885. The 1880s and 1890s were an era when Southerners heralded the "New South" of industrial progress. Southern cities tried to outdo each other with bigger and better industrial expositions. Atlanta was the first, with its International Cotton Exposition in 1881 followed by Louisville's Southern Exposition in 1883. New Orleans' exposition opened a year later, but Atlanta was not to be outstripped by New Orleans. In 1887 Atlanta held the Pied-

As the South's largest city in the 1880s, New Orleans' future was promising. (THNOC)

mont Exposition. Again, eight years later, in 1895, Atlanta boosters opened the even bigger Cotton States and International Exposition. Two years later Nashville hosted its Centennial Exposition.

In 1884 New Orleans' businessmen and boosters were putting other cities on notice that they were ready to compete. The 1884 (which supposedly marked the 100-year anniversary of America's first export shipment of cotton) exposition was designed to be the Crescent City's calling card to the world, demonstrating its commercial and industrial potential.

The exposition was organized by state treasurer and New South booster, Major Edward A. Burke. Burke, an affable Confederate veteran, epitomized the Gilded Age entrepreneur. He was a railroad executive, a prime mover in state politics, and publisher and editor of the New Orleans *Times-Democrat,* one of the South's leading newspapers. Moreover, Burke was among the first to envision the great potential wealth the South and Central American trade and investments could have for New Or-

leans and other Gulf Coast ports.

To raise the huge amount of money needed to finance the exposition, Burke convinced Congress to grant a $1-million loan, plus a $300,000 gift to build government exhibits. The New Orleans city government donated $100,000 and private stock sales provided the rest.

The grounds of the World's Industrial and Cotton Centennial Exposition were located on 249 acres of Upper City Park — now Audubon

Left
This monument standing 106 feet, 8 inches tall with a 42-square-foot base, honors Confederate hero Robert E. Lee. It was dedicated in 1884 in a circle at the intersection of St. Charles and Howard avenues. (THNOC)

Below
The University of Louisiana was renamed for benefactor Paul Tulane in 1884. Several years later the campus was moved from its downtown location to its present site on St. Charles Avenue across from Audubon Park. (THNOC)

The opening ceremonies of the World's Industrial and Cotton Centennial Exposition included a reading of a speech by President Chester A. Arthur. President Arthur officially opened the exposition from the White House by pressing a button that turned on the electric lights at the fair. (THNOC)

Below
The exposition, which had the character of a World's Fair, was held on the grounds now occupied by Audubon Park. (THNOC)

Park — that had once been part of the plantations of Pierre Foucher and Etienne Bore. Construction was far from completed, however, on December 17, when President Chester A. Arthur pressed a button in the White House which rang a bell at the fairground as a prearranged signal to start up the generators and the festivities. New Orleans was enjoying one of its famed carnival events. In the tradition of Mardi Gras, the exposition began with a grand parade, complete with steamboat processions, the Mexican army band and military units, and welcoming artillery.

Despite the carnival atmosphere of opening day ceremonies, the exposition was plagued with problems from the start. Besides poor management, the initial difficulties in obtaining financing, and the building delays, many of the exhibits failed to show up on time. Often when they did arrive, the exhibits sat around on loading docks in unpacked crates. Foreign exhibits were tied up in bureaucratic wrangles. Although Congress had exempted them from import duties, this was not communicated to local customs officials in time to prevent further delays of weeks or months. The popular Belgian exhibit did not get completely unpacked until late February, 1885.

The items that were in place at the exposition grounds must have been a great disappointment to the approximately 14,000 people who flocked to the opening day. They certainly did not get the promised "unrivaled" and "unparalleled" sights and scenes. The 31-acre Main Building, which had been built of wood under the direction of Swedish-born architect G. M. Torgerson, was almost empty. New Orleans' historian and archivist D. Clive Hardy described its architecture as "typical nineteenth-century eclecticism," but a contemporary account called it an "eyesore." A trade journal of

the day further declared: "The result calls to mind the effect of looking behind the scenes at a theater when all the beautiful solidity of masonry disappears, and is replaced by dirty canvas and very small scantlings."

Attached to the Main Building was the Factories and Mills Building which contained 67,500 square feet of floor space, and the United States Building which covered over a half-million square feet but lacked flooring. Other major buildings included Horticultural Hall, which housed only a few plants provided

Right
The buildings that housed the exhibitions at the W.I.C.C.E. were among the largest in the world. Most of them were dismantled shortly after the exposition and its extension (known as the North, Central, and South American Exposition) ended. Pictured here is the Main Building. (THNOC)

Below
The exposition's 116,400-square-foot Horticultural Hall was left standing in the park after the conclusion of the exposition. It was used as a greenhouse. This last remnant of any significance pertaining to the W.I.C.C.E. was blown down by a hurricane early in the 20th century. (THNOC)

by local gardeners at the last moment, the Art Gallery, the Grand Rapids Furniture Pavilion, and the Mexican National Headquarters. Numerous smaller buildings scattered around the grounds were connected by walkways, actually muddy mires that made it nearly impossible for people to walk from building to building.

By most contemporary accounts, the buildings and the exhibits themselves were lackluster. One foreign consul described the exhibits built by various American manufacturers as not "representative" of the "perfection" American enterprise had obtained. British manufacturers also were poorly represented, but apparently only Belgium made any real effort to send a quality exhibit. Conspicuously absent were the industrial manufacturers of leading European powers. France sent among other things artificial flowers and perfumes, while Germany and Russia displayed textile samples. Japan, China, Siam, Turkey, Jamaica, Hawaii, Honduras, Venezuela, Brazil, Guatemala, Colombia, Nicaragua, Costa Rica, San Salvador, and Asia Minor also sent exhibits of their industries, natural resources, and folk crafts. Of the non-European nations, Japan and Mexico sent the most elaborate exhibits. Moreover, Mexico constructed two buildings on the exhibition grounds. The Mexican Pavilion was built in a Moorish design and the other was a barracks for the Mexican band and cavalry.

Despite the city's efforts to promote the exposition, newspaper reports chronicled its increasing problems. Sightseers expected from all over the world did not materialize in the expected numbers. The "conservative estimate" of four million visitors eventually amounted to little more than a million. A month after the World's Industrial and Cotton Centennial Exposition opened its gates, it was $250,000 in debt. In February the deficit had increased to $360,000. Congress appropriated an additional $335,000 in federal funds, but the

SHOWING RELATIVE SIZE & IMPORTANCE OF THE

Right
In an attempt to recapture financial losses from the World's Cotton Centennial Exposition, it was continued under the name of North, Central, and South American Exposition. (THNOC)

Below right
Artist C. Upham sketched the illumination of the fountain inside Horticultural Hall. (THNOC)

exposition was forced to close on June 1, 1885. An attempt to reopen was made — under the title "North, Central, and South American Exposition" — but the exhibits were closed down for good in April of 1886. The assets eventually hit the auctioneer's block to help offset debts which reached a final tabulation of $470,000.

Almost nothing of the exposition's buildings and vast halls remain today. A large chunk of iron ore from the Alabama exhibit (which local legend holds to be a meteorite) is the only survivor of the grounds themselves. Exposition Boulevard — then little more than a walkway — still exists, lined by beautiful residences facing Audubon Park. Not far from the boulevard on Hurst Street is a small, attractive house that served as a railway ticket office. Another survival, and all but forgotten is the small statue of the goddess Ceres, which stands atop a grossly oversized terra cotta base in Gayarre Place on Esplanade Avenue near Broad Street.

Historian Joy Jackson has ventured several possible reasons for the failure of the exposition. Besides gross mismanagement by exposition officials, the opening festivities, held in the dead of winter, were less well attended than they might have been in the summer months, when transportation from the North would have been easier. The distance of New Orleans from the major population centers of the East and Midwest was also a factor in the poor attendance, especially since land routes to the city were still few and badly kept up. Although James B. Eads had completed his system of

jetties at the mouth of the Mississippi River in 1879, deepening the ship channel and greatly aiding traffic, the first railroad linkup to the West Coast had not been finished until 1882 and had yet to become a familiar route of access to New Orleans. Most important in keeping people away, however, was probably the city's reputation for yellow fever epidemics. The memory of the last major epidemic, in 1878, was still fairly fresh.

Although the exposition, at least financially, was virtually an unqualified disaster, it did help spread the word that progress had been made in New Orleans and further improvements were underway. The 1880s had witnessed an economic revival that would be solidified and increased in the coming years. The city was slowly working its way out of the financial morass of Reconstruction. In 1880 it had had 11 state and national banks with total capital and surplus of just over $5 million. By 1895 New Orleans would boast 19 state and national and 4 savings banks, which came into being during this era, with capital and surplus exceeding $8 million and deposits of more than $26 million. In addition, 24 homestead associations were formed between 1880 and 1896.

Manufacturing concerns also improved their return with new investments and greater productivity. The value of goods manufactured in the city rose from a little more than $18 million in 1880 to almost $64 million by 1895, while the number of manufacturing establishments went from about 900 in 1880 to nearly 2,000 in 1890, when they actually began to drop again. By 1900 there would be only about 1,500 manufacturing concerns in New Orleans.

This dropoff did not indicate a slowdown in economic growth, however, only the tendency of smaller companies to be absorbed into larger corporations. The rise of the corporation, which had begun in the North after the Civil War, was a nationwide phenomenon of the period, and not just a local trend. It was an era of mergers, consolidations, associations, and organizations of all sorts. John A. Garraty explored some of the reasons for this development in his *The New Commonwealth: 1877– 1890.* "Industrialization," he writes, "with its accompanying effects — speedy transportation and communication, specialization, urbanization — compelled men to depend far more than in earlier times on organizations in managing

their affairs, to deal with problems collectively rather than as individuals." New Orleans was no exception to this: merchants and businessmen organized, as did the work force into labor unions.

Before the war, most business dealings in local commodities were conducted on street corners or on levees. According to Louisiana historian Joy Jackson, a commercial revolution took place in New Orleans during the 1870s. Moving from the street corners, saloons, and levees, merchants formed commodity exchanges to transact their business. Factors dealing in cotton futures formed the Cotton Exchange in 1871 to boost cotton business, to draw up regulations for the cotton trade, to exact standards, and to provide cotton men meeting rooms where they could discuss business. Bankers organized into the New Orleans Clearing House Association in 1872, in order to stabilize finances and business dealings between banks. The Produce Exchange, in which produce merchants came together to represent their interests, was begun in 1880. The following year the Mechanics, Dealers, and Lumbermen's Association was organized. The Sugar Exchange came into being in 1883, to publish information about the sugar industry and to provide meeting rooms. And, in 1889, members of the Produce Exchange, the Chamber of Commerce, and the Merchants and Manufacturers' Association formed the Board of Trade to expand their influence. They were later joined by representatives of the Cotton Exchange and Maritime Association.

In the area of city government, the Board of Liquidation was formed in 1880 to oversee the city debt. By the end of the century, management of the Port of New Orleans became a controversial issue. Toward the end of Mayor John Fitzpatrick's administration, the city council, with the support of the city's commercial establishment, enacted an ordinance placing the wharves under the control and management of a public body. The ordinance later was repealed by the council during Mayor Walter C. Flower's term. Businessmen then formed a special committee and, with Flower's nod, drew up special state legislation to create the Board of Commissioners of the Port of New Orleans, popularly known as the Dock Board. The legislature created the board in 1896 and four years later gave the Dock Board control of the

The commodities of sugar and cotton were important to the economy of New Orleans. The buying and selling of these, and other items, were carried out in the exchange buildings built for those purposes. The exterior (right) and interior (below right) of the Cotton Exchange building are shown here. (THNOC)

This tranquil scene of the levee, depicted by W.A. Walker in 1883, was shattered a decade later when the wharves became the scene of violent labor disputes. (THNOC)

wharves.

In the political arena, the Democratic political machines, which had directed their affairs with organizations of their own, such as the Crescent Democratic Club and its successor, the Choctaw Club (1897), also encountered organized opposition. City reformers joined together to form the Committee of One Hundred in 1885, the Law and Order League in 1886, the Young Men's Democratic Association in 1887, and the Citizen's League in 1896.

The rise of the corporation and its need for large numbers of skilled workers also brought the rise of organized labor. The Central Trades and Labor Assembly, numbering over 30 member unions, was created in 1881 to coordinate and support the goals of both black and white labor unions in the city. National labor unions, especially the American Federation of Labor (AFL) established in 1886, also made inroads. Scores of other local unions also started up in the 1880s and 1890s. "Trade unionism had become so popular by this time that even shoe-shiners and horseshoers organized," historian Joy Jackson wrote.

As in many other American cities during this period, however, the demands of laborers for better pay and working conditions often met with resistance. The ensuing conflicts between striking workers and business and government officials sometimes resulted in violence.

A nine-day strike by New Orleans streetcar drivers in May of 1892 was followed by a general walkout by teamsters, screwmen, packers, longshoremen, pressmen, and gas and utility workers in November. The city's 42 AFL unions issued the strike call in support of the Triple Alliance of teamster, screwmen, and packer's unions which were demanding a 10-hour workday, overtime pay, and closed shops. When negotiations broke down between the unions and the Board of Trade, almost 20,000 laborers walked off their jobs. The city was dark at night, activity on the wharves ceased, and drays went unharnessed. The workers returned to their jobs only after Louisiana Governor Murphy J. Foster threatened to send in the state militia to break up the strike. The strike had been only partly successful: the Triple Alliance got its 10-hour work day and overtime pay, but not its demand for closed shops.

The militia was actually called out again three years later for a more serious labor upheaval on the city wharves, with considerably graver consequences. The Panic of 1893 had left some segments of the New Orleans economy depressed and built up frustrations among merchants and workers alike. These frustrations erupted into violence that revealed the ugly underbelly of racial resentment that had changed little since Reconstruction. During times of economic prosperity, black and white unions cooperated with each other. They divided up the work between the two and often struck together as in the general strike of 1892. But during hard times, such as the Panics of

1873 and 1893, racial tensions increased as employers generally tended to hire lower-paid black workers. Competition for jobs often became bloody. When a British ship attempted to replace white screwmen, the high-paid aristocracy of all dock workers, with lesser-paid black screwmen in October 1894, the white screwmen rioted. They raided the ships hiring their black counterparts, and several blacks drowned when they jumped overboard to escape the angry mob. Fights, beatings, burnings, shootings, and killings continued well into March of 1895. Governor Foster called in the militia to protect blacks returning to work, and the violence was finally quelled.

Another violent incident — the assassination of Police Chief David Hennessy — resulted in strained relations with another of New Orleans' ethnic communities, the Italians and Sicilians, and eventually attracted international attention.

By 1890 the city's Sicilian and Italian population had grown to 25,000 or 30,000. As modern-day historian-journalist John Wild recently wrote: they were "strangers in a not-too-friendly land, scrounging for an existence, they were ripe for exploitation by leaders who came from an environment in which terrorist gangs and secret societies flourished."

While a detective on the New Orleans police force, Hennessy had gained a national reputation in 1881 by capturing the infamous Sicilian bandit, Esposito. Facing numerous charges in his homeland, including murder and kidnapping, Esposito had fled to the United States. Eventually landing in New Orleans, he opened up a fruit and vegetable business and went by the name of Randazzo. He named his boat *Leone* after his Sicilian mountain band.

When Hennessy and his brother, Mike, received word that Esposito was in the city, they tracked him down and informed the New York City police of his whereabouts. The Hennessys and two New York marshals captured him in Jackson Square on July 5, 1881, and he was quietly slipped aboard the steamer *New Orleans* bound for New York. Esposito was extradited to Italy, where he was indicted for 18 murders and scores of kidnappings, but a death sentence was later commuted. Vendettas were waged against people thought to have informed on Esposito and blood flowed in certain segments of the New Orleans Italian community.

David Hennessy in 1889 was named chief of police as part of Mayor Joseph A. Shakspeare's reform campaign to rid the city of the criminal underworld. In 1890 Shakspeare publicly denounced the secret Sicilian criminal gangs as "horrid associations: No community can exist with murder associations in their midst. These societies must perish, or the community itself must perish." Esposito's betrayal had not been forgotten, but the continuing war between the Provenzano and Matranga families was primarily over control of the produce business on the city's wharves. Chief Hennessy met with the warring families and demanded the violence be stopped, stating, "The Mafia cannot flourish while I am chief of police." Despite Hennessy's warning, the blood feud continued. On May 1, 1890, members of the Matranga family were attacked and one was severely wounded. Several Provenzano gang members were later convicted and jailed for the assault. Hennessy, considered to be a friend of the Provenzanos, managed to secure a new trial for them.

Then at 11 p.m., on October 15, 1890, Chief Hennessy was shot down while walking home along Girod Street. "Oh, Billy, Billy. They have given it to me and I gave it back to them as best I could," Hennessy reportedly whispered to a friend, who had rushed to his side shortly after the shooting. His friend told newspaper report-

The rail link to the West Coast from New Orleans was opened in 1882. This provided still another method for goods to reach the Port of New Orleans. (THNOC)

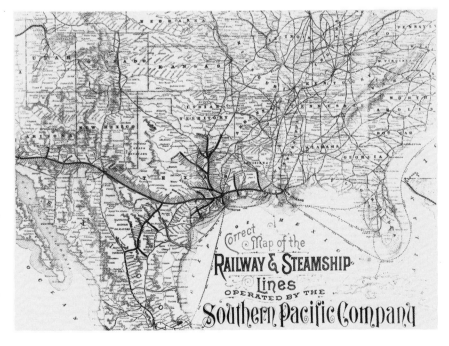

ers that Hennessy had been shot by "Dagoes." The police chief died the next morning.

On the night Hennessy was shot, Mayor Shakspeare ordered the arrest of every Italian found in the streets. Nineteen Sicilians and Italians were later indicted for the shooting, but only ten were actually charged. Nine others were also indicted as accessories before the fact.

The trial began on Feburary 16, 1891, and after 11 days a jury was finally selected. During the next two weeks a parade of witnesses took the stand for both the defense and prosecution. Eyewitnesses, both reliable and questionable, placed several defendants at the scene of the shooting, while several leading citizens, testifying for the defense, provided alibis for others on trial. On March 13 the jury acquitted seven of the defendants and declared a mistrial for the remaining three.

The next morning, the *Daily States* prepared an extra edition with a front-page appeal to the people of New Orleans to turn out in force to take justice into their own hands:

Awake. Arise. Rise in your might, People of New Orleans. Rise, citizens of New Orleans. When murder overrides Law and Justice, when Juries are bribed, and suborners go undetected and unwhipped, it is time to resort to your own natural indefensible right of self-preservation.

Local newspapers carried notices exhorting the people to turn out for a mass meeting at the Henry Clay statue on Canal and Royal streets. They were told to come prepared for action. After inflammatory speeches were made by several prominent civic leaders, the armed mob moved on to the parish prison located near Treme and Basin streets.

After being denied entry to the prison by officials, the mob battered down the door to the Treme Street entrance. Meanwhile prison guards had released the Italians to let them hide wherever they could. Two of those who had been tried for the Hennessy murder were shot to death in a locked cell. A third one was shot in the back of the head as he tried to leave the cell. A member of the mob put a shotgun to the chest of the wounded man, blowing off the Italian's hand when he grabbed for the barrel. Trying to shield his face with the remaining stub of his arm, a second load of buckshot was emptied into his chest. Six other Italians ran into the prison yard and begged for mercy, but they were shot on the spot. Two of the defendants were dragged into the streets and hanged. When one of them grabbed for the rope with his hands, he was lowered, his hands bound, and raised again. Shots ripped through his body and bystanders took pieces of his shirt as souvenirs.

New Orleans newspapers generally praised the mob's work. The reaction around the nation was mixed. Some large metropolitan newspapers condemned the mob action, but others, especially those in cities with large Italian populations, tempered their censure, referring to similar "secret societies" in their own cities. The United States eventually had to pay the Italian government about $24,330 in reparations to soothe its feelings and to put an end to the growing international reaction. On May 5, 1891, an Orleans Parish grand jury concluded that the Mafia existed in New Orleans and that Hennessy had been murdered by its members. It further stated that the lynchings had been justified.

The incident resulted in an unjust indictment of the entire Italian community. Perhaps no other segment of the city's population was held with so much suspicion during those years as the Italians.

New Orleanians in the Gilded Age continued their zestful pursuit of factional politics, as the Democratic and Republican parties struggled for dominance, and sometimes even survival. New, more complicated scandals were added to the problems of Reconstruction, although there was one controversial holdover from that especially corrupt era — the Louisiana State Lottery Company.

Founded in 1868 by Baltimore-born Charles T. Howard, the Lottery Company's tentacles reached into every segment of the New Orleans community and even into the national power structure. It had gained its 25-year charter from the state legislature through bribery and it always kept powerful city, state, and national politicians on its payroll. To maintain a beneficent image, the company donated miniscule amounts of its huge profits to various charitable, educational, and cultural institutions, such as the Charity Hospital and the French Opera House. The Lottery Company was also always ready with a helping hand to victims of floods, hurricanes, and other disasters.

New Orleanians from all walks of life, with an affinity for lotteries since colonial times, were ever ready to pour their money into the Lottery Company's coffers, purchasing 25-cent, 50-cent, and $1 tickets. If someone really felt lucky, he could buy a $20 ticket for the $300,000 prize or the $40 ticket for the big prize of $600,000. The company had more than 200 shops in New Orleans with branch offices in New York, Kansas City, Chicago, Washington, and other major cities.

The New Orleans *Democrat* estimated that a ticket holder had one in 76,076 chances to win, stating further:

The man who buys a ticket every day at every drawing will have only one chance in 84 years to draw even the $243.35 prize. Old Methusaleh himself had he bucked up against the lottery from his earliest childhood to the day of his death and bought a ticket every day, would have found himself winner of $2678.85 after about $250,000 having been spent on the lottery.

To give an air of respectability to the drawings, the Lottery Company hired two former Confederate generals — the "Hero of Fort Sumter," P.G.T. Beauregard, and the crusty old Jubal Early. Both worked for the company for 16 years with reported annual salaries ranging from $10,000 to $30,000. The drawings were gala events: huge crowds turned out, each person with his dreams on a single ticket clutched tightly in his hand. When the wrong number came up, there was always tomorrow and a new ticket.

The Lottery participated heavily in politics simply to ensure its own survival. It supported and was supported by many Republicans and Democrats. During the post-Reconstruction period it was able to retain its monopoly and survived several attempts to revoke its 25-year charter, which was due to expire on January 1, 1894.

The Louisiana State Lottery was formed in 1868 with a 25-year charter. It was an institution fraught with scandal and, despite the advertisements to the contrary, only small portions of the profits went to help needy institutions. (THNOC)

Right
The drawing of the winning lottery numbers, held at the Academy of Music, was a big event. Civil War hero General P.G.T. Beauregard worked for the Louisiana Lottery Company for 16 years. The company assumed that Beauregard's association would give its operation a semblance of legitimacy. (THNOC)

The Lottery issue was continually at the forefront of political debates during the era, especially in the 1892 elections. In the gubernatorial election of that year, Democrat and anti-Lottery candidate Murphy J. Foster narrowly defeated fellow Democrat and pro-Lottery candidate Samuel D. McEnery. The Republicans also fielded their pro- and anti-Lottery candidates for governor. The Republican party was split between two former governors of Reconstruction fame — P.B.S. Pinchback and Henry Clay Warmoth. Pinchback supported the company, while Warmoth had opposed the Lottery from its inception. With the Populist candidate in the field, there were five candidates for governor. Foster, however, carried the day.

In New Orleans in 1892, John Fitzpatrick and his pro-Lottery forces defeated incumbent Mayor Joseph A. Shakspeare and the Anti-Lottery League. Fitzpatrick and the Crescent Democratic Club (Regular Democrats) would face a tough four years in office with Foster, an avowed political opponent, in the governor's office.

By election day, however, the future existence of the Lottery Company was already a dead issue; but neither side would admit it. The resentment and hostilities were too deep-seated. The U.S. Supreme Court had struck the Lottery's death knell when it upheld a lower court's decision affirming the right of Congress to prohibit the Lottery's use of the mail in its advertising. The Lottery Company continued in the state until its charter expired in 1894. It then moved to Honduras, but operated illegally in New Orleans until its complete suppression in 1907. With the Louisiana State Lottery Company crushed, one more remnant of Reconstruction came to an end. The state was gradually being "redeemed."

After the long and hard-fought mayoral campaign, Mayor Fitzpatrick's problems were far from over. In addition to the national financial panic of 1893 and the labor troubles mentioned earlier, Fitzpatrick's administration was thoroughly discredited by the "Boodle Scandals."

In 1894 the Citizens Protective Association of New Orleans, while investigating graft and corruption in city government, uncovered a major scandal in the construction of the courthouse and jail on Tulane Avenue and Saratoga Street. The investigation and scandal went all the way to the city council and mayor's office. The contract to build the courthouse had been awarded during Shakspeare's reform administration, but the actual construction was completed during Fitzpatrick's term. Even though no evidence could be found against the mayor, the citizens' group and the district attorney filed suit in civil court, asking for the impeachment of Fitzpatrick for "nonfeasance, malfeasance, favoritism, corruption, and gross misconduct." Fitzpatrick won the suit. The investigation eventually led to the indictments of 10 councilmen, the city engineer, and a former tax assessor. Three of the twelve were later convicted of misconduct in office.

By the end of Fitzpatrick's administration in 1896, the Crescent Democratic Club (CDC), riddled with scandal, began to fall apart. There were mass defections to the newly formed Citizens' League. During the 1896 municipal elections, Governor Foster refused to support the League's candidate for mayor — New Orleans businessman Walter C. Flower. Foster backed instead the CDC's candidate, Congressman Charles F. Buck. Fitzpatrick was refused the machine's nomination because of the scandals during his term and because of Foster's deep resentment toward Fitzpatrick dating back to the 1892 Lottery fight. After a bitter campaign, Flower defeated Buck. The CDC disintegrated after the election, but out of its ruins the Choctaw Club of Louisiana was formed the following year. This political organization would in three years take control of city government and hold it for over three decades, until the ascendency of a powerful political force from Winn Parish — Huey Long.

Mayor Flower, although he lasted only one term in office, provided the city with an efficient and progressive administration. Many of the municipal improvements begun during his tenure would not be completed until well into the next century. Among the accomplishments listed by his administration were reduction of city employee salaries to a level comparable to

private industry, the regaining of control of municipal services that had been franchised to private companies, and the beginning of construction of sewerage and water systems that were still in use by the 1980s. The Flower administration also reorganized the city government under a new charter, which provided for a councilmanic form of government and civil service. Perhaps the most well-known "reform" during his time in office was the creation of Storyville—the infamous red-light district which gave the city such colorful characters and places as Lulu White, Tom Anderson, Josie Arlington, the Countess Willie Piazza, Mahogany Hall, and Basin Street.

Popular legend, both in print and in the movies, has credited Storyville with being the birthplace of jazz. But jazz historian Al Rose considers Milneburg, Old Spanish Fort, Little Woods, Bucktown, and West End as the "hallowed" grounds of the birth of jazz. "To a limited and lesser extent Storyville . . . served as a forge in which some of the pure gold jazz was smelted," Rose said. Rose also traces the origins of jazz to Canal Street, South Rampart Street, Bourbon Street, Perdido Street, the legion of small dance halls on both sides of the Mississippi River, and to the Tango Belt, "an almost unbroken line of cabarets, dance halls, and honky-tonks" surrounding Storyville.

The purpose for creating Storyville was not to legalize prostitution but to confine it to one section of the city. This was not the first attempt to regulate "the world's second oldest profession," that had existed in Louisiana since colonial days. Only 14 years after the Louisiana Purchase, the city fathers had passed an ordinance that fined a prostitute if she "shall occasion scandals or disturb the tranquility of the neighborhood." In 1837 another ordinance was added to the books that enabled the mayor to evict a harlot from any premises upon the signature of three respectable citizens. Two years later prostitutes were forbidden to occupy and ply their trade in the ground-floor buildings in the Vieux Carre. In 1845 ladies of ill-repute were prohibited from visiting or drinking in coffee houses and cabarets. During the 1850s Know-Nothing businessmen initiated two reform drives to rid the city of harlots; and in 1857 the city made its first attempt at licensing the trade and restricting it to certain types of structures. The harlot paid annually a $100

license fee and the keeper of a house of prostitution paid $250 annually. Although the ordinance prohibited them from one-story edifices, they could live and conduct business in any multistory building in the city. The ordinance was an attempt to placate both anti-prostitution crusaders and powerful factions in the city that supported the practice.

Throughout the century prostitution was a lucrative source of income for corrupt politicians, government officials, policemen, lawyers, and landlords. The well-known philanthropist John McDonogh, who had extensive landholdings all over the city, was often berated in the newspapers for renting property to harlots.

After the 1896 municipal elections, Mayor Flower and the Citizens' League were ready to deal with the problem. On January 29, 1897, the city designated a certain "restricted district" to which prostitutes must confine their business. The district shortly gained the name Storyville, much to the displeasure of City Councilman Sidney Story, author of the ordinance creating it. Story's measure, called Municipal Ordinance 13,032 CS, read in part:

From the first of October, 1897, it shall be unlawful for any public prostitute or woman notoriously abandoned to lewdness to occupy, inhabit, live or sleep in any house, room or closet situated without the following limits: Southside of Customhouse (Iberville) from Basin to Robertson Street, east side of Robertson Street from Customhouse to St. Louis Street, south side of St. Louis Street, from Robertson to Basin Street.

The city government believed that restricting prostitution to a certain area was the best way to deal with the situation, since attempts to outlaw it had proven futile. The ordinance did not legalize harlotry, but simply made the practice of it outside the district illegal. Even

Left
Joseph Shakspeare and his anti-Lottery forces were defeated in the 1892 municipal elections. The Lottery operated in Louisiana until 1894, when its charter expired. It continued to operate clandestinely from Honduras until 1907. (THNOC)

Below
Storyville was a district of the city set aside for the houses of prostitution, which flourished at the time. Blue Books contained directions to the brothels, saloons, and clubs in the district named after the city councilman Sidney Story. (THNOC)

though Storyville was created by a reform administration, it would soon come under the attack of more zealous reformers until its eventual "elimination" during World War I.

The Citizens' League itself lasted only one term. In the 1900 municipal elections the League's successors, the Jacksonian Democrats, were handily defeated by the resurgent Regular Democratic Organization. The Regular Democrats rallied to the new Choctaw Club.

The same year that Flower and the Citizens' League began their campaign to ready New Orleans for the 20th century, the U.S. Supreme Court handed down the *Plessy v. Ferguson* decision which would have a devastating impact on race relations throughout the nation. The high court upheld Louisiana's 1890 separate railroad coach law and fostered the "separate but equal" standard in the nation (until it reversed itself in the 1954 *Brown v. Board of Education of Topeka* decision).

Homer Adolph Plessy, who brought the suit, described himself as "seven-eighths Caucasian and one-eighth African blood." He bought a ticket on June 7, 1892, aboard a train bound from New Orleans to Covington, north of Lake Pontchartrain. Plessy sat in the "white only" coach despite a clearly marked Jim Crow car. Plessy had resolved to test the constitutionality of the state law, which stated that "all railway companies carrying passengers in their coaches . . . shall provide equal but separate accommodations for the white and colored races." The law also required blacks and whites to ride in the coaches designated for their races. Criminal Court Judge John H. Ferguson was the original trial judge in the case.

In handing down the majority decision for the U.S. Supreme Court, Justice Henry Billings Brown declared that state legislatures can pass laws "with reference to the established usages, customs, and traditions of the people, and with a view to the promotion of their comfort, and the preservation of the public peace and good order." Delivering the minority opinion, Justice John Marshall Harlan said that separation was but a mere "badge of servitude."

While the "separate but equal"ruling had a damaging effect on black civil rights, an even more severe blow was struck two years later when the writers of the state constitution of 1898 disfranchised the vast majority of black voters through an ingenious exception to the literacy qualifications clause. During the 1890s Southern states rewrote their constitutions to disfranchise Negro voters. States such as Louisiana adopted the literacy test, property qualifications, and poll taxes in their new constitutions to achieve that end. These consitutions, however, included certain "escape" clauses to enable whites, who could not meet the literacy and property qualifications, to register to vote.

The states tried various means and wordings to accomplish this, and Louisiana's 1898 constitution included a "grandfather clause" as an exception to these two requirements. The grandfather clause stated in part that no male could be denied the right to register to vote if he, his father, or grandfather, had been eligible to do so on January 1, 1867, or before. The year 1867 was important because it was not until the Louisiana "Black Reconstruction" constitution of 1868 that blacks in general were extended full "civil, political, and public rights." The new constitution achieved its aim. In 1896 there were 126,822 Negroes registered to vote. By 1900 the number had dropped to 5,320. Other states copied Louisiana's grandfather clause until the U.S. Supreme Court declared it unconstitutional in 1915. The 1921 Louisiana constitutional convention adopted Mississippi's "understanding clause," that required a potential registrant to be able to read parts of the state constitution, or be able to give a reasonable interpretation of it when read to him.

The 1898 constitution came as a hard blow to many black Louisianians who realized that progress — both social and economic — was in direct proportion to their political strength and having the right to vote. One of the last major advancements of Radical Reconstruction was gone.

During the 1800s the Crescent City had risen from a relatively insignificant colonial outpost to one of the major cities and ports in the nation. Like the progress of the nation itself, the growth and changes were phenomenal. Men and events like Thomas Jefferson, the Louisiana Purchase, the Battle of New Orleans and Andrew Jackson, the Mexican War, yellow fever, Ben Butler, the Civil War and Reconstruction, and the Louisiana State Lottery Company had been important in shaping chapters in the city's history. A new chapter and century with new names and events was about to commence.

The 1896 municipal elections caused the breakup of the Crescent Democratic Club. Other organizations were formed from the disintegration of the CDC: the Citizens' League, whose candidate Walter Flower was elected mayor; and the Choctaw Club, which was to become the organ of the Regular Democratic Organization and would dominate local politics for three decades. (THNOC)

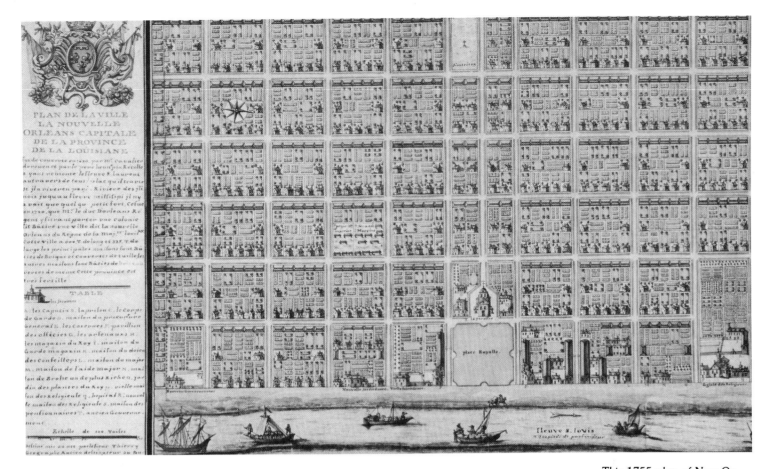

This 1755 plan of New Orleans by Thierry seems a bit fanciful in its depiction of neat houses and parterre gardens, but accounts by inhabitants of the city at that period attested to the physical charm of New Orleans. (THNOC)

137

Facing page
With his success against the British at Pensacola, Galvez received recognition for his exploits from the king of Spain. The monarch allowed him to add to his coat of arms the words "Yo solo" (I alone) for his heroism against the British. The addition appears in a scroll above the ship in the lower right quadrant of the shield. (THNOC)

Above
The Battle of Lake Borgne, depicted in this oil painting, was a naval skirmish which preceded the final Battle of New Orleans early in 1815. (THNOC)

A motley group of troops that included regulars, recruits, and volunteers commanded by General Andrew Jackson achieved a victory over British forces in January 1815. The Battle of New Orleans was painted by Dennis M. Carter. (THNOC)

These lithographs from the 1870s depict the New Orleans establishments of George Merz, proprietor of the Old Canal Brewery, and C. Cavaroc, wholesale liquor dealer. The end of Reconstruction government in Louisiana marked the beginning of a new era of prosperity in New Orleans business. (THNOC)

Steamboats were important movers of commercial goods, passengers, and mail throughout the Mississippi Valley, and New Orleans was the most important port on the route. This painting is by Hippolyte Sebron. (THNOC)

Entitled New Orleans: Die Canal Strasse, *this view depicts Canal Street circa 1850–1860. The street has always been a fashionable and important one to New Orleans. Despite many changes in its appearance throughout the years, the street has retained the essence of its former character. (THNOC)*

143

Lafayette Square was the main public square of the American Sector and a popular place for people to congregate for an afternoon of relaxation. This drawing is from an 1850s edition of Ballou's Pictorial Drawing-Room Companion. *(THNOC)*

This oil painting depicts the destruction that occurred when the Federal fleet passed the forts below New Orleans. (THNOC)

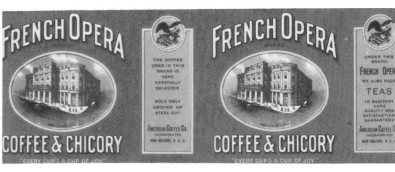

Importing, roasting, and packaging coffee has been an important industry in New Orleans since the early 1800s. These colorful, decorative labels are only a part of the lore associated with the coffee trade. (THNOC)

Construction and installation of the buildings and exhibitions at the World's Industrial and Cotton Centennial Exposition experienced many delays, and the exposition had to be opened in a partially completed state. Pictured here are some of the workers at the site. (THNOC)

As shown in this brightly colored poster announcing the opening of the W.I.C.C.E., several large buildings were constructed to house the event's many exhibits. Audubon Park was the site of the exposition. The Main Building at the W.I.C.C.E. (right) covered 33 acres. (THNOC)

Mardi Gras invitations and posters during the "golden age" were often very elaborate, being intricately colored and/or die-cut into complicated and unusual shapes. Themes for the parades and balls that followed were often drawn from ancient history or mythology. (THNOC)

CHAPTER VII
A MODERN CITY EMERGES

New Orleans entered the 20th century with great optimism. The nation had just emerged victorious in its war with Spain and at home in Louisiana, the Democrats had become by far the dominant political party, while New Orleans boosters were busily trying to sell the city's attributes to the nation's business community.

During the first three decades of the new century, the face of the city began to change. Uptown New Orleans continued to grow and new and more lavish mansions joined their predecessors on the prestigious St. Charles Avenue. New and higher skyscrapers jutted through the skyline of the Central Business District, dwarfing the 19th-century structures of the old American Sector. It was a period of dramatic building activity, especially multistoried commercial edifices.

Three Presidents — William McKinley, Theodore Roosevelt, and William Howard Taft — visited the city during the first decade. McKinley was the first President ever to come to the Crescent City while in office.

During these early decades, New Orleans jazz moved north and eventually to the hearts of jazz enthusiasts around the world. The famous Galatoire's Restaurant first opened its doors in 1905 and four years later an automobile speed record was set in the city by Ralph de Palma, traveling 50 miles at an average speed of 60 m.p.h. These were the

Overleaf
*The Maritime Building and the
Pere Marquette Building were
two of the larger structures
built in the downtown area in
a spurt of building activity that
occurred in the first three
decades of the 20th century.
(THNOC)*

Left
*This panoramic view of the
growing city of New Orleans
was made circa 1900.
(THNOC)*

Below, far left
*The Hibernia Bank Building
on Carondelet Street is one of
the architectural landmarks of
the Central Business District.
(THNOC)*

Below left
*The Gypsy Tea Room, seen
here circa 1937, was one of
the many small clubs in New
Orleans where jazz was
played. (THNOC)*

beginning years for many of the city's cultural,
entertainment, and educational institutions.
The New Orleans Symphony Society was
founded in 1906, as was the Louisiana State
Museum (located in the Presbytere and
Cabildo). In 1910 the first motion-picture house
opened its doors and in the years following
"movies" would join vaudeville marquees in
the city's major theaters. A year later Loyola
University was established and the Isaac Delgado Museum of Art opened in City Park. Another center of higher learning came into being
in 1916 with the founding of Xavier University.
Another French Quarter institution, Le Petit
Theatre du Vieux Carre, began its long career
of delighting New Orleans audiences. During
the 1920s the French Quarter became a popular place for young artists and writers to meet
and to create. In 1921 the short-lived *Double
Dealer* began publishing the early works of the

then little-known William Faulkner and others who would gain fame.

In this period many of the city's antiquated and inadequate public utilities were replaced. New drainage and sewerage systems were built and a modern water purification plant took the place of individual rainwater cisterns. Perhaps the most important achievement during the first decade of the new century was the elimination of the city's dreaded perennial visitor — yellow fever.

By the turn of the century, however, New Orleans still did not show many of the signs of growth exhibited by other American cities. While Atlanta, Memphis, Cleveland, and Baltimore almost doubled in population, New Orleans increased by only 25 percent. Its national standing according to population dropped from ninth to twelfth in 1900 and to sixteenth by 1918. New Orleans' greatest business asset,

its port, had fallen into decay and disrepair during Reconstruction and the decades following it. But with the activities of the Dock Board (formed in 1898) and the building of the Public Belt Railroad in 1908 the annual revenue from the port increased from approximately $215,000 in 1902 to $430,000 in 1912.

The city's economic growth during these years was sporadic. From 1899 to 1904 the city rolled on a tide of national prosperity, as was reflected in the increase of its capital assets. But good fortune was short-lived. New Orleans, as well as the rest of the nation, suffered from a general economic depression in 1907. From that year until 1913 the city's economy steadily deteriorated; capital assets fell by almost 5 percent and the market value of its products fell by 12 percent. With 1914 and the war in Europe, New Orleans and the nation once again began to prosper. By 1920 the city's

Above
In the early 20th century, jazz became quite popular. It was played in clubs and aboard luxury steamboats. This band aboard the steamer Sydney *was led by Fate Marable. (THNOC)*

capital had more than doubled and the total market value of products tripled 1914 figures.

New Orleanians looked to the new century with almost childlike optimism, but of course events did not always justify it. The first year of the century, three major events took place that would have a profound impact on political and social matters for several decades. It was the year that the Regular Democratic Organization, usually referred to as the Choctaw Club or Regular Democrats (later Old Regulars), took the reins of city government and would hold them for almost three decades. It was also the year of the streetcar employees riot and the Charles riot — one of the most violent race riots in the city's history.

Robert Charles, a black native of Columbus, Mississippi, came to New Orleans as a member of a movement to encourage blacks to return to Africa. He and a cousin rented rooms near Washington Avenue and Dryades Street where they resided and worked toward their cause. White neighbors became suspicious and reported the two black men to police. When police officers came to their apartment on July 23, 1900, Charles and his cousin opened fire, seriously wounding one officer. The cousin was captured, but Charles escaped. The next day Charles shot and killed a police captain and corporal as they approached an abandoned house where he had taken refuge.

News of the policemen's deaths spread rapidly through the city. Mobs of young white men roamed the streets randomly beating

blacks. Mayor Paul Capdevielle, the last of the Creole mayors, cut short his vacation and returned to the city. He immediately ordered the mobs off the streets and sent out a call for 1,500 volunteers, whom he deputized as special police. Seven blacks, who were overheard to praise Charles' "war on the whites" were jailed.

Charles was later trapped in a house on Saratoga Street. A policeman or one of the hundreds of volunteers surrounding the house set fire to the structure to force the fugitive into the open. As Charles tried to escape the smoke and flames, he was shot to death. The resulting riot lasted four days, causing the deaths of three policemen and approximately ten private citizens (white and black).

Three months after the Charles riot, labor

Right
During the streetcar workers' riot of 1901, Mayor Paul Capdevielle tried to mediate between management and labor, but was unsuccessful. The state militia eventually intervened, and the strike ended. Capdevielle was replaced as mayor by Martin Behrman in the 1904 election. (THNOC)

Far right
Citizens erect a barricade of streetcars and billboards on Canal Street during the 1901 riot. Courtesy, Louisiana State Museum.

troubles began among the city's streetcar workers. In October the carmen went out on a two-day strike, but their grievances were quickly resolved. The following September 27, however, they called a general strike and effectively stopped every streetcar in the city for over a month. The workers demanded an eight-hour workday at 25 cents an hour. The strikers had the support of the populace and several trade unions. Canal Street businessmen and merchants and Mayor Capdevielle tried to arbitrate the dispute. An offer of a 10-hour workday and 23 cents an hour was made, but turned down. On October 8 violence broke out when the company tried to operate four cars on Canal Street with strikebreakers from St. Louis. Despite police protection, the strikers attacked and stopped cars at Galvez and Canal streets. Three strikers were arrested.

Having little confidence in the emergency capabilities of the police department, Capdevielle called for volunteers to act as special police, but few responded. So at the mayor's request, Governor Heard ordered out the militia. But before they could arrive, violence erupted between strikers and police on Canal and Dorgenois streets. Two policemen and ten civilians, including striking carmen, were injured. A police wagon hurrying reinforcements to the scene was overturned by strikers, also causing a number of injuries. On October 9 Heard arrived in the city with 700 militiamen and forced the strikers to accept 20 cents an hour for a 10-hour workday. The strike lasted about 14 days and ended with considerable loss of life and injury on both sides.

After the settlement of the streetcar strike,

New Orleanians turned to a game they were more familiar with — politics. The municipal elections of 1904 and the victory of Mayor Martin Behrman, the Regular Democratic Organization's candidate, was the beginning of 16 years of uninterrupted Tammany Hall-styled machine politics in New Orleans. The reform-minded New Orleans *Times-Democrat* (which became the *Times-Picayune* in 1914) strongly opposed Behrman's candidacy:

A man of pleasant personality and popularity . . . Mr. Behrman does not rise to the standards but represents the very elements that would assure misgovernment of the city and seriously hinder and check its prosperity. . . . When New Orleans falls into the hands of the ring, when the arch masters of the politicians, the bosses, get possession of its government and administer it in the interest of the ward workers, hangers on and all of the others of the great army of janissaries who make up the machine, it suffers in every department, in every branch of government and in its business as well.

The Regular Democratic Organization (RDO) — also known in New Orleans as the Choctaw Club, the Ring, machine, Regulars, and after 1922, as the Old Regulars — represented all walks of life in the city: workers, businessmen, attorneys, physicians, bankers, gamblers, clerks, and professional politicians. According to a study of the organization in the early 1930s by a Columbia University graduate

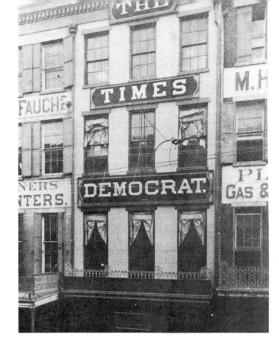

student, the success of the organization was due to the simplicity of its structure and to patronage. The RDO was divided into the caucus and the club. The caucus — the ruling body of the machine — was composed of the ward leaders from the city's 17 wards. All policy decisions were made by the "Council of Seventeen" and it decided who would run for office with the Regular's endorsement. Anyone in the organization who did not go along with its decisions could have his patronage cut off.

The machine was, in effect, a federation of ward organizations in which the ward boss had complete charge of his organization. He chose his precinct captains and dispersed all patronage in his territory. Behrman once claimed that the success of a ward boss was due to "personal traits, hard work, uneven distribution of patronage, and luck."

The nucleus of the organization was in the precinct clubs. The machine's success was in direct proportion to the efficiency of the precinct captain and his workers in getting out the vote on election day. Precinct leaders had to possess an encyclopedic knowledge of the people in his area: their problems, jobs, hobbies, likes and dislikes, and ambitions provided clues to getting their votes.

Running the RDO and winning elections was expensive. Club members paid a dollar a month in dues and everyone on the city payroll was required to belong. During a political campaign, city department heads had to collect "contributions" from the employees in their sections. A political candidate, seeking the RDO's endorsement, had to pledge to kickback 10 percent of his salary to the organization, and in some cases, depending on the candidate and the office, larger percentages would be levied. Corporations and small businesses, as well as gambling dens and bordellos, had to contribute to the "war chest."

Left
The Times-Democrat, *a New Orleans newspaper, was opposed to Martin Behrman's candidacy for mayor, seeing him as a typical "boss" type. (THNOC)*

Below
The key to Behrman's controlling city politics was a system of patronage and kickbacks to the political machine. The machine was the Regular Democratic Organization. Behrman is shown here with some of the members who made the system work. (THNOC)

The RDO's success was also partly attributable to its good relationship with the business community, which it considered "normal, necessary and in the interest of the city." Behrman's own motto was that "nothing would be done to hurt business and business was to be judge." He worked closely when he could with such booster organizations as the Progressive Union (formed in 1902) and its successor, the New Orleans Association of Commerce (formed in 1913).

Behrman's relationship with business was not uncommon. Historian Harold Zink concluded in his 1930 work, *City Bosses in the United States,* that most city bosses of the late-19th and early-20th centuries had some form of business connections. For examples, "Colonel" Ed Butler of St. Louis, "Honorable" William Tweed of New York, and Abraham Reuf of San Francisco were either presidents or directors of numerous corporations, while "Old Boy" George Cox of Cincinnati, Christopher Magee of Pittsburgh, and Roger Sullivan of Chicago controlled banks, street railways, and gas companies.

Businessmen, like any other group of people, could not always agree among themselves and often Behrman was caught in the middle. One such occasion occurred in the 1915 session of the state legislature. The Louisiana sugarcane growers introduced a number of "anti-corporation" bills hoping to free themselves of the sugar trusts. The American Sugar Refining Company, the New Orleans Association of Commerce, the New Orleans Clearing House Association (banks), the Sugar Exchange, and labor groups employed in the refineries (yielding to the corporations) led the opposition to these measures. The Association of Commerce warned that these bills were the first step on a path toward "socialism." As mayor and leader of the strongest faction in the state legislature, Behrman was in a difficult position for he had to decide whether to back the sugar growers or the business interests within his own city. Aware of the growing tendencies in the state and country toward regulations of monopolies, Behrman backed the growers.

This was just one of the highlights of Behrman's first 16 years in office (1904–1920). Others included the 1905 confrontation with the colorful Dominick O'Malley — publisher of the New Orleans *Item* — over control of the police department; the city's last yellow-fever epidemic the same year; and, the creation of the Public Belt Railroad in 1908. The city tried unsuccessfully to get the 1915 Panama-Pacific Exposition; and a police superintendent was assassinated in 1917. Although Behrman wore the badge of political boss, many important improvements were made in the city during his tenure, such as extensive street-paving, a modern sewerage system, new schools and playgrounds, and increased fire and police protection.

Throughout his mayorality, Behrman faced constant opposition from such "reform" groups as the Home Rulers (1904), Independents (1908), Good Government League (1912), and Governor John M. Parker and his Orleans Democratic Organization (1920). Cries for government reform in New Orleans usually took the form of progressive democracy — abstract *versus* practical politics. The reformers were middle class and generally lawyers, businessmen, social uplifters, and editors; there were as many Catholics as Protestants, and included Jews. A look at those who supported Behrman revealed they were also middle class, with the same religious and ethnic diversity. Behrman characterized the reformers as a disgruntled combination of discontented Regulars, idealists, opportunists, and "uptown silk stockings." The silk-stocking reformer, the mayor claimed, was one "who knew all about municipal government because he read magazines and books . . . and did not know where to file his complaint if the garbage man did not come early enough to suit him." This perennial op-

position, he said, was nothing more than "the outs wanting in." Only the professional politician, Behrman declared, "knew how to get the job done."

The most successful attack against Behrman and the RDO was made during the 1920 mayoral elections. Reform Governor John M. Parker and his New Orleans-based Orleans Democratic Association (ODA) — a political offspring of the RDO — succeeded in getting Andrew McShane elected mayor. The contest between the Behrman-RDO faction and the Parker-ODA-McShane alliance had been the most heated mayoral election in decades.

In an attack on Behrman's administration on August 7, 1920, Governor Parker appointed a committee led by prominent businessmen and labor leaders to investigate the city's municipal government. The ODA worked diligently for months compiling incriminating evidence against Behrman. Behrman, in a countermove, obtained a court injunction to postpone the investigation until after the election. The ODA, stunned, pointed to the injunction as an admission of guilt to the charges. Esmond Phelps, chairman of the McShane campaign, claimed that Behrman had pleaded guilty to "inefficiency, extravagances, and poor business methods . . . by enjoining an examination of the city's affairs." Behrman told the ODA that he did not oppose an investigation of his administration, but asked that it be held after the election. When the ODA refused, Behrman ac-

cused the organization of using the investigation to create political jobs.

McShane campaigned on a ticket calling for "public decency, free politics and civil progress," while accusing Behrman of being "irreconcilably for public vice, political bossdom and social and civil stagnation."

The *Times-Picayune* kept up a constant and unrelenting attack on Behrman. From August 25 to September 14, 1920, it carried daily front page spreads attacking Behrman's record, especially concerning vice, poor street conditions, and the city debt. Damaging articles and photographs appeared daily on the front pages showing neglect in street-paving, drainage, and garbage collection: "Anywhere off the 'show streets' there is the same dreary picture of neglect." In defense Behrman asked, "Why don't these damnable, slimy, unfair newspapers print pictures of the avenues and pretty places?"

The *Times-Picayune* also charged that policemen were stationed in the city's "dives" to protect gamblers and underworld characters. In a series of articles entitled "Under the Shadow of Vultures' Wings," *Picayune* reporters exposed saloons, gambling parlors, and houses of prostitution allegedly permitted to exist by the police and Behrman. In his memoirs Behrman denied the *Picayune's* charges. After the passage of the National Prohibition Enforcement Act, or the "Volstead Act," in 1919, there were no saloons in New Orleans or illegal liquor, he claimed. Any liquor that may have been on hand was purchased legally before the law. "Besides," he said, "I didn't have time to go around investigating such foolishness." Alcoholic beverages could be gotten with little difficulty in the city that boasted of its unique history, sophistication, and cosmopolitan attitudes toward good living. As historian Joy Jackson wrote: "Although bars, restaurants, groceries, and fruit stands were highly likely spots to purchase alcoholic beverages, it could be bought in poolrooms, from bellhops, taxi drivers, and the neighbor down the street who operated a still or winery in the drop-shed adjacent to his house. Making home brew became almost a universal practice among Orleanians."

During the campaign Parker and the ODA accused Behrman of using the infamous Storyville as a source of political power. Behrman reminded Parker that Storyville was already in existence when the Choctaws had gained power in 1900. He also reminded Parker that Storyville had been created in 1897, during Flower's administration, by the Citizen's League of which Parker had been a member. The ODA characterized Behrman as the "King of the Tenderloin" (another name for Storyville) in that he fought to keep the district open during World War I, an accusation that Behrman denied, saying he had done all he could to close Storyville during the war.

A Liberty Bond parade takes place on Canal Street in 1917. That year Storyville was ordered closed as a threat to military men. Quite a number of military personnel were billeted in and near New Orleans during World War I, and the presence of a red-light district was seen as too much of a problem. (THNOC)

Just after the war mobilization had begun, both public and governmental attention focused on the prevention of social diseases among servicemen. Behrman, after discussing the matter with the military commanders of army camps surrounding the city, decided to place Storyville off limits to soldiers, and military commanders were requested to place a ring of guards around the district to keep out uniformed personnel. Behrman thought that this would take care of the problem. However, in 1917, Raymond Fosdick arrived in New Orleans and ordered the district closed. Fosdick, a member of the Navy Department's special Federal Commission on Training Camp Activities, was sent to the city to investigate and eliminate places of vice near military bases. Behrman told Fosdick that he did not intend to close Storyville until he had heard from Secretary of War Newton D. Baker. Fosdick demanded that the Tenderloin District be closed, but Behrman again refused to comply with Fosdick's order until he could confer with Baker.

Before traveling to Washington, Behrman called a special meeting at City Hall. Present at the meeting were John M. Parker and the editors of the *Item, Times-Picayune,* and *States.* Behrman told them of the situation and his intentions and they all agreed that the district would remain open until after Behrman's conference with Baker.

In his meeting with the secretary, Behrman

argued that closing the district would cause prostitution and vice to spread throughout the entire city. But Baker, a former mayor of Cleveland, Ohio, drawing from his own experience in cleaning up that city's "red-light district," disagreed with the idea that restricting prostitution to a specified district was the best way to handle such a "difficult situation." Baker, however, instructed the "king" to maintain the "status quo" until further word. Behrman assured the secretary that he would abide by any decision the government made.

A short time later Behrman received an order to close Storyville from the Secretary of the Navy "Tea Totaling" Josephus Daniels. Behrman offered no more resistance: "I had gone as far as I thought I ought to go in impressing my opinions on one member of the Cabinet and I did not care to go further." In compliance with Daniels' instructions, Behrman introduced a bill to the city council directing the closing of the district. The bill passed and Storyville was "officially" closed; however, it continued to operate illegally until the 1940s when it was razed to make way for a federal housing project.

Toward the end of the campaign, the *Times-Picayune* made an appeal to Behrman's supporters to defect and join the ODA. It warned that Behrman and his machine were on the way out:

On the road to ODA: The plaint of the Long-Suffering "Regular"
In the City Hall, while idling, thinking anxiously the while,
There's a Regular a-gazing at his fading salary pile,
And the wind above the rafters seems to whisper, soft and low:
"The Behrman ship is sinking; don't you think it's time to go?"
Hurdle to the ODA
Where you'll get an even play.
Can't you feel the ring a-slippin'
As it totters on its way?
On the road to ODA
You can keep your monthly pay,
With no Choctaw Club a-waitin' for it's just across the way.

The relentless attacks by Governor Parker, the ODA, and the *Times-Picayune* were suc-

cessful; McShane defeated Behrman 22,986 votes to 21,536. The ring was smashed, at least temporarily, and the ODA captured four of the five seats on the city council. The fifth, the only seat won by a Choctaw, went to Paul Maloney. Obviously pleased with the results, Parker reminded the victors that it was not the time for "crowing" but to get busy and make the most of the opportunity.

In searching for the causes of his defeat in 1920, Behrman looked to World War I and its effects on the nation's attitudes:

It happened that the people were in the frame of mind of being against everything. They seemed to be against the war itself, in their hearts. . . . My defeat in 1920 was due to many causes. The very fact that I had been mayor for so long means that I had accumulated enemies. No matter what you do in office, you still make enemies. Sixteen years of enemies is a lot of them.

Behrman, however, failed to admit that the majority of the voters were convinced that vice and corruption in the city were being tolerated by his administration.

The combined efforts of Governor Parker and the Orleans Democratic Association defeated Martin Behrman and the Choctaw Club in 1920. But the ODA had been a loosely knit organization composed of many different factions with the common goal of defeating Behrman. Once this objective had been achieved the coalition degenerated into petty factionalism and quickly returned the Old Regulars to power. Behrman did not retire from New Orleans politics after his rejection in 1920. He stepped aside, rebuilt his machine, and planned his comeback. The Old Choctaw's first step back into public life was his election to the 1921 state constitutional convention.

During the 1919 gubernatorial campaign, both Parker and his opponent, Colonel Frank Stubbs called for a new constitution. Parker referred to the 1913 constitution as a "patchwork" document containing more amendments than all of the other 47 state constitutions combined. With an eye on the 1920 New Orleans municipal elections, Parker thought that it would be a mistake to convene the convention until after the city elections. Otherwise

he said, "It would be a political convention."
He believed that only through the machine
could society in general prosper. Business was
an essential part in the scheme but subordinate
to the machine. During the constitutional convention of 1921, the ex-mayor was content, as
mentioned earlier, to be merely a part of the
proceedings, rather than a leader. The most
important result of the convention, for Behrman at least, was that it gave him a new aura of
victory which he desperately needed after his
defeat in 1920.

The Old Regulars' comeback was temporarily halted on Wednesday, October 4,
1922, when Behrman announced that he was
retiring from politics because of poor health.
The Choctaws then dubbed as their new leader
Paul Maloney, commissioner of public utilities.
Actually Behrman's announced reasons for retiring were not quite the whole truth. Behrman
resigned at the urging of the Choctaw Caucus

because of his defeat in 1920, failing health,
and rising ambitions of younger members. The
war bonnet was passed to Maloney because of
the Choctaw's custom of naming as its leader
the official holding the highest office. In the
1920 municipal elections, he was the only Old
Regular not to go down with Behrman. Reporters asked Maloney if his selection meant that he
would be the 1925 Old Regular candidate for
mayor. Maloney, coyly refusing to commit himself, told them that the election was too far in
the future to comment, although he undoubt-
edly believed that he would be the Old Regulars' candidate. (Maloney's life was a traditional
success story. He began his career in 1892 as a
$15-a-month office boy for the Crescent Trans-
fer and Shipping Company; by 1917 he was
the full owner.)

But Behrman would not be content with retirement after so many years of wielding
power. Though illness forced Behrman into retirement, his ego and love of a campaign could
not keep him there. He helped elect judges to
two New Orleans benches in 1922, assisted in
the 1923–1924 gubernatorial campaign, and
made another bid for mayor in 1925, all of
which attest to his political nature.

The 1923–1924 gubernatorial race was
probably the most controversial campaign for
that office in 20th-century Louisiana history.
By the end of the summer of 1923, three main
candidates and their supporters had committed
themselves. They were Henry L. Fuqua, a Protestant from southern Louisiana; Hewitt Bouanchaud, a French-Catholic from the southern
parish of Pointe Coupee; and Huey Long,
chairman of the Public Service Commission
and a Protestant from northern rural Louisiana.
The main issues during the campaign, regardless of efforts to avoid them, were religion and
the Ku Klux Klan (KKK), which had become an
ever-increasing power in state and national
politics.

Fuqua, the general manager of the state pen-
itentiary at Angola, had the endorsement of
former governors Sanders and Pleasant. Although Fuqua had been an important member
of Governor Parker's administration, he did not
receive the governor's support. Parker en-
dorsed Hewitt Bouanchaud, his lieutenant governor and a Catholic. Catholics, at that time at
least, had practically no chance of being elected
in statewide contests because of northern Loui-

siana's predominantly Protestant population coupled with Protestant voters in the southern part of the state.

Most political observers found it difficult to understand why Parker would back an almost certain loser. Historian T. Harry Williams, writing in his Pulitzer prize-winning *Huey Long,* ventured several possible reasons for Parker's commitment. First, he may have felt a sense of personal loyalty to his fellow "good government" reformer. Secondly, he wished to demonstrate that he could elect his own hand-picked successor over the opposition of Sanders, Pleasant, and the Old Regulars of New Orleans. Thirdly, the reform governor, believing that both Fuqua and Long were afraid of alienating the Klan vote, felt that at least one candidate had to stand staunchly against the hooded order. Actually Parker had little choice.

He could hardly back Long because of his attacks against Parker's pro-Standard Oil stand during the constitutional convention of 1921. Nor could he back Fuqua who had received the enthusiastic support of Behrman.

Behrman and the Old Regulars were impressed with Fuqua's strength in the country parishes. Fuqua was Protestant and anti-Klan, but not as vigorously as Bouanchaud. Behrman could not support Long because he believed Long to be a "radical opponent of business," and he could not join forces with Parker and back Bouanchaud. Besides, he did not think the lieutenant governor had a chance to win. The Old Regulars put their entire organization to work for Fuqua and formed "Fuqua clubs" in each of the city's 17 wards. Although a Catholic himself, the Old Choctaw chief realized that a Protestant from southern Louisiana had a far

Canal and Rampart streets in the 1920s, with the turrets of some of the Storyville brothels in the distance on the right. The transitions apparent in the city at the time are clearly seen in this photograph. Visible are many types of vehicles: electric streetcars, gasoline-powered automobiles, and horsedrawn wagons. The Southern Railway terminal is at the center of the photograph and just to the right is the Saenger Theatre. (THNOC)

greater chance than a Catholic. Furthermore, Fuqua's moderation toward the Klan did not alienate its members or sympathizers as did Bouanchaud's vehement attacks.

Long attacked everything and everyone. The *Item,* he said, was owned by Wall Street and the *Times-Picayune* by New York bankers; Fuqua and Bouanchaud were both Parker's men; Behrman and Colonel John Sullivan, both agents of Wall Street, were actually working together. "If Behrman took a dose of laudanum," he charged, "Sullivan would get sleepy in ten minutes." But regardless of how hard he tried, Long could not evade the real issue of the campaign — the Klan.

In the beginning of the campaign each candidate expressed his position on the hooded order. Bouanchaud said that he stood for law and order and was opposed to the "Invisible Empire of the Ku Klux Klan." If elected governor, he promised, he would go to the limits of the federal and state constitutions to protect the people from the Klan. Fuqua stated that masked and secret societies bred violence and mistrust. If elected, he promised to push for an anti-masking law, one that would require all secret societies to file at regular intervals with the secretary of state lists of their memberships. Long, on the other hand, attempted to evade the issue. The campaign, he said, should be free from religious agitation. He gave a long discourse on the principle of separation of church from state, saying he hoped everyone would live by the "Golden Rule." Later, when pressured for a clearer statement of his views on the Klan, the Winn Parish candidate evasively said that he was "against any unlawful practices by the Klan or anyone else." He doubted that Fuqua's plan for an anti-masking law would work. He pointed out that there was already an anti-masking law in the statutes: "We don't need two, just enforce the first." Bouanchaud challenged his opponents to come out against the Klan "as an un-American organization that cannot exist because it is opposed to constitutional forms of government." Fuqua accused the lieutenant governor of trying to make the Invisible Empire an issue in the campaign in order to distract attention from the "real issues." The real issues for New Orleans, Long asserted, were natural gas, free textbooks for *all* school children, improved workmen's compensation laws, paving Claiborne Avenue,

reduction of taxes, and elimination of governmental extravagances. Long accused Bouanchaud and Fuqua of having no issue but the Klan. The only difference between the two, he remarked, was "that Bouanchaud wanted to hang them before the election and Fuqua wanted them to vote for him first then hang them."

According to most predictions in New Orleans, at least among Bouanchaud supporters, Long did not have a chance. Both the *Item* and the *Times-Picayune* predicted that the lieutenant governor would win, Fuqua would finish second, and Long, a miserable third. The results, however, proved them only partially correct: Bouanchaud received 82,910 votes; Fuqua, 82,177; and Long, a surprising 73,275. The most dramatic results were in New Orleans: Bouanchaud, the Catholic, received 23,232; Fuqua, the Protestant, 32,999; and Long, 12,303. Behrman and the Old Regulars delivered 15 out of the 17 wards to Fuqua. In the second primary Long's supporters swung over to Fuqua giving him the final victory and the governorship.

The most ominous results of the 1924 gubernatorial campaign in New Orleans were the rise of Huey Long in the city's politics and the return of Behrman. The Public Commissioner from Winn Parish realized that great inroads would have to be made in New Orleans if he was to have any future success in the state or national political arenas. This strategy set the pact and drew new political lines in New Orleans politics for the next two decades.

In his campaign for governor in 1924, Huey Long from Winn Parish ran a nonstop race. Although he drew the fewest votes of the three major candidates, fewer than 10,000 votes separated him from Hewitt Bouanchaud, the winner of the primary. (THNOC)

Behrman's next step in his comeback was at the 1924 state Democratic convention which followed the gubernatorial election of that year. The party met in June to select delegates for the national convention. The state convention was merely a formality as it had been the practice for many years in Louisiana that the governor would meet with other state leaders and New Orleans bosses to select the delegates. Fuqua and Behrman saw no reason why 1924 should be any different. In a secret meeting 20 delegates were chosen, 16 on a geographical basis and 4 at-large. After a bit of political manipulation the delegates-at-large were decided upon: Fuqua, Behrman, former Governor J.Y. Sanders, and Lee E. Thomas, mayor of Shreveport. Huey Long denounced the secret agreements as a fraud, stating that Sanders and Behrman had both been rejected by the voters in their last attempts at political office. The Winn Parish upstart vowed that he would go to the convention and help select a new slate.

Actually, Long did not get a chance to change anything. From the moment the convention was called to order, Behrman and Sanders assumed complete control of the proceedings. Behrman was chosen permanent chairman of the convention and in turn appointed Sanders head of the resolutions committee. They ruled the meeting with as heavy a hand as any South or Central American dictator. They tabled and allowed to be shouted down all proposals with which they did not agree, such as the resolution denouncing the KKK. One delegate advocating support for the 18th amendment was physically thrown off the stage by Behrman. Huey Long jumped on the stand and proposed that the number of delegates-at-large be increased from four to eight. That way, he said, the "has beens," referring to Behrman and Sanders, could keep their seats while four more reflecting the "will of the voters" could be chosen. Huey's resolution was tabled by a voice vote. He had been beaten and New Orleans newspapers gleefully wrote the obituaries: "Huey Long is finished."

As the 1924–1925 New Orleans mayorality election approached, Behrman was ready to take advantage of his startling series of political successes since 1920. In a special meeting of the Choctaw Caucus, Behrman was selected to head the Old Regular ticket. The caucus was not unanimous, however; Paul Maloney re-fused to step aside. He walked out, taking many supporters with him. Behrman dubbed those Old Regulars who backed Maloney as deserters and called Maloney a champion of "mediocrity." On January 4, 1925, Maloney announced his ticket and platform.

On the same day Maloney announced his platform, Huey Long was seen meeting with the Williams brothers, John Sullivan, and Colonel Ewing, owner of the New Orleans *States*. Long was taking advantage of the unprecedented division in the Old Regular organization to gain a foothold in New Orleans' politics. Shortly after their conferences they announced that they were supporting Maloney. The *Times-Picayune* asked why, with so much against him, would Behrman run again for mayor. Francis Williams declared that the Old Choctaw was politically sick and would be "politically dead within 30 days." He charged that Behrman, while telling labor of what a good friend he was, had his "loyalists" in the state legislature killing labor bills. Behrman, Williams said, took the working men and women of New Orleans to be a "bunch of boobs."

The two main issues of the campaign were "bossism and labor." On bossism, Behrman's two main opponents were Miss Jean Gordon, a nationally known New Orleans reformer, and the *Times-Picayune*. Miss Gordon supported Maloney. "This was not the time," she said, "to take chances and be sorry afterwards." She reminded voters of Behrman's trip to Washington in 1917 to save Storyville and of his efforts to suppress enforcement of the Sunday closing laws.

The *Times-Picayune* said that Behrman could no more change than the "Ethiopian can change his skin." His methods, it continued, and attitudes were fixed by a lifelong practice of "autocratic" leadership. He was too old and opinionated to change his views. "Behrmanism," wrote the *Picayune,* was the nearest thing to despotism remaining in the United States and was the common enemy of all those who believed "in independent political thought and in public administration which serves primarily and above all else the common will of the whole community." A surprise announcement by Governor Fuqua hit Behrman hard. Fuqua stated that he was going to stay out of the New Orleans campaign and not give state patronage in the city to anyone until

Facing page
Mayor Martin Behrman controlled almost every aspect of political life in New Orleans in the years he held office. He also had considerable influence in state politics. (THNOC)

after the election. Fuqua warned that any promises made by either faction were without foundation.

Organized labor leaders were divided between Behrman and Maloney. David Marcusy, president of the Central Trades and Labor Council, gave his full support to the incumbent McShane. John F. Bowen, chairman of the state legislative board of the Brotherhood of Railroad Trainmen, who had made the opening speech in Behrman's 1920 campaign, backed Maloney. Bowen accused Behrman of not being loyal to the Choctaws. If he had been loyal, Bowen claimed, he would have worked to keep the organization together and not left that job to the rank-and-file. Fuqua's election in 1924, he said, was due to their efforts and not Behrman's. The Choctaws were strong again, he continued, because they had backed Fuqua and now they could win the local election by backing the "logical candidate" — Maloney.

Behrman, borrowing a stratagem from Huey Long's 1923–1924 campaign, used the radio to broadcast his political rallies. Before a crowd at the Folly Theater in Algiers and a radio audience, Behrman made his opening address. "Let's get together," was the keynote of the speech. He pleaded with the voters to give the "battle scarred veteran of many political campaigns" the chance to move New Orleans ahead.

In the same broadcast, Behrman commented on the two newspapers opposing him. He said that he knew Colonel Ewing, of the *States,* about as well as any man in the community. At times, he continued, there had been cordial relations between them, but only when "Behrmanism . . . (was) in full accord with Ewingism." But when they did not agree, Behrmanism was "as wicked a thing as the works of Satan himself." The only comment he had for the *Times-Picayune* was that it was "the prime example of consistency." The former mayor expressed the hope that the campaign would be conducted with more dignity than in 1920. "The reckless display of unjust and untruthful publicity," he asserted, "served (no other) purpose but to injure the standing of the city."

During the campaign an editorial feud developed between the *Item* and the *Times-Picayune.* The *Picayune* accused the *Item* of "lending itself . . . to the baldest and oldest strategy of despots and bossdom." "For

years," said the *Picayune,* "the *Item* did not have a kind word to say about Behrman and during the 1920 campaign called him King of the Tenderloin and an undesirable citizen as well as public official." But during the 1925 campaign, continued the indictment, it was Behrman's strongest supporter and defender. The *Item* denounced the *Picayune* and other Maloney supporters for using smear and character-assassination tactics against Behrman.

The *Picayune* said that it did not have anything against Behrman personally but that he was too old and "broken under the strains of ambition." "For the safety of the city," it pleaded, "his desire to come back must be denied." His type of government, it argued, was based on patronage: "An employee has two masters, the city, who pays his salary, and the boss who gives the jobs." Loyalty to the ring superseded the welfare of the city and it was this type of situation that caused his downfall in 1920. The *Picayune* claimed that Behrman was at his "peak" in 1912, for then he had "vision and drew about him alert and competent men." But as time progressed Behrman turned to machine politics to protect his power: "Behrman the mayor talked about playgrounds and schools while Behrman the boss facilitated the marriage of the lowest strata of the 'ring' with the darkest elements of the underworld of corruption and commercial vice, that poison youth and taint all society." From 1916 on, continued the denunciation, Behrman had been in a state of visible decay and had fallen victim to the strain of high office.

As the campaign neared its conclusion the *Picayune* became more vehement: "Out of the slough of degrading bossdom New Orleans clambered four years ago. Much of the mud of it, the slime of it, still clings to our governmental garments. . . . But we have climbed out." In the same edition it pleaded with voters in an editorial, entitled "Think It Over," to consider their votes. Behrmanism and ring government, it wrote, were a thing of the past. Behrman, in rebuttal, said he believed the people wanted "an administration with party obligations and party responsibilities — for it is only through party government . . . that true progress has ever been made in government." The *Picayune* said what Behrman really meant was that he believed in government by faction and that had to be completely under his control. "Papa," it

continued, believed that he was the "anointed, indispensable and infallible shaper of human desires. . . . Behrman's ethics were ethics of gangdom."

Many voters apparently disagreed with these accusations and denunciations. Behrman received 35,731 votes to Maloney's 33,631. Since "Papa" did not receive a clear majority, a second primary would have been in order, but Maloney withdrew.

Behrman's reelection in 1925 was accomplished over almost insurmountable odds. His opponents thought him politically dead and wondered why he had run at all. Though his reelection was due in part to the lack of coordination among his rivals, his own energies and the effectiveness of the Choctaw's organization were the decisive factors. Behrman's reelection marked the climax of his political career and he immediately began working to fulfill his campaign promises as if inwardly he knew what fate awaited him. On January 12, 1926, one year after his reelection, Martin Behrman died. He died of *chronic myocarditis*, "which was a degeneration of heart muscles due to over work," his physician claimed. Governor Fuqua in a tribute to Behrman said he "pushed himself to become mayor and it killed him." "He died in harness," continued Fuqua, "as he would have liked to die." Governor Alfred E. Smith of New York said he had lost a personal friend.

The *Picayune* in a special editorial ironically stated that Behrman's death would be regretted by all. He was a politician, it said, who liked a good fight, and had fewer personal enemies than one with a lesser public life. His critics, continued the editorial, could never question his sincerity in wanting to do what was good for New Orleans: "His growth in vision and understanding, his broadening concepts of public service and duty, proved something better than the ordinary type of successful politician." It continued its laudatory but hypocritical tribute to Behrman in describing him as "a kindly citizen, a forceful leader and a municipal servant who made the most of his opportunities for service to the city he loved." Behrman's death marked the end of a lengthy political career of over 40 years. It also left a void in New Orleans politics that would soon be filled by Huey Long, who was elected to the governor's office in 1928.

New Orleanians awoke Friday morning October 25, 1929, to read about tremors in the stock market the day before. Black Thursday would affect their lives for the next decade, for the Great Depression had begun. Beside "Stock Exchange Panic," were headlines stating that President Harding's Secretary of the Interior Albert B. Fall had been convicted of bribery, and a report from the YWCA's National Council of Business Girls that "a painted face" was not a woman's guarantee of a good job. Also in the news that morning was Governor Huey P. Long, who had just reorganized the New Orleans Dock Board, eliminating his opposition.

Huey Long, often called the 'Kingfish,' was a force in Louisiana that affected the lives of New

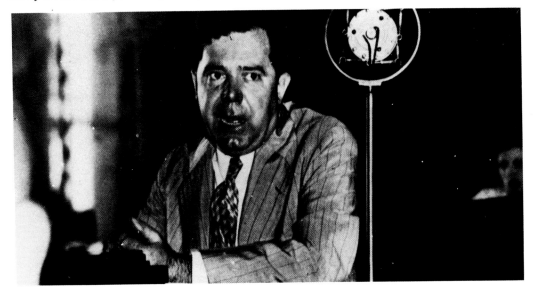

Left
Huey Pierce Long was elected governor of Louisiana in 1928. He was a dominant force in state politics for many years afterwards, with his influence being felt even after his assassination. (THNOC)

Facing page
A street in the French Quarter as it appeared in the early years of the Depression. (THNOC)

Though the Depression had begun, Canal Street looks as busy as ever in this photograph. (THNOC)

Orleanians to a greater extent than even the Depression. On Black Thursday 1929 former Governor John M. Parker warned a gathering of the Young Men's Business Association in New Orleans, that we should not "permit ourselves to be the toy and the plaything of the greatest Mussolini the United States has ever seen."

Huey Pierce Long's election to the governor's office in 1928 marked a break in the political history of Louisiana. Until that time governors were products of the old Bourbon and "aristocratic" class of planter-merchants that had ruled the state since antebellum days (with the exception of Reconstruction). Long in fact campaigned for the office on the promise that he would sweep the Bourbons out. When elected Long set about destroying his opposition — particularly the machine in New Orleans that had so vigorously fought his candidacy — through tight control of the state legislature and by acquiring complete power over state patronage in New Orleans.

Political power in New Orleans up to and during the 1930s was synonymous with patronage — the ability to provide jobs to rank-and-file voters was the lifeblood of the Old Regulars, and this is what Long immediately set out to seize and use for his ends. (Long, however,

believed that his purposes were in the best interest of the poor of Louisiana, and his campaign program — featuring pledges of better roads, better schools, free textbooks for children, and a better court system — was at least partially the reason for the success of his campaign.)

In his first year as governor Huey Long was able to shift patronage for state jobs in New Orleans to his direct control. But in doing so, he met stiff resistance in the state legislature. He reorganized the Orleans Levee Board and the state Board of Health. Opposition in the legislature, however, blocked his attempts to reorganize Charity Hospital in New Orleans and the Orleans Courthouse Commission, as well as his attempt to replace the elected assessors in Orleans Parish with his own appointee.

In the spring of 1929, Long's opponents made a frontal assault, attempting to destroy him politically through impeachment. Nineteen charges were filed against him ranging from misuse of appointive powers and attempted bribery of legislators, to illegally using the state militia to raid New Orleans gambling houses and engaging in immoral behavior in a New Orleans night club.

"The reason for this is that he [Long] is temporarily and otherwise unfit to hold the office,"

said the *Times-Picayune.* "His tactics and methods reveal him to be a cruel political tyrant, willing to resort to almost any expediency to carry out his own wishes and purposes. Long cleverly defeated a conviction in the state senate by having 15 senators sign the infamous "Round Robin," saying they would refuse to convict Long no matter what evidence was presented.

In his successful 1930 bid for the U.S. Senate, Long formed his own political organization, the Louisiana Democratic Association, to counteract the Choctaws in New Orleans. In January 1932 Long took the oath of office for the U.S. Senate. His successor to the governor's office was his hand-picked candidate, Oscar K. Allen. Robert Maestri, later mayor of New Orleans, was appointed head of the Louisiana Democratic Association in the city. Before assuming his Senate seat, Long finally achieved an uncomfortable peace with the Choctaws: in exchange for their support in the legislature for several of his pet bills, Long promised New Orleans state money to pave and repair city streets, pay the debt of the Port of New Orleans, and build a free bridge across the Mississippi River at New Orleans.

While Huey Long's reign was detested by liberals across the country, at home his campaign on a platform of helping the "little man" seemed to work well as the Depression was hitting New Orleans very hard. Five New Orleans banks collapsed in 1933 as did many homestead, or building and loan, associations. Unemployment lines grew longer as the ability of the city to provide jobs became increasingly difficult. In 1934 11 percent of the people of Louisiana were on federal relief. By 1939 federal spending on relief agencies in New Orleans totaled more than $50 million.

Employment opportunities were so hard to acquire that riots erupted at several places in New Orleans when hundreds of job seekers showed up answering job announcements in the classified sections of newspapers. In 1930 Mayor T. Semmes Walmsley, who served from 1930–1936, announced a new job program for the city's unemployed: selling oranges. The needy bought boxes of Louisiana oranges and peddled them on the streets at two for a nickel. According to Louisiana historian Roman Heleniak, local newspapers urged people to buy "Louisiana's golden oranges," with the slogan "Health for you — Help for the Needy." New Orleans even had its pathetic variation of the apple vendor standing in the snow to make a few nickels. Bertha McMahon, a 27-year-old orange peddler, although gravely ill continued to sell oranges during bad weather because her family needed the money. She later died of influenza.

To deal with the Depression as it was affecting New Orleans in 1931, Mayor Walmsley took a bold new step. He formed the New Orleans Welfare Committee to find jobs for the unemployed and relief for the destitute. At

• THE LONG PLAN •

To Spread the Wealth of the Country Among All the People!

There is no need of hunger in the land of too much to eat; no need of people crying for things to wear in the land of too much cotton and wool; no need of homelessness in the land of too many houses.

With the one law which I propose to submit the minute Congress meets, I think most of our difficulties will be brought to an almost immediate end. To carry out President Roosevelt's plan as announced in his inaugural address for redistribution and to prevent unjust accumulation of wealth, I am now including roads, navigation, flood control, reforestation, unemployment, farm relief, canals, irrigation, etc. And with this law passed, no one can ever again say that our government has not a satisfactory basis for an adequate and sufficient currency. All such can be amply financed by the government without

first, funds were collected from private individuals and businesses. But in 1932 New Orleans voters approved a $750,000 bond issue to support the Walmsley program. This project would be a preview of President Roosevelt's New Deal programs and especially the Works Progress Administration.

Walmsley's Welfare Committee also marked a transition in New Orleans' political and economic history. Except for a brief period during the Civil War, it was the first time New Orleans city government got into the business of relief. City government here had always provided jobs, but for different reasons. Now it was doing so for the survival of the people and the political system. But according to historian Roman Heleniak of Southeastern Louisiana University in Hammond, Walmsley's committee could not begin to solve the problem.

More help came for beleaguered New Orleanians and Louisianians that same year when Huey Long formed the State Unemployment Relief Committee to provide part-time work programs for the unemployed with funds from the federal Reconstruction Finance Corporation. But because of the on-and-off-again antagonisms between Long and the Old Regulars, New Orleans usually took a back seat to the rest of the state in getting the relief programs.

By mid-1933 the cooperation between Long and the Choctaws began to break down, especially when Long attacked President Franklin D. Roosevelt's New Deal programs pending in the Senate. Long had vigorously supported Roosevelt in the 1932 Presidential election but that was short-lived. The following year Long launched his national campaign of "Share-The-Wealth" in what many believed would be his bid for the Presidency in 1936 or 1940. Roosevelt, meanwhile, awarded all federal patronage in Louisiana to Long's opponents and in 1935 the President sent the Internal Revenue Service to investigate the senator's past income tax returns.

The enmity between Long and the Old Regulars erupted into bitter warfare between August 1934 and September 1935, when Long personally orchestrated a drive in the legislature to strip New Orleans of its autonomy. Open hostilities between Long and the Old Regulars broke out in the 1934 elections. Long ordered an investigation of vice and corruption in the city on the eve of the election in an effort to embarrass the city administration. Fearing that the Old Regulars might use the city police force to falsify the election returns, Long ordered Governor O.K. Allen to send the National Guard to New Orleans, where the guardsmen seized the city's voter registration offices. Long also warned the city that if one policeman was seen at a polling place, he would send in a squad of troops. Mayor T. Semmes Walmsley, enraged, denounced Long: "I warn you, Huey Long, you cringing coward, that if a life is spent in defense of this city and its right of self-government, you shall pay the penalty as others have done before you."

By the time of his assassination in September 1935, the Old Regulars had been soundly defeated. After his death, Huey Long's influence was felt in New Orleans politics for another decade. Particularly during the Depression, New Orleans' economic stability depended upon its relations with the state

Far left
New Deal politics in New Orleans took many forms, one of which was a Writers Project conducted under the auspices of the Works Progress Administration. (THNOC)

Left
Robert Maestri (bottom row, center) replaced T. Semmes Walmsley as mayor of New Orleans in 1936. (THNOC)

Below left
Maestri was an active mayor who was not content to stay cloistered in his office. He was very conscious of the need for physical improvements in the city, such as the repair of streets. (THNOC)

administration. At the time of Long's death in 1935, the Old Regulars were ready to surrender. They had been thoroughly defeated, according to historian Edward F. Haas of New Orleans.

Governor-elect Richard Leche, the Kingfish's political heir, accepted their surrender with the understanding that Walmsley and the Old Regulars would have to step down. Walmsley reluctantly agreed to leave office only if the legislature restored to the city some of the powers it had lost to Long in 1935.

At a secret meeting in Hot Springs, Arkansas, Leche named Robert Maestri, one of Huey Long's financial backers, to be mayor of the city in August 1936. Maestri, described by Haas as "earthy" and a "financial wizard," is probably best known for his famous question to a visiting President Roosevelt: "How ya like dem ersters?" and for a city wide open to corruption, prostitution, and gambling. Historians,

however, have been kinder to Maestri. According to Haas, Maestri reorganized the city's financial structure and made it more efficient. In addition his administration took an active interest in bolstering the city's cultural and recreational programs.

For the duration of the Great Depression, Maestri and Leche worked closely together, Haas said, to create jobs for the city's work force. They were also able to get millions of dollars from the federal Works Progress Administration to employ many New Orleans writers, artists, musicians, laborers, and craftsmen.

Maestri and his "ersters" remained in office until 1946 when he was defeated by a young veteran returning from World War II who preached reform and promised to turn out the rascals. De Lesseps Story "Chep" Morrison symbolized a new era of politics and prosperity and a break with the old order of New Orleans political history.

CHAPTER VIII
THE POSTWAR CHALLENGE

World War II brought a prosperity to New Orleans and other Southern cities that they had not seen in almost a century. "World War II activated another cycle of change in the South. To a greater degree than the previous war it put people on the move: to shipyards, war plants, training camps, and far-flung battlefields," according to historian George B. Tindall. "It intensified established trends: in economic development, race relations, and politics."

As the war effort cranked up, the South began to receive a great percentage of the war-production contracts, especially in shipbuilding and assembly plants. By the end of the war the South's 17 major shipyards had received 23 percent of federal expenditures for shipbuilding. Shipyards like Ingalls in Pascagoula and Higgins in New Orleans provided jobs for the residents, dollars for the community, and naval vessels for the war effort. New Orleans — like other Southern cities — also got a share of the aircraft assembly and components plants.

Although the war boom was only temporary, "still [it] created permanent assets," wrote Tindall. "If the South later slid back from the wartime peaks, it remained on a plateau higher than ever before." New Orleans used the war years to launch its quest for commercial and industrial prosperity. For example, in 1943 a group of businessmen in the city formed a trade club to encourage foreign nations, especially in Latin

America, to use the port of New Orleans. Two years later, the International House opened its doors in the downtown area. Today the International Trade Mart is a cornerstone of the city's foreign commerce. In the years following the war, New Orleans would also assume a leading role in the petrochemical industry. Many of the major oil companies established large offices in the city to be close to the on- and offshore oil fields and refineries. New Orleans also became one of the important centers for the nation's efforts to explore outer space during the 1960s. The Michoud Assembly Facility, which built the Saturn S-1 booster rockets for the Apollo program, was responsible for the development of eastern New Orleans and the nearby community of Slidell in neighboring St. Tammany Parish. Thousands of acres of marshland in eastern New Orleans gave way to residential subdivisions, shopping centers, motels, gas stations, and restaurants.

After the war New Orleanians, fresh from cheering the downfall of dictators in Nazi Germany and Facist Italy, were ready for a change in local politics. The city's national reputation for political corruption, wide-open gambling, and prostitution had become an embarrassment. Reminiscent of the voting after World War I, a wave of civic morality dictated a change in city government. Mayor Maestri had given the city a good and efficient administration during his early years in office; but in later years, the mayor's office became a friendly ally to the *demi-monde*. Reformers demanded a change and they turned to a 34-year-old returning veteran, Colonel de Lesseps Story "Chep" Morrison, to lead the crusade in the 1946 mayoral campaign.

Morrison was able to unite behind his candidacy all of those people who had grown complacent under 46 years of machine politics. During Morrison's campaign, the "new broom sweeps clean" became the rallying slogan to rid the city of corruption. When the votes were counted, Chep had narrowly defeated Maestri. Commissioner Fred A. Earhart was one of the few members of the old order to survive Morrison's "clean sweep."

According to Morrison's biographer, Edward Haas, the new mayor had the rare ability of being many things to different people. To the national press, and most New Orleanians, Chep was an efficient and capable young politician who was delivering New Orleans from corruption. To New Orleans, Chep Morrison

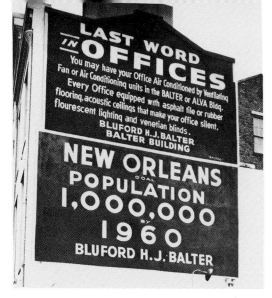

brought new industry; a Union Passenger Terminal; a network of overpasses in the city; the nationally acclaimed New Orleans Recreation Department (NORD); the Civic Center; an expressway system to connect the city with its suburbs; and, national attention. On the other side of the ledger, Morrison's building and streets programs threw the city's bonded debt into chaos; the expressways facilitated white flight to the suburbs during the 1960s; and, the national attention was not always good. Morrison and some members of his political organization—the Crescent City Democratic Association—allied themselves with the old machine politicians and gambling and vice interests in the city, Haas wrote.

Although Morrison allegedly had some political ties with gambling interests in the city, he played an important part in the federal government's nationwide campaign against organized crime. In 1949 and 1950 Morrison, who was then president of the American Municipal Association, called for a concerted local, state, and federal investigation of organized crime and later for passage of the Kefauver bill to investigate interstate gambling.

Meanwhile in New Orleans public clamor against wide-open gambling and vice had reached such a point that a grand jury inquiry was arranged in July 1949. Two days before the grand jury met, Superintendent of Police Joseph Scheuering, in a transparent move, ordered handbook operations to close down. After the jury completed its task, the gamblers were permitted to resume their trade. The jury later recessed with no indictments or any plans for future actions.

New Orleans hosted a national spectacle in January 1951, when Senator Estes Kefauver held nationally televised public hearings on the

Far left
This advertisement for the Balter Building embodies the spirit of general optimism ushered in by the "Chep" Morrison administration. Post-World War II New Orleans was characterized by a flurry of building activity. (THNOC)

Above
The Michoud Assembly Facility in eastern New Orleans had a great impact on the area and was one of the major factors that spurred development there. (THNOC)

Below left
The young "Chep" Morrison was a reform-minded candidate who was a different type of politician than his predecessors. (THNOC)

corruption in the city police department and city government. The wife of a former chief of detectives claimed that her husband as a patrolman had received $150,000 from gambling and prostitution figures during a six-month period. The hearings also revealed that an association of pinball machine operators had one of the city attorneys on its staff as a legal adviser. Testimony also connected some members of Morrison's Crescent City Democratic Association with gambling operations in the city.

Between September 1952 and February 1953, the city administration was embarrassed once again when the state police, under the direction of Colonel Francis Grevemberg, conducted a number of raids on New Orleans gambling and prostitution houses operating under the eyes of the police department. In March 1953 Morrison came to the defense of the city police and his administration, claiming the city "has in seven short years achieved the greatest degree of law enforcement we have ever had." But the city's commission council was not convinced by Morrison's claims. It appropriated $50,000 and called for a special investigation of the police force by a three-man team, representing the Bureau of Governmental Research, the Metropolitan Crime Commission (formed in 1952), and the Society of Former FBI Agents. Morrison publicly supported this team called the Special Citizens Investigating Committee (SCIC), but privately he opposed it.

In June SCIC hired Aaron Kohn to manage the police probe. Kohn, a lawyer and former FBI agent, previously had conducted a similar investigation of the Chicago police force. Despite obstructions placed in his way by police and city officials, Kohn energetically and tenaciously went about exposing corruption at all levels of the department. Between November and the following January, public hearings on police corruption were held once again. During the hearings the Orleans Parish grand jury went to work and indicted the police superintendent and chief of detectives for malfeasance. But a month later a criminal district court judge dismissed the indictment and returned the men to office. On January 7 a court injunction reportedly initiated by top police officials ended the hearings. Three months later SCIC published the results of its investigation which included nine pages of recommendations for reorganizing the police force and for curbing vice in the city.

Haas wrote that Morrison was caught in the middle between the "reform morality and the human nature of the average man":

The Union Passenger Terminal, located near the Civic Center, was the starting and ending point for over a dozen passenger trains that served New Orleans in the 1950s. (THNOC)

*Morrison . . . could not overlook those
New Orleanians who held different
hopes. Over the years gambling,
prostitution, and various forms of vice
had become pleasurable aspects of
Crescent City life that many residents
enjoyed and wanted to preserve. . . .
This dichotomy in urban mores and local
ideals found the new mayor in the
middle. Caught between reform morality
and the human nature of the average
man, Morrison had to find a suitable
approach to law enforcement that would
not alienate any segments of New
Orleans society, even those who were
less than respectable.*

Morrison's most disappointing political defeats came in the 1956, 1960, and 1964 gubernatorial elections. In the first campaign (1955–
1956), Morrison met his old political nemesis,
Governor Earl K. Long, Huey's younger
brother. The younger Long was backed by the
Old Regulars in New Orleans and by the rural
supporters who had been instrumental in elect-
ing Huey. "Uncle Earl" carried out a comical
but successful attack on Morrison. "I'd rather
beat Morrison than eat any blackberry huckle-
berry pie my mama ever made. Oh, how I'm

praying for that old stump-wormer [Morrison]
to get in there," Long said before the campaign
got under full way. "I want him to roll up them
cuffs and get out that little old tuppy [toupee],
and pull down them shades, and make himself
up." While "Uncle Earl" was mocking "de
Lasoups" and the mayor's toupee, Morrison
attacked the governor's record in office between 1948 and 1952.

After his victory Earl Long turned to wooing
New Orleans with the honey of the state treasury. He gave the city Louisiana State University in New Orleans (now the University of New
Orleans); Southern University in New Orleans;
and, expanded the Delgado Trade School. In
addition, the Long-controlled legislature approved large appropriations to the Orleans Parish Teachers' Retirement Fund; Charity Hospital; Ochsner Foundation; and Touro Infirmary.

In the 1959–1960 gubernatorial campaign
Morrison lost to former "Singing" Governor
("You Are My Sunshine") Jimmie H. Davis,
who capitalized on New Orleans' integration
problems and the mayor's associations with
movie-star Zsa Zsa Gabor and Senator John
Kennedy. Davis also had the invaluable assistance of Judge Leander Perez of Plaque-
mines Parish and William Rainach of Claiborne
Parish. Perez and Rainach, who were leaders of
the White Citizens' Council, traveled the state
feeding racial hatred in support of Davis' candidacy. Davis' workers claimed Morrison was
an integrationist working hard to end segregation in New Orleans. Morrison was a segrega-
tionist, but not a rabid racist. When ordered by
the federal courts to desegregate public transportation in the mid-1950s, he did so.

Morrison's greatest political crisis came with the school desegregation order of 1960. For almost a decade school integration was litigated in the nation's courts. Then came the order from federal Judge J. Skelly Wright to integrate public schools in New Orleans by November 1960. City officials had given little thought or preparation to handling this problem. Governor Davis and the state legislature jumped in and passed 47 acts and 17 resolutions in an attempt to circumvent the court order. But one by one, the federal courts struck down the legislature's feeble attempts. Then on November 4, 1960, six-year-old Ruby Bridges, led by her mother and U.S. marshals, entered the previously all-white William Frantz School amid the shouts, threats, and torments of white hecklers. Three other black children attended McDonogh No. 19 that same day. The swift action by the New Orleans Police Department spared the city a bloody racial confrontation. Some rioting took place during the daylight hours by white students and after dark by blacks, but these were minor considering the impact of integration on the entire social order. Integration had arrived and even threats by the New Orleans White Citizens' Council, men like Leander Perez, and the state-supported white private "segregation" schools, could not stop it. "During the desegregation crisis, Mayor Morrison received criticism from all sides," Haas wrote. "Civil Rights advocates blasted the mayor for his reluctance to take a firm stand on school integration, and segregationists argued

that he favored racial mixing."

In the spring of 1961 Morrison took a middle-of-the-road course on the racial issue. He ordered the arrest of civil-rights workers staging sit-ins in downtown lunch counters; as well as a busload of George Lincoln Rockwell's American Nazi Party "stormtroopers" when they caused a disturbance in front of a downtown theater. One of the city's primary industries — tourism — suffered as a result of the bad publicity the city got in the national news media. People were hesitant to visit New Orleans for fear of racial violence. The Citizens' Council's most vocal members were constantly on the nation's stage. Not until the city's business community finally spoke up for an end to violence and for open schools, did the precariously tense situation begin to ease.

But Morrison's political future looked bleak after he failed to have the city charter amended to enable him to have another term as mayor. However an old acquaintance, then President John F. Kennedy, came to his rescue. In July 1961 Morrison resigned to become the U.S. ambassador to the Organization of American States. Morrison ran for governor a third time against "Won't you please help me!" John McKeithen and lost again. A year later, the former mayor and his younger son died in an airplane crash.

Morrison's successor at city hall was the short, balding, but bouncy and affable Victor Schiro, whose favorite slogan was, "If it's good for New Orleans, I'm for it." Schiro unlike Morrison took a firmer stand on the school integration issue. The court had ordered it and Schiro, through the police department, enforced it with proper planning. Among his many accomplishments, Schiro and police Superintendent Joseph I. Giarusso restored public confidence in the police force. Schiro also has been given little credit for the business revitalization in the Central Business District. Over much criticism, Schiro widened and beautified Poydras Street,

Far left
John J. McKeithen took over the Louisiana governor's office in 1964 after defeating "Chep" Morrison, former New Orleans mayor. Courtesy, New Orleans Public Library, Louisiana Division.

Left
Victor H. Schiro succeeded "Chep" Morrison as mayor of New Orleans and served the city at a time of considerable social strife. Courtesy, City of New Orleans, Public Information Office.

which is rapidly becoming the business center of the city. Many New Orleanians will never forget the television program that appeared only days before the 1965 mayoral election in which Schiro, recovering from an appendectomy, announced plans for a domed stadium in the city. Many say the announcement won him the election.

Schiro was able to hold together a declining political coalition that kept him in office until 1970. During the 1960s, New Orleans had experienced dramatic demographic changes. The lure of suburban subdivisions with colorful names, coupled with real and imagined fears of racial integration, caused many whites to flee to the predominantly white suburbs surround-ing the city. The Brooklyn and New Jersey-style accent of the old Third and Ninth Wards, with their "choiches" (churches) and "zinks" (sinks), moved to nearby "Metry" (Metairie), Chalmette, and Slidell. One was more likely to hear the familiar greeting "Where y'at!" in the suburbs than in the Irish Channel or St. Claude Avenue, which are populated now mostly by blacks, Vietnamese, and Cuban refugees.

These suburban expatriates built their own style of New Orleans living. Restaurants and bars abound along the major suburban thoroughfares separated only by residential subdivisions, apartment complexes, and vast shopping centers. In neighboring Jefferson Parish, local entrepreneurs built Fat City—a Bourbon

This page

Below left
Suburban growth around New Orleans was extremely rapid in the 1950s and 1960s. Subdivisions were laid out by land developers and "modern"-style homes were built on the lots. (THNOC)

Bottom left
Victorian "shotgun" cottages and other types of 19th-century residences have become quite popular among renovators in New Orleans in recent years. While this trend has served to rejuvenate areas of the city, it has also caused problems of displacement.

Facing page

Left
Mayor Ernest "Dutch" Morial, the first black person to hold the office of mayor of New Orleans, was elected in 1978. His administration has sought to increase city revenue through an increased sales tax and road use and property service charges, which have proven to be unpopular, but necessary in order to provide much-needed city services. Courtesy, City of New Orleans, Public Information Office.

Right
Widespread demolition in the Central Business District caused some of New Orleans' architectural treasures to be lost. Demolition is more tightly regulated today, but the wrecking ball is not totally inactive downtown. Courtesy, John H. Lawrence.

Street-style assemblage of saloons and night spots. One can even participate in one of the many new Mardi Gras parades now rolling in the outlying areas. Left behind in the city were decaying neighborhoods, poverty, and spiraling crime rates.

While thousands of blue-collar and some middle-class whites were fleeing to the suburbs, many of the more affluent middle to upper-middle class whites began buying and renovating the gingerbread-draped Victorian cottages in the Uptown and University areas. Entire neighborhoods, which had been populated by blue-collar whites and then blacks, have given way to the restoration craze. The restored cypress cottages, which once sold for a few thousand dollars, have fetched prices in the six figures. The almost pioneer spirit of the renovation movement has given older sections of the city new life.

Even in the Central Business District (CBD) — the old American Sector of the early-19th century, where many architectural treasures have been lost to fires or "progress" — the restoration of commercial buildings has been economically feasible. Individual preservationists and preservation groups in the city had a difficult struggle during the 1960s and 1970s convincing property owners and the municipal government of the importance of preservation to the economic health of the Canal Street area. Widespread destruction of the 19th-century buildings in the CBD was occurring so rapidly in these decades that preserva-

tionists were able to get Mayor Landrieu and the city council to declare a moratorium on further destruction. Convincing city government to take such a bold step did not come easily. Preservationists waged a long but stubborn campaign to win over city officials who at first were less than enthusiastic. Despite the great losses in the old Faubourg St. Mary, many 19th-century edifices, which have been restored with internal modifications, mingle quietly but magnificently among their 20th-century neighbors.

Since World War II, New Orleans has continued to slip in rank as compared to other Southern cities. Between 1940 and 1950 the city's population increased from 494,537 to 570,445. But despite this almost 20-percent increase, it dropped in rank from the South's largest city to the second largest, falling behind Houston. By 1970 New Orleans would be only the fifth largest and the 1980 census showed the city falling even further behind other Southern cities. Preliminary census figures for 1980 placed the city's population at 556,913. When these "startling" numbers were released city officials protested vigorously, insisting the population was actually closer to 643,000. City officials issued a press release in September 1980, declaring that "since about 1977, people have been moving into New Orleans after nearly 10 years of migration out of the city." Another important change surfaced in the 1980 census: more than 55 percent of the city's population was black.

Reflecting on the white flight to the suburbs, Mayor "Moon" Landrieu (1970–1978) said New Orleans "lost 125,000 people — mostly white and affluent — moving out to the suburbs, and in their place, 90,000, mostly poor and black, moved in."

The rapidly changing demography brought increased tensions between the races. The upwardly spiraling crime rate in the black communities spilled over into the white communities. Many middle-class whites have become so afraid of the violence, they have formed neighborhood vigilance committees and hired off-duty policemen and private security guards to protect themselves. In September and November 1970 bloody battles took place between the police and an arm of the Black Panthers in the vicinity of the Desire Street Housing Project. On January 7, 1973, Mark Essex — a young,

demented black sniper from Kansas — paralyzed the city as he ran about the downtown Howard Johnson Motel with his high-powered rifle, randomly killing and wounding. Before police machine-gun fire finally brought him down, Essex managed to kill nine people and wound almost a score of others.

The changing demography in the city coupled with the 1965 Voting Rights Act and the voter registration drives of the 1970s also drew new political lines in the city. For the first time since Reconstruction, blacks were a political force, if not the dominant force in the city's political arena. Blacks have gained new economic opportunities that have reinforced and expanded the black middle class. Like their white counterparts, many of the affluent young black families have fled to the suburbs of eastern New Orleans.

In 1970 the able and politically astute "Moon" Landrieu formed his own political organization and actively solicited the help of the influential black political groups in his bid for the mayor's office. Blacks held high-level jobs during Landrieu's administration. While in office Mayor Landrieu gained national attention because of his leadership role in the U.S. Conference of Mayors. After relinquishing his mayoral seat he was appointed by President Jimmy Carter to head the federal Office of Housing and Urban Development.

In the 1977–1978 mayoral campaign, New Orleans made a major break with the city's political past. Blacks, with sizable support from whites, elected the city's first black mayor, Ernest N. "Dutch" Morial. Morial, who had been one of the leaders of the civil rights movement of the 1950s and 1960s, inherited a city plagued with financial and social problems, and labor unrest among city employees (for example, the 1979 police strike crippled the city and caused the cancellation of most Mardi Gras Parades that year).

Even with the economic uncertainties and the growth of violent crime during the 1970s and early 1980s, New Orleans has shown remarkable resiliency. Since 1970 the skyline changed dramatically as new skyscrapers rose above the foundations of the 19th-century old American Sector. The awe-inspiring $180 million Louisiana Superdome — despite the controversy that surrounded its construction — launched a building boom and economic

Below
The Louisiana Superdome, opened in the mid-1970s, is a sport and multi-purpose auditorium and stadium. Its presence is one reason for the building boom that has occurred along Poydras Street. (THNOC)

Below right
Some of the new high-rise construction (office towers and hotels) completed in the 1960s and 1970s can be seen in this view of the Central Business District. (THNOC)

revitalization in the Central Business District, while the French Quarter took on the trappings of a tourist-oriented economy. The oil industries have invested millions of dollars in CBD construction and towering hotels have risen from the ruins of run-down tenements and warehouses. In 1980 city officials announced the development of the Almonester-Michoud Industrial District in eastern New Orleans as a new source of prosperity for the city.

In late 1980 Mayor Morial expressed intensive optimism for the city's future. Waving a hand toward the CBD, he claimed there had been more commercial construction in that area since 1978 than in the previous 20 years. Large corporations were moving to New Orleans, he said, because they were convinced the city had a new-found vitality. The city has charm, the mayor said, but "it is more than a Bourbon Street or Fun City U.S.A." To attract more businesses to the Crescent City, Morial formed a committee of 100 businessmen to wage an intensive public-relations drive to sell the city.

It required a great deal of persuasive skill to convince the Bureau of International Expositions in Paris that permitting New Orleans to host the 1984 World's Exposition was a good idea; but it was done. The exposition was organized by a group of private corporations under the title the Louisiana World Exposition, Inc., which raised over $40 million in pledges from the business community to make the fair possible.

The site for the exposition, which took for its theme, "The World of Rivers: Fresh Water as a Source of Life," is an 80-acre stretch of land in the old riverfront warehouse district in the CBD. At the center of the exposition grounds, the taxpayers financed a 820,000-square-foot exhibition hall at a cost of over $88 million. An economic study projected the exposition would draw 11 million visitors and generate $2 billion in business activity, not to mention 39,000 temporary jobs and 14,000 new permanent jobs once the fair is closed.

That the 1984 World's Exposition is to be held in New Orleans epitomizes New Orleanians' determination that their city will remain prosperous and vibrant into the 21st century and beyond. But the future is not their sole concern. New Orleanians are working as never before to preserve their heritage, as Mary Lou Christovich explains in the following chapter. So while the towering structures of the Central Business District may seemingly dwarf the remaining edifices of the 18th and 19th centuries, an appreciation of both can ensure that the Crescent City's future will be no less remarkable than its past.

CHAPTER IX
A NEW CUSTOM IN NEW ORLEANS:
PRESERVING THE PAST

BY MARY LOU CHRISTOVICH

As a 20th-century concept, historic preservation in New Orleans did not commence until almost 200 years after the city's founding. Although there were isolated instances of vocal concern — objections to demolition and alteration of place — serious appreciation of the city's cultural and physical environment began only at the end of the 19th century.

Perhaps the first locally documented objection to city planning is to be found in the September 5, 1722, journal entry of Jean Baptiste-Martin d'Artaguiette d'Iron. At that time Adrien de Pauger, a French military engineer, laid out the original city according to the plan of his superior, Pierre Le Blond de La Tour, in the French, fortified manner with an enclosed grid-street pattern.

A few years earlier a Monsieur Traverse had built a residence not in alignment with the newly planned streets; he was ordered to move his house or tear it down. Private motivation prompted him to seek preservation or restitution for his home. Infuriated by Traverse's stubborn appeal to the French Superior Council, Pauger attacked him with a stick, administered a thorough thrashing, and summoned the *gendarmes* to cast him into jail. The house was summarily expropriated and demolished to complete what may have been preservation's most one-sided setback.

Writing about New Orleans in 1722, Jesuit Father Charlevoix said:

"The eight hundred fine houses and the five Parish Churches that Le Mercure [a French newspaper] gave it two years ago is today reduced to about a hundred huts placed without much order, a large warehouse built of wood, two or three houses that would not grace a French village and half a wretched warehouse that they had been good enough to lend to the Lord."

There is some concern for the validity of the *Le Mercure* description of the early settlement. Glowing and romantic tales that had little relationship to actuality often encouraged emigration. In reality life in the colony was a constant struggle against the elements. A flood in 1717 was followed by hurricanes in 1719, 1722, and 1723; the settlers' hold on property was at best a precarious one.

The dramatic vicissitudes of the semitropical New Orleans climate were not expected by early French architects and builders and their plans did not take them into account. Unstable, spongy land caused massive foundation problems; only after the structural failure of the original soldier's barracks designed by architect Ignace Broutin were the problems of soil conditions solved. Armed with experience in 1745, Broutin designed the Ursuline Convent, which survives as one of the earliest French colonial buildings in the Mississippi Valley.

Although soirees, banquets, and even balls

occurred during the governorship of Pierre Rigaud de Vaudreuil in the 1740s, New Orleans essentially remained the river town and trading post founded by French-Canadian Jean Baptiste Le Moyne, Sieur de Bienville in 1718. New Orleans' fate was sealed and her direction altered when the French king, Louis XV, gave the entire Louisiana territory to his Spanish cousin, Charles III in 1762. Four years later Spanish officials arrived to claim the colony thus beginning a Spanish domination that lasted until 1803.

Numerous tile-terraced houses, employing the creole-cottage floor plan of the four square rooms, were constructed along the planked *banquettes* of the French town; patios were integrated into important outdoor activity areas in the Spanish style. Evidence of most of these buildings remains only in notarial property descriptions because fires — one in 1788 and another in 1794 — destroyed 856 and 215 buildings, respectively. Although fewer buildings were lost in 1794, the value of the property lost was far greater. These disasters removed permanently most of the tangible evidence of New Orleans' 18th-century architecture and prevented the possibility of effort toward its preservation.

New Orleanians built and rebuilt without a conscious concern for the past. They replaced the houses lost in the 1788 fire with similar frame ones in the amalgamated French and Spanish styles. Salvaged materials — bricks, iron, flooring, and structural timbers — were reworked into the fabric of the new buildings. There is evidence that, after the 1788 fire, structurally sound surviving walls and floors often were incorporated in new construction. Despite these conservations, many of the new buildings were lost to fire just six years later.

After the 1794 fire the Illustrious Cabildo (the Spanish governing body of the city) prohibited frame construction and ruled that all buildings from then on would be of brick or brick-between-posts and plastered over with at least a one-inch layer of cement stucco. Frugality prompted Don Andres Almonester y Roxas to use the demolished brick walls from around the old St. Peter Street cemetery for rebuilding of the St. Louis Parish Church and the Cabildo building which were destroyed in the fire of 1788. The new Cabildo structure of 1795 utilized the walls and brick floor of the 1750 French *corps de garde* which can be viewed

Courtyards and patios have provided quiet, privacy, and a degree of coolness to Vieux Carre residents almost from the beginning. Many, such as this one at Brennan's, are lavishly landscaped, containing trees and fountains. Photo by Robin Boylan.

Built in 1795–1799, the Cabildo, perhaps New Orleans' most historically significant building, served as city hall from 1803 to 1853, as the Louisiana Supreme Court building from 1853 to 1911, and as part of the Louisiana State Museum since 1911. Within its walls the formal transfer of Louisiana from France to the United States took place in 1803. Photo by Robin Boylan.

today in that building.

Further tolls on New Orleans' early architecture were taken by hurricanes, such as the one that struck in 1811, destroying the new French Market. The river was always a potential threat; a break in the levee system in 1816 caused the inundation of the entire city from eight miles upriver to the Marigny section below the Vieux Carre. One wonders, however, why the city didn't develop an effective fire-control system very early. In the fall of 1816 another large block of buildings in the Vieux Carre was lost; this time 60 buildings turned to ashes.

With the destruction of these buildings and the advent of the American period following the Louisiana Purchase in 1803, the architectural character of the Vieux Carre became a mixture of retardate French and Spanish colonial styles and the newer Eastern Seaboard English townhouse.

The city expanded beyond the Old Quarter both up- and downriver and back-of-town as the population in the early 19th century reached almost 15,000. Bernard de Marigny had his downriver plantation subdivided in 1805, and Claude Treme sold his land behind the city for the first municipally planned suburb in 1810. With the development of Canal Street and the American Sector (known as Faubourg Ste. Marie or St. Mary), the French Quarter began to lose business and residents, and many of the buildings became rentals.

Other changes were occurring in the French Quarter; an 1823 appeal from the Widow Carrick vividly illustrates the advent of a destructive practice. Mistress Carrick inherited 90 feet of property on Levee (now Decatur) Street between St. Philip and Ursulines from her late husband who, she declared, had purchased the property and buildings from Elie Beauregard in 1800. She claimed that the property was ac-

quired with privileged frontage to the river, including all other servitudes and advantages incidental thereto, such as a free, direct, and uninterrupted view of and intercourse with the river. These rights in the past had been considered in conformity with the title deeds and sanctioned by the Spanish government. The city, however, had just erected a vegetable market on the vacant ground, thus depriving Mistress Carrick of all her rights and diminishing the value of her property. She publicly protested against the mayor and aldermen and sought financial redress. The city denied her claim.

A few years later in 1830, no fewer than 25 leading residents and property owners in Faubourg Ste. Marie wrote to the mayor and city council:

The experience has taught them, that the erection of cotton steam presses in the faubourg St. Mary, is a nuisance of the worst description, at once interfering with the comfort of the inhabitants and tending greatly to lessen the value of their property. The contiguity of a steam press to the dwelling of individuals, not only increases the rate of Insurance, but greatly jeopardizes those dwellings by means of the vast masses of cotton constantly on hand and liable to conflagration, both from the nature of the article, and from external causes. To those grievances may be added, the disagreeable and unremitted noise of the machinery, and the constant emission of smoke, which penetrates every aperture of our dwellings, and soils and destroys every article of furniture within them. We are aware of the great importance of the cotton trade to the City of New Orleans; but they do not admit it as a right of any individual, community or even, government itself, to take, injure, destroy or deteriorate the property of individuals without their consent, or at least without giving them an equivalent for such taking, injuring, destroying, or deterioration.

On the fringe of the French Quarter in 1832, the homeowners facing North Rampart Street petitioned the city council in objection to a railroad in the center of their street. They claimed that they had purchased their lots with the as-

surance that they would peacefully enjoy the advantages of a public walk. Theirs, too, was another citizens' battle lost; the St. Claude "Railroad" ran down to the parish line terminating at the Jackson Barracks.

It was not the loss or alteration of any part of their physical setting that stirred the founders of the Louisiana Historical Society to organize in 1836. It was the expressed desire of these learned men to record over 100 years of events, providing posterity with a documented history of their city and state. To this end, they searched the archives of France and Spain returning with much of the information that still affords present-day historians with the basis for historical recollection.

The society's third president, Charles Gayarre, elected in 1860, served the next 28 years giving numerous lectures and papers on both the colonial periods. These were later bound into two of a four-volume series entitled *Louisiana History*. In 1850 when the wardens of the St. Louis Cathedral planned the demolition of Almonester's Cathedral, it was Gayarre who publicly objected to the plans and outspokenly condemned the designs by Jacques N.B. de Pouilly. With injured dignity Gayarre proclaimed: "This venerable relic of the ancient past was demolished in mere wantoness of vandalism and replaced by this upstart production of bad taste."

Rampart Street, pictured here from Canal to Esplanade Avenue, marked the extreme western boundary of New Orleans as originally laid out. The land approaches to the city were defended by two forts from which Rampart Street takes its name. Though homeowners along North Rampart fought to keep a railroad from running down the center of their street in 1832, they lost the battle and tracks (pictured here on the far left) were laid for the St. Claude "Railroad."

The Baroness Micaela Almonester de Pontalba and city officials concerned themselves with a rejuvenation of the Place d'Armes as early as the 1830s. Actual alteration began at the same time as the new cathedral, when mansard roofs were added to the Cabildo and Presbytere overlooking the Place d'Armes (which was renamed Jackson Square in honor of General Andrew Jackson, hero of the Battle of New Orleans). There may have been some displeasure when the Baroness Pontalba tore down her parents' buildings flanking Jackson Square in order to replace them with the symmetrical rows of the Pontalba Buildings; if so, it was not recorded. But when she turned Jackson Square into a baroque garden, destroying the old sycamore trees placed in rows of three on both sides of the square, there was an uproar; undaunted, she continued her improvements.

The Civil War cut deeply into the psyche of New Orleans. Occupied from 1862 until 1877 — when Federal excesses were ended — the citizens suffered survival without the luxury of future planning. The saga of the St. Louis Hotel in the French Quarter demonstrated essential elements of these political events and the citizens' position.

For many years social and political conflict grew between the Creole (meaning native born) community and that of the new Americans. Financial differences in banking, real-estate expansion, commodity futures — almost everything — reached an apex of antagonism in the early 1830s. When French architect Jacques N.B. de Pouilly came to New Orleans from Paris freshly inspired by its latest influences, he was engaged to design a commercial exchange in the French Quarter. The Americans immediately hired Irish architect James Gallier, Sr., (ne Gallagher) who planned the St. Charles Exchange Hotel to house business transactions in the American Sector.

De Pouilly's plan encompassed an Exchange Passage beginning at Iberville Street and continuing down to and through the St. Louis Hotel to the Citizen's Bank on Toulouse Street. A rhythmic harmony of arched facades was arranged to reach a crescendo at the entrance of the hotel. Completed in 1836, the hotel burned but was immediately rebuilt in 1841. Sweeping stairways, domed ceilings, and crystal chandeliers were the opulent setting for the Creole *creme de la creme*.

The St. Louis, like its rival the St. Charles Exchange Hotel in the American Sector, was

occupied by Federal troops during the war. In 1877 Louisiana overthrew the Reconstruction government and reclaimed the state politically. It purchased the old St. Louis Hotel and there established the capital; but in 1882 the capital was finally moved to Baton Rouge. An architectural and social renaissance was attempted for this building when it opened two years later as the Hotel Royal. The venture failed, and again the New Orleans climate whirred a destructive fate, critically damaging the structure in the hurricane of 1915. The remnants were demolished in 1916 despite the plaintive appeals and objections of N. Courtland Curtis, Dean of the Tulane School of Architecture. The site ironically became the home of Kross Lumber and Wrecking Yard. Classic marble columns and some of the granite sections were salvaged, redressed, and "utilized for architectural beauty and traditional interest for excellent effect" on the Railway Passenger Terminal at South Rampart and Girod streets.

The demolition had been preceded by a poorly conceived attempt at beautifying the French Quarter. The entire square directly in front of the old St. Louis-Hotel Royal was destroyed. Private homes were replaced with a giant Civil Courts Building. The design — in grandiose white marble and terra cotta, rendered in the popular eclectic style of the period — disregarded all consideration of scale. The *Journal of the American Institute of Architects,* referring to the white elephant, carried an editorial entitled "Speaking of Ugliness." Nevertheless today the building is valued as a bona fide architectural expression, constructed with fine materials and with excellent execution of detail; these mark it as a building worthy of preservation. (Interior spaces are commodious and the Louisiana Supreme Court justices desire to return, having grown crowded and discontented with their new quarters.)

The "American" style of architecture was ushered in by architects like James Gallier, Sr., and his son, James Gallier, Jr., and the firms with which they were associated. This elevation of a building on Camp Street, which Gallier and Turpin designed, dates from about 1835. Photo by John Lawrence.

CAMP STREET.

New Orleans historian Grace King had not only lamented the demolition of the square but also had photographed the buildings. The glass negatives produced a positive treatise to the superiority of the original buildings *in situ*. Her enlightened appreciation of scale, texture, and design inherent in the Vieux Carre may have been sparked by New Orleans' 1885 World's Cotton Exposition.

Formally known as the World's Industrial and Cotton Centennial Exposition, the fair is treated more kindly by history than it was by contemporary observers. Grace King wisely demurred, saying that the exhibit in the Women's Department ". . . was incredible, astounding. Indeed, it was the opening of the past history of the city, not only to strangers, but to the citizens themselves." D. Clive Hardy in his monograph on the exposition claimed that what the local citizens "had taken for granted was in fact their own unique and rich culture. Ultimately, this awareness would be the most important legacy of the exposition."

It was at this time that the embryonic notion of New Orleans preservation was conceived. Nourishment was obtained through an art movement fostered by the Woodward brothers, William and Ellsworth, at Newcomb College Art School, and was further developed by the superb writings of Lafcadio Hearn, Lyle Saxon, Sherwood Anderson, and scores of others who became literary greats. Arnold Genthe in 1926 produced a magnificent photographic essay that won praises for his talent and for the French Quarter.

Historians joined the movement with the formation of the Louisiana Historical Association in 1889; its purposes paralleled those of the earlier-formed Louisiana Historical Society. The latter organization received a boost from the St. Louis Exposition of 1904. When the exposition ended, all the artifacts gathered for Louisiana's participation were placed in the Cabildo and Presbytere, forming the nucleus of the Louisiana State Museum collection. The need for a museum building was fortuitous because members of the city council had actually proposed the demolition of the Cabildo. Fortunately, members of the society and association were ready to defend the continued existence of the historically significant building.

The growing appreciation of architecture as an element deserving preservation was allied with visual images, letters, and later, the theater. The Arts and Crafts Club, organized in 1921 and located in the old Broulatour Court (Seignoret House on Royal Street), continued in community service until its dissolution in 1957. It provided a forum for young architects as well as artists. Charles B. Hosmer, Jr., in his book *Preservation Comes of Age* (1981), lists short-lived organizations that were certainly forerunners of Vieux Carre preservation groups; among them was *La Renaissance du Vieux Carre,* chaired in 1930 by historian and author Stanley C. Arthur. It saved sections of the French Market from demolition thus scoring its lone victory.

There was no unevenness about what is now understood to be a continuum of the preservation movement. It was certainly a straight-line activity and commitment by the feminine element of New Orleans. If the ladies did not act directly in promoting events connected with preservation, they inspired the male community to do so. This was true in the Arts and Crafts Club, *Le Petit Theatre du Vieux Carre, Le Petit Salon,* and particularly in the attainment of a state constitutional amendment enabling the city council to establish the Vieux Carre Commission.

The organization, *Le Petit Theatre,* hired architects Armstrong and Koch in 1922 to adapt a building near Jackson Square for their theater. They purchased buildings on St. Peter Street, and Koch conceived one of the first buildings consciously designed to blend with the surrounding Vieux Carre buildings. *Le Petit Salon,* a literary group of socially prominent ladies led by Mrs. Elizabeth M. Gilmer (who wrote a syndicated column as Dorothy Dix), Mrs. Charles F. Buck, and its first president, Grace King, bought the Victor David House next to the Little Theater. This renovation was an extremely brave venture for the Old Quarter's slum conditions made their act socially daring. When the same architectural firm adapted the Wogan House at 711 Bourbon Street into apartments, still another milestone in architectural preservation and reuse was reached.

Despite her busy writing schedule, Grace King founded the Society for the Preservation of Ancient Tombs in the early 1920s. By 1923 a newspaper article revealed that the organization had the support of the Louisiana Historical

Society and listed luminaries from throughout the city among its members. Its stated purpose was to save for future generations the historic tombs that were crumbling away. Sixty years later, this battle continues under Save Our Cemeteries despite the disappearance of many tombs and family histories once etched on marble tablets. The intent of this modern preservation group reiterates that of the earlier one.

Ironically, two of New Orleans' most active early 20th-century proponents of preservation came from outside their adopted city. Elizebeth Thomas of Bay City, Michigan, had studied voice in England and France for four years before making her first visit to New Orleans in

1908. She met and married Philip Werlein six weeks later, thus continuing a dual love affair with her new family and city. Her first home was the historic Flowers-Morrison House in the Lower Garden District. Through her European exposure, she recognized the charm and ambiance of the Vieux Carre, and until recently was the only person who attempted a catalog of rare and exquisite wrought-iron balconies in the Vieux Carre, many of which vanished even before her monograph could be published.

Mrs. Werlein's enthusiasm over the architecture and atmosphere of the Old Quarter was encouraged as the city began to teem with experts gathering data about the past. The American Institute of Architects had participated in the sponsorship of the Historic American Buildings Survey, a nationwide architectural survey that by 1941 had yielded thousands of drawings and negatives. However, this rich strike of researched materials remained hidden like a rare ore itself; its availability was limited and impact on local preservation nonexistent.

The ambitious Mrs. Werlein interpreted the importance of the Historic American Buildings Survey study and strove for implementation through preservation. She won a victory for the city and the nation when in 1936 she convinced the Louisiana legislature to pass a constitutional amendment authorizing the city to create the Vieux Carre Commission. The mayor was empowered to appoint members to this commission with some selected from the Louisiana Historical Society and the Louisiana State Museum board, and three qualified architects. Among its powers, encompassing signs and alterations to all exterior elevations, the Commission could cite and fine violators and even levy taxes.

Through the decade of the 1930s, Elizebeth Werlein was to battle not only bars and brothels but often the Vieux Carre commissioners who were not always entirely scrupulous and dedicated to the law. By this time she was living on St. Ann Street, and had helped to organize the Vieux Carre Property Owners, becoming its president in 1938. The American Institute of Architects, recognizing her invaluable tenacity, fortitude, and leadership in the preservation of the Vieux Carre *tout ensemble,* made her an

honorary member. Mayor Robert S. Maestri, trading humor and support for the prestige of her association, crowned her Mayor of the French Quarter.

Mrs. Werlein — and consequently the city — lost several skirmishes against businessmen whose encroachment caused gerrymandering of the French Quarter to exclude their projects

from Vieux Carre Commission controls. The Monteleone Hotel, the river side of Decatur Street, and the lake side of North Rampart were excluded from its jurisdiction. After years of litigation and demolitions, the Vieux Carre Property Owners with Jake Morrison's leadership, carried the case to the state supreme court. It was held that the exclusion of these properties was unconstitutional. But by that time there was little left to save on either Decatur or Rampart streets.

William Ratcliff Irby adopted New Orleans over his home state of Virginia. He was a pioneer preservationist and philanthropist who purchased Vieux Carre properties and bequeathed them to educational institutions. To the Louisiana State Museum in 1927 went the lower Pontalba Building and the Jackson and Creole houses; to Tulane University, the Bank of Louisiana and the Old French Opera House. The upper Pontalba Buildings were purchased in 1921 by other financiers who sold them to the Pontalba Building Museum Association in 1930, who in turn donated the buildings to the city.

New Orleanians of prominence and prestige began to interest themselves, not only in buying Vieux Carre properties, but also in actually liv-

The Historic New Orleans Collection occupies buildings on Royal and Toulouse streets purchased in the 1940s by General and Mrs. L. Kemper Williams. The structures include the Merieult House (built in 1792 by Jean Francois Merieult and one of the few buildings to survive the 1794 fire) and the very fine 1889 house known as the Williams Residence, adopted by the Williamses as one of the Quarter's "hidden houses" and now maintained as it was when they lived there. General and Mrs. Williams established the Collection in 1966. It was opened to the public in 1974. This view of the courtyard and Williams Residence is from the Merieult House. Photo by Robin Boylan.

ing there. Matilda Geddings Gray bought the magnificent Gauche House on Esplanade and Royal streets, as well as surrounding properties. General and Mrs. L. Kemper Williams purchased the Royal Street Merieult House and three connecting Toulouse Street buildings. Many years later the Williams' buildings would house the Historic New Orleans Collection, one of the city's small elegant museums and finest research centers. The *Vieux Carre Survey,* 130 volumes of 108 squares within the area, is available to the public in the Historic New Orleans Collection library. The accumulation of this material was the result of a collaboration between Tulane University, the Schleider Foundation, and the Collection beginning in 1961; research continues with a special grant from architect Collins Diboll and assistance from the Historic Preservation Seminar of Tulane University.

Architectural historian Samuel Wilson, Jr., began teaching a class in Louisiana architecture at Tulane University in 1949. Shortly thereafter, the Olivier House, an early-19th century raised, galleried house was threatened with demolition by the New Orleans Roman Catholic Archdiocese. Mr. Wilson and most of his class — including Angela Gregory, Mrs. S. Walter Stern, Clem Binnings, and author T. Harnett Kane — along with Martha Gilmore Robinson and J. Raymond Samuel, organized the Louisiana Landmarks Society in 1950 to save that plantation. They did not succeed, but other victories would provide the group with the strength to prevent many demolitions and to become a statewide organization. As its first president, Mr. Wilson continued to guide preservation through principles established on sound architectural and archaeological

research.

The Louisiana Landmarks Society's first lady, Martha Robinson — lovingly known as "Miss Martha" and "the Senator" by friends and foes — carried the banner of preservation New Orleans-style to Washington, D.C., when she, with hundreds of concerned citizens, defeated the Riverfront Expressway in the 1960s. A tireless, lovely lady, she won by charm, astute judgment of human nature, excellent preparation, and timing. She knew and loved her city; her contributions to preservation are exhibited in structures and environment saved and in the inspired spirits of thousands.

This major preservation-versus-city planning conflict in New Orleans had its inception with New Yorker Robert Moses' Transportation Plan. Limited-access super highways with elevated sections were the rage in engineering and city planning immediately after World War II. To get America on the road was an at-any-cost ambition. In New Orleans a Riverfront Expressway was first proposed in the 1950s. Members of the Vieux Carre Property Owners were probably the first preservationists alerted to the planned roadway cutting the Vieux Carre off from the Mississippi River and permanently damaging the historic area with an elevated

Above
These stately homes are located on Esplanade Avenue. Known as the "Promenade Publique" in the 1830s, Esplanade Avenue became the fashionable place to live for New Orleans' socially prominent residents in the late 1800s. In this century, it became the scene of many restorations undertaken by concerned residents. Photos by Robin Boylan.

Below left
The French Market is highlighted in this view down Decatur Street. Though originally built in 1791, the market was rebuilt in 1813 and modernized in 1937–1938. The structure's basic Spanish Colonial characteristics have been preserved. Photo by Robin Boylan.

roadway.

The Louisiana Council for the Vieux Carre was formed in 1960. Its first president was Harnett Kane; he was succeeded shortly after by Martha Robinson. The organization soon became a vehicle to oppose the Riverfront Expressway. More than 35 organizations joined, creating one of the first preservation conglomerates in the country. Armed with a cause, they put a stop to the expressway in 1969 when Secretary of the Interior John A. Volpe withdrew federal funding. This issue polarized the city as no other; its victorious conclusion remains to be written as further studies and plans for city development continue to include a Riverfront Roadway.

The expressway was one of many Vieux Carre issues that siphoned time and energy from Mary and Jake Morrison after their move to New Orleans in 1937. Together they worked toward its physical improvement by actively organizing the Vieux Carre Property Owners, whose corporation purposes were synonymous with the Morrisons: ". . . the awakening, fostering and cultivating of a feeling of civic pride around the residents and property owners of that section of New Orleans, bound by the Mississippi River, Rampart, Esplanade, and Iberville — known as the Vieux Carre — and to encourage and assist in the preservation, resto-

ration, beautification and general betterment of said section."

Combining his roles as attorney and preservationist, in 1957 Mr. Morrison wrote *Historic Preservation Law,* a comprehensive nationwide study on the subject. In 1974 the Morrisons received the Crowninshield Award from the National Trust for their activism and devotion to preservation. The Friends of the Cabildo, honoring Mr. Morrison for his past presidency and constant contributions to the organization, dedicated the fifth volume of the *New Orleans Architecture* series to him in 1977. The always-vigilant Mary Morrison serves on the Vieux Carre Commission, alert to the recurring topic of the Riverfront Roadway and infractions against the law in her beloved Quarter.

The Friends of the Cabildo, formed in 1954, was organized to assist the Louisiana State Museum in the maintenance and preservation of its buildings and collections. As a membership auxiliary, it is "a catalytic organization, with its exhibitions, lectures, guide programs, and books serving as effective instruments of education and even propaganda for preservation. By relating the past to its present, the Friends hopes to remove history from institutional isolation and encourage citizen awareness of our historic environment." This quotation from the first of six volumes entitled *New Orleans Architecture,* introduced the sponsoring Friends of the Cabildo to city leaders as well as to individuals desiring information. The organization

Wealthy New Orleans residents of yesterday spared no expense in constructing their beautiful St. Charles Avenue homes which are still a source of delight today. Photos by Robin Boylan.

has become a powerful and respected voice for preservation. The series is the most influential publication on the architecture of New Orleans neighborhoods and has been directly responsible for many allied studies and monographs. As a result of the mammoth, all-volunteer Friends effort, the following organizations were formed for the protection of individual neighborhoods: the Coliseum Square Association (1972), the Central Business District Improvement Association (1973), Save Our Cemeteries (1974), Save Our Riverfront (1975), Faubourg Marigny Association (1976), the Esplanade Improvement Association (1977), Historic Faubourg St. Mary Corporation (1976), the Improvement Association of the Irish Channel (1974), Mid-City Improvement Association (1975), City Park Mid-City Improvement (1971), the Canal Area Service Association (1978), and many small neighborhood groups, all of which belong to the Preservation Resource Center (1974).

Sixty preservation and neighborhood organizations belong to the Preservation Resource Center. The potential wisdom and effectiveness of a consolidated preservation organization are obvious. In addition to sponsoring meetings, programs, tours, mailings, and publications, its successes include the proposed and partial restoration of Julia Row, an 1830s set of 13 rowhouses; the publication of a

monthly newspaper carrying citywide preservation news from Algiers Point to New Orleans East; and its combined efforts to save the "Warehouse District" in the Central Business District. Such accomplishments promise the transposition of preservation from "pioneer defender" to "promoting planner."

Often when New Orleanians are found to plead for preservation, they apologetically eschew many of their true ideals such as historicity, human scale, patina, and texture; it is defended, as in the case of the Vieux Carre, as being only economically important. Economics alone will never be an effective preservation motive. Apartments were once hailed in the Vieux Carre as a viable economic solution to preservation, but time-sharing condominiums and their evils may well sound the final doom of many structures.

John Kenneth Galbraith, Harvard University professor emeritus of economics, in his essay in *Preservation: Toward an Ethic in the 1980s* wrote:

Above left
This shotgun house—so called because its long, narrow design would allow one to stand at the front end of the house and shoot a bullet straight through the back door—is located in the Irish Channel. Photo by Robin Boylan.

Above
Along Bayou St. John stand many charming older homes such as the one pictured here. Photo by Robin Boylan.

Preservationists must never be beguiled by the notion that we can rely on natural economic forces or that we can rely on the market. If we do, a large number of important art objects, artifacts and buildings will be sacrificed. The reason is that the market works on a short-time dimension, and the people who respond to the market are different from those who ultimately gain from conservation or preservation. The market works against social economic interest as well as the larger interest in the artistic and educational rewards of conservation. This is not a question of ideology and should not be thought of as an argument between liberals and conservatives. It is a simple fact that the market will always favor the short-run solution. . . . It will always favor the people who are in immediate possession, as against the large social and economic interests of the community. Preservationists must never doubt that they are engaged in a public and philanthropic and social enterprise and should never, whatever their political faith, be in the slightest degree apologetic.

When Dr. Margaret Mead, anthropologist, psychologist, and one of the world's most respected intellectuals, was interviewed in 1978 by *American Preservation* magazine, she was asked, "How do you see the preservation movement today?" Her response, after stating that she thought the bicentennial celebration in 1976 had been a great stimulus for preservation, was: "I think it's another of the many ways we're beginning to compensate for ruthlessness towards the past, this country's past. We're ruthless towards the past, we're ruthless towards the old, we're ruthless towards the environment. . . . Tearing down, destroying—it does have an effect. . . . The destruction of things that are familiar and important causes great anxiety in people."

Preservation in New Orleans, to be effective, can not be a piecemeal process. New Orleans needs not only the Vieux Carre and Garden District, but it also requires the contrast of low-scale buildings to high-rises within the Central Business District. The city needs all of its 19th-century neighborhoods, those along the river's edge, as well as those that lead back toward Bayou St. John and Lake Pontchartrain.

The appreciation of the past had a slow beginning in New Orleans, but it has arrived. Today its forces fortunately include the talents of the entire spectrum of the community. The fields are less those of battle, more those of computed probabilities, preferably liberally combined with the esthetics of man and his relation to his environment. New Orleans' spirit is enriched by its living past; its body is enhanced in a humane urban setting; its wealth is invested in its perception of both.

The U.S. Mint, now restored, was built in 1835 on the site where Fort St. Charles once stood. Photo by Robin Boylan.

One of the dominant subjects of this book is the way in which New Orleans has been seen, by its residents and visitors, in succeeding periods in the past. This section, however, divided into seven groups, is devoted exclusively to the look of the city today, with an emphasis on some of the enduring landmarks and institutions that give New Orleans its special character.

These pages and overleaf *Some of the older homes that line many of New Orleans' streets, avenues, and boulevards. Fascinating in the variety of their settings, design, and details, it is hardly surprising that so many of them have been beautifully maintained. Photos by Robin Boylan.*

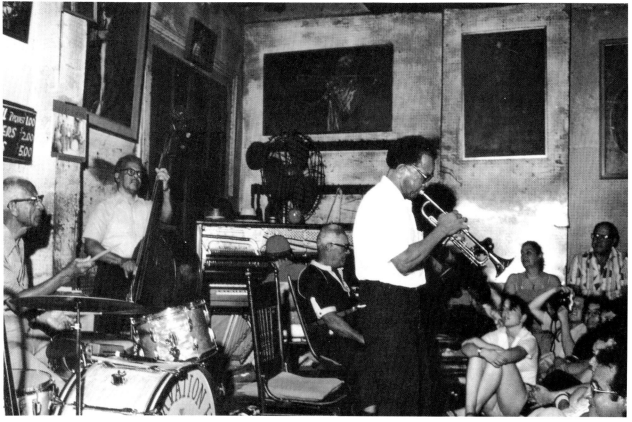

New Orleans is, in the American imagination, almost synonymous with unrestrained gaiety and the celebration of being alive—and for good reason. Shown here and on the following pages, festivities associated with music, pageantry, or both. Facing page (top) and this page (below and far right), scenes from the New Orleans Jazz and Heritage Festival; facing page (below) Preservation Hall; right, street entertainers in the French Quarter. Photo at right by John Lawrence. Rest by Robin Boylan.

213

Mardi Gras is on Shrove Tuesday, the day before Ash Wednesday (the beginning of Lent). The peak of the period of celebration that begins soon after New Year, Mardi Gras is the day thousands of residents and visitors make merry in the streets of the city.

Photos on facing page, bottom right, and this page, left, by Robin Boylan. Rest by John Lawrence.

215

The form New Orleans' early tombs took was the result of two factors: the Catholic prohibition against cremation and the water-soaked ground residents encountered. After 1800 it became mandatory to build tombs above ground, which also marked the point at which the city's cemeteries became famous. Like the early houses, the early tombs were usually built of brick and plaster. The small white buildings and the narrow passageways that divide them create a strange, melancholy beauty that reminds us of the attitude toward death of the earlier residents: while death was mourned, it was also idealized in these cities of the dead. Photos by Robin Boylan.

New Orleans has a deep fondness for its heroes, as is reflected in the many monuments that grace the city. Far left, the remarkable statue of Andrew Jackson in Jackson Square by Clark Mills. Left, a view of the monument to Robert E. Lee. Below, the participants in the Battle of New Orleans are honored at Chalmette. The 110-foot-high structure marks Andrew Jackson's position during the battle.

Parks make an important contribution to the quality of life in New Orleans. Pictured here are (above) the entrance to Audubon Park, named for ornithologist and artist John James Audubon; a scene of the Louisiana Nature Center (above and right); and New Orleans Museum of Art in City Park (right). Photos (both pages) by Robin Boylan.

The churches of New Orleans have tended to the spiritual needs of residents from the city's founding. Facing page, St. Louis Cathedral is the fourth structure to bear the name. The first two were destroyed by a hurricane and a fire, respectively, and the third, constructed by Don Almonester y Roxas in 1794, had to be rebuilt in the mid-19th century.

On this page, the breathtaking interiors of St. Patrick's Church (above), designed in the 1830s by James Dakin and completed by James Gallier, Sr.; and St. Louis Cathedral. At right, an exterior view of St. Mary's Assumption. Photos by Robin Boylan.

Facing page, Bottom
The first attempt to establish an institution of higher learning was made in 1811, with the short-lived College of Orleans. But it was not until 1835 that the Medical College of Louisiana began educating students. It started with only 16 students and grew slowly until it became part of the University of Louisiana thanks to the state legislature in 1847. In 1883 a large bequest by Paul Tulane caused the university to further expand. It was then that the name was changed to honor him. A significant part of Tulane is Newcomb College, founded by Josephine Le Monnier Newcomb for women, with an extremely generous endowment in 1886.

Top
Loyola University of the South began its existence as Loyola Academy in 1904. In 1910 the academy, now known as Loyola College, merged with the College of the Immaculate Conception and in 1912 the college was incorporated as a university. Photos by Robin Boylan.

Right
The cargoes, look, and techniques of importing and exporting goods at the Port of New Orleans have changed somewhat over the last two centuries, but this is still very much a port city, whose location on the Mississippi is still of great importance. At bottom right, the New Orleans skyline and the Mississippi River Bridge from the west bank of the river. Photos by Robin Boylan.

223

As this 19th-century view emphasizes, New Orleans has always owed its prosperity to the port. And yet, the business community that has evolved since this illustration was done is diversified to an extent that hardly could have been foreseen then. (THNOC)

CHAPTER X
RECESSION, REVIVAL AND RENAISSANCE

New Orleans entered the 1980s with the optimism of a young priest on the first day of Lent after Mardi Gras. Good times were coming. Construction on the new Louisiana Superdome was complete, the Poydras Avenue corridor was attracting new high-rise office buildings, oil companies were moving in with new district headquarters, and the 1984 Louisiana World Exposition "The World of Rivers" was taking shape along the city's 19th Century riverfront above Canal Street. Business and political leaders were upbeat and convinced that the city's best years were just ahead.

"Laissez les bon temps rouler!" ("Let the Good Times Roll") was the unofficial theme for the 1984 World Exposition held in New Orleans from May 12 to November 11. The official title was "The World of Rivers: Fresh Water as a Source of Life." The theme was selected to show an awareness of international concerns over the world's depleting freshwater supplies. But that was about as serious as New Orleanians wanted to get. The world's fair, as it was called locally, was to be a party with all the intensity of a six-month-long Mardi Gras. The fairgrounds was a fantasyland with passenger gondolas stretching back and forth across the Mississippi River, monorails, cascading fountains, lagoons, floating stages with live entertainment, parades, steamboats, jazz, food and the 2,400-foot long, polychrome "Wonderwall," a psychedelic New Orleans apparition of Giambatists Piranesi's famous 18th Century

Above: The countdown for opening ceremonies of the Louisiana World Exposition took place on May 12, 1984 amid much fanfare. The LWE opened one year later, a century after the last world's fair in New Orleans. Though visitation fell short of projections, the event was one of several that spurred development of New Orleans's Warehouse District. Photography by Judy Tarantino, Courtesy, THNOC (1991.144.48)

where they were greeted by a massive papier mache and buxom Mardi-Gras-like mythological river deities wrestling with alligators. At night, search lights, fireworks and green laserbeams traced across the sky. The International Pavilion housed exhibits from at least two dozen foreign countries. The Jazz Tent along with the Afro-American, Vatican and Louisiana pavilions were particularly popular. Even the New Orleans Museum of Art (NOMA) and the Louisiana State Museum in the French Quarter got into the act with special exhibitions. NOMA featured Leonardo da Vinci's Codex Hammer and the Louisiana State Museum organized one of the most important historical exhibits to visit the city: "The Sun King: Louis XIV and the New World."

drawings of Rome. It was an eye-dazzling mixture of Byzantine, Moorish, Gothic, Classical Greek and Art Deco with built-in shops, food stands, arcades and rest stops. Its creator, UCLA architecture professor Charles Moore, called the father of architecture's post-modernism, described it as a "sensory overload." A *New York Times* reporter said "the issue here is not whether the Wonderwall is appealing, but whether it is enough to save one of the strangest world's fairs in history."

Flags, banners, balloons and street musicians lead visitors to the main entrance

Although popular with most New Orleanians, the exposition got off to a rough start and received mixed reviews from the local and national news media. When opening day came along, workmen tried feverishly to complete construction. People stepped over cables and wires and many exhibits did not open until weeks later. A Chicago newspaper reporter described the fair as "a decadent Disneyland." Somehow, the exposition's troubles were an omen of troubles ahead for the city.

The optimism of the early 1980s was short lived. The mid to late 1980s and early '90s were chaotic years for New Orleans. When the oil-producing OPEC nations dramatically increased oil production in the early 1980s, the state's once rich oil and gas industries collapsed, sending the city into an economic

Above: When the oil industry went into a slump in the 1980s, the effects were felt in many quarters. Construction of offshore platforms abated, with a subsequent loss of jobs. Other suppliers and service providers felt the decline as well. The industry has been recovering through the 1990s. Photo by John H. Lawrence

Right: The fire at the Spanish-era Cabildo on Jackson Square in April 1988, occurred during the process of renovating the historic structure and refurbishing its displays. Efforts of the New Orleans Fire Department, and subsequent assistance from volunteer conservators prevented what could have been a much greater disaster. The Cabildo reopened in 1994. Photo by James Dent, courtesy THNOC (11989.80.31)

Facing page, left: The Wonderwall, designed by Charles Moore, was one of the identifying features of the Louisiana World Exposition of 1984. Photo by Judy Tarantino, courtesy THNOC (1985.178.13)

Facing page, right: Traditional Mardi Gras organizations were affected by the City Council's anti-discrimination ordinance. Some agreed to abide by the new regulations; others ceased parading in public. Photo by John H. Lawrence

industry, a point-shaving scandal by Tulane University basketball players, the crash of Pan Am flight 759 in July 1982, the Brilab insurance racketeering scandal involving a local crime boss and state official, and the May 1988 fire that almost destroyed the two-hundred-year-old Cabildo on Jackson Square —one of the city's three most famous buildings. Even the old-line Mardi Gras clubs came under attack in a city trying to deal with old racial tensions. According to the 1990 census, the city dropped from the nation's twenty-second largest city in 1980 to twenty-fifth, just behind Cleveland, Ohio. The city also ranked third in the nation in child poverty with more than 46 percent of its 135,000 children living in poverty.

Even cartoon character Bart Simpson took a shot at New Orleans in 1992 with a satirical song titled "New Orleans!" that described the city as "home of pirates, drunks and whores ...Tacky, overpriced souvenir stores...the Sodom and Gomorrah on the Mississippi." A 1990 article in *Money* magazine aimed squarely at the city's soul—it's food. The magazine ranked the New Orleans restaurant scene eighth in the nation behind Boston and Seattle with Los Angeles first. "The facts are cruel: [New Orleans] is no longer a wealthy city capable of supporting many fine restaurants without relying on the kindness of strangers. Some of its oldest names...have lowered their standards and cater to tourists by the busload." This was the unkindest blow of all since most New Orleanians rank the city's cuisine sacred and right up there with the Trinity and Mardi Gras.

Despite an economic resurgence in the mid 1990s, outside observers could not help but reflect on the city's miseries. A writer for *The New Yorker* noted his findings in a 1997 visit to the city: "New Orleans is a heartbreakingly poor city; economically, it bottomed out during the oil bust of the eighties. It has rebounded since, but the poverty rate is still the third highest of any major city in America. Louisiana consistently competes with Mississippi for the lowest rank in crucial statistics like education. There is hardly any middle class in town: there are, in the main, the wealthy and the upper-middle class, who thrive on tourism and oil, and the poor and the lower-middle class, who work

depression not seen since the Great Depression of the 1930s. The 1984 World Exposition was an artistic success but financial flop, forcing many major and small investors into bankruptcy. The dramatic increase in inner-city crime and drug use chased thousands of middle-class families to the suburbs east and west of the city and north of Lake Pontchartrain to St. Tammany Parish.

Daily headlines told sobering stories of a dwindling population, poverty, corrupt policemen, record-breaking murder rates, shady politicians and cronyism, political shenanigans in the city's new gambling

Right: New Orleans's renowned cuisine maintains its classic signature dishes while exploring new ways of combining traditional ingredients in innovative ways. Both established chefs and a generation of younger ones were part of this culinary reassessment and expansion. Photo by John H. Lawrence

Below right: Two programs operated by the New Orleans Preservation Resource Center had central roles in the renovation of the city's historic neighborhoods. Christmas in October relies on corporate sponsorship and hundreds of volunteers to refurbish residences of elderly and/or indigent homeowners. Operation Comeback assists buyers in targeted neighborhoods with technical advice and other incentives to foster renovation and residency. Courtesy, Christmas in October/New Orleans Preservation Resource Center

in the hotels and restaurants for minimum wage. This sad gumbo of ingrained corruption, violence, and poverty has been a constant in the city for so many years that most people take it for granted as an immutable law of local existence."

But not all was so gloomy in the 1980s and 1990s. The New Orleans Saints made the National Football League playoff for the first time in 1987, but lost its first game, and Pope John Paul II visited the city in September 1987. Ironically, *Money* magazine's 1989 survey of best places to live placed New Orleans 12th in the nation among three hundred major American cities. In 1994 the city regained its gastronomical honor in a *Conde Nast Traveler* magazine poll that ranked New Orleans, with world-renowned chefs such as Paul Prudhomme, Emeril Lagasse, John Folse and Leah Chase, among others, as the best food city in the world with New York and Paris coming in second and third. By late 1996 and early 1997, the city and state's economies, which had greatly diversified during the oil and gas bust, began coming back strong. The price of oil, which hit a high of $32 a barrel in 1981 and a low of $10 by 1986, rebounded to $19 a barrel by the spring 1997. Downtown real estate sold at premium prices. Tourism was up,

manufacturing increased steadily, oil and gas prices rose sharply and other industries showed healthy growth. In April 1997, the *Times-Picayune* won two Pulitzer Prizes—their first ever. Later that month, University of New Orleans economist Timothy Ryan forecasted continued economic growth and at least 10,000 new jobs, mostly in the service industries, by the end of 1998. The following month, the city's unemployment rate had dropped to 4.4 percent, one of the lowest in the state. Rising oil and energy prices continued to pump renewed life into large and small businesses from Belle Chasse to Lake Charles.

In June 1997, U.S. Representative Bob Livingston of Louisiana announced federal plans to build a major U.S. Navy computer center at the University of New Orleans Research and Technology Park. The center could translate into 1,500 big-salary jobs and a $272 million impact on the state's economy. That same month, two steamship cargo companies announced efforts to expand links between New Orleans and Latin America. According to reports, trade between the city and Latin America has grown 44 percent since 1994. Also in June, Jazzland Inc. and partners unveiled elaborate and ambitious plans for "Jazzland," a $76.5-million-dollar music theme park scheduled to be built by the year 2000 on a 220-acre site in eastern New Orleans. Developers are hoping the New Orleans experience will draw 1.4 million visitors annually. On July 1, Avondale Industries announced a $332 million contract to construct two crude-oil tankers with an option for three more. This contract was in addition to two major U.S. Navy multi-billion-dollar contracts for war ships.

Little things also reinforced the local psyche. Earlier in 1997, a small eastern New Orleans company that manufactures and distributes water quality instruments was named the Small Business Administration's nationwide small business exporter of the year. This past summer, the National Park Service, working with the New Orleans Jazz Commission, sponsored a summer-long series of jazz concerts in Armstrong Park to attract and make people feel good about coming back to the inner city. Hotel revenues were

up twenty-plus percent over last year, the Saints got a new start with "Iron" Mike Ditka, and business activity was so strong in the Central Business District that parking had become a major problem. Even a run-down stretch of St. Charles Avenue gained renewed attention among preservationists and business people when vampire queen Anne Rice went for chicken king Al Copeland's jugular in a highly publicized verbal street fight over the gaudy-versus-chic design of his new restaurant on the avenue.

During the 1980s and early '90s, New Orleans also experienced a cultural and artistic renaissance that it had not seen since its glory days in the 1850s. The World's Exposition was a failure but it revitalized the city's decaying 19th Century warehouse district and stimulated conversion of Victorian-era factories and storefronts into plush apartments, art galleries and upscale cafes and restaurants. Despite mind-numbing urban decay, major renovation efforts were made in the city's oldest neighborhoods by organizations, such as the Preservation Resource Center, families and young professionals who refused to leave the city . The Jazz and Heritage Festival, Tennessee

Ernest "Dutch" Morial was elected mayor of New Orleans in 1978. He was the first African American to hold the office, and served two terms. Though not without detractors or political opponents, his death in 1989 was mourned citywide. In this photograph, Mayor Sidney Barthelemy (to right of cameraman) and Reverend Jesse Jackson, accompany the funeral procession. Photography by Cornelius Regan, courtesy, THNOC (11994.24)

Below right: Sidney Barthelemy served two terms as mayor of New Orleans, beginning in 1986. Barthelemy's support extended from the mansions of St.Charles Avenue to the blue-collar neighborhoods of the Ninth Ward. His administration actively lobbied for and secured legislation permitting a land-based casino in New Orleans. Photo by John H. Lawrence

Williams Literary Festival, and Essence Music Festival attracted tens of thousands of people from all over the world to the city. New Orleans now had more art galleries, working artists and writers, world-class restaurants and hotels than in any other time in its almost three-century history.

Despite hard times, or perhaps because of them, New Orleanians continued to pride themselves for their endless striving for good times. New Orleans, a *Time* magazine reporter wrote in 1991, is the "epicenter of hedonism." The late jazz banjoist and guitarist Danny Barker described that hedonism this way: "New Orleans people are unique. Somebody goin' to jail? Give him a party. Somebody died? Give him a party. They'd throw a party for a dog's birthday. Here you have a million people raised with a habit to celebrate."

At the center of New Orleans hedonism is politics, a game New Orleanians play with the gusto of New York's Tammany Hall seasoned by a Gallic, Hispanic, Mediterranean and Caribbean ancestry. During the 1980s and early 1990s, political power in the city shifted from the white to the African-American communities. Mayor Ernest "Dutch" Morial was the city's first black mayor followed in 1986 by former city councilman Sidney Barthelemy and in 1994 by Dutch's son, Marc Morial. The political change reflected the city's new demographics. Despite the increasing number of Vietnamese and Latin Americans moving to New Orleans from Cuba, Honduras, Nicaragua and El

Salvador, practically every section of the city, excluding the Lakefront area, held a black majority.

Dutch Morial, who had a long and distinguished career in city and state civil rights movement before coming mayor in 1978, was the most capable and yet most controversial mayor in the city's recent history. In 1985 he rose to national prominence when he was elected president of the U.S. Conference of Mayors. When he left office eight years later, he left a record of major city improvements, extensive street paving, construction projects such as the $93 million Riverfront Convention Center, and a legacy of bitter confrontation. His was a government of inclusion in which he placed more blacks and women in top jobs and policy-making positions than any mayor before him. He appointed Warren Woodfork as the city's first black police superintendent and created scores of volunteer committees and task forces that brought blacks and whites together like never before. Yet, a week before he left office in 1986, the *Times-Picayune* noted that "Morial's confrontation style produced a turbulent eight years that divided the city and slowed its progress."

Even his friends and foes alike noted his often bitter confrontations with the news media, city council, state legislature, white business establishment, officials from surrounding parishes and, at times, black political organizations such as COUP and SOUL that had supported him. "These battles," wrote the *Times-Picayune*, "isolated Morial and his supporters, placing them in the position of fighting most of the traditionally powerful interests in the city and state. The city was put on the defensive in Baton Rouge; efforts to develop tourism, the port and the general economy were fragmented. Virtually every gain involved a

fight." Morial's support from the upper-middle class community continued to dwindle during his administration. He beat his white opponent, Councilman Joseph DiRosa, in a 1977 runoff with 20 percent of the white vote. That percentage dropped to 13 percent in his 1982 runoff against white opponent Ron Faucheux. The mayor's support in the white community dropped to 5 percent the following year when he tried to change the city charter to enable him to seek a third term. That same year he broke with what little white support he had left when he opposed their efforts to make Audubon Park a state agency. "I always felt that Dutch could have settled the issue with them quietly," Councilman James Singleton told a *Times-Picayune* reporter. "But he was angry and apparently wanted to teach them a good lesson about power. He did, but it cost him his last sizable pocket of support among white voters."

That loss of support became even more evident in the 1986 mayoral election when Councilman Sidney Barthelemy, a Morial opponent, went up against the candidate Morial supported, state Senator William Jefferson, who would later go on to represent the New Orleans area in Congress. "The more he tried to hurt me," Barthelemy told the reporter, "the more people, especially in the white community, saw my consensus approach to government as a viable alternative to Dutch's antagonistic style." In the runoff, Barthelemy defeated Jefferson with 86 percent of the white vote and 30 percent of the black vote. Ed Renwick, a political analyst at Loyola University in New Orleans, told a reporter that Barthelemy was elected "in large part because of his nice-guy style [which] is in contrast to Dutch's style. If Sidney succeeds, many people will conclude that Dutch's problems were the result of an abrasive style. But if Sidney fails, the consensus will be that it takes a tough mayor to run a tough city." Morial, denying he was as contentious as painted by the news media, said he was accessible and able to work with anyone "but was unable to overcome unfair labels about his alleged adversarial style."

Renwick's words, however, may have been prophetic. Barthelemy, a former Catholic seminarian and social worker, was extremely popular during his first administration,

especially among white voters. He inherited a city in "economic free fall" and had to lay off at least a quarter of the city's workforce. He handily won re-election in 1990, despite the oil and gas bust and unemployment in double digits. Two years later, a University of New Orleans poll showed the mayor's popularity had dropped rapidly. Although most people considered the mayor to be a genuinely good person, New Orleanians were pessimistic about the city's future and the mayor's handling of the job. The *Times-Picayune* pointed out that the mayor promised a major shakeup in his administration and forced the resignation of 255 appointees. He later rehired all but two. Barthelemy blamed his declining popularity not on his own job performance but on crime, unemployment and the Reagan-Bush administration's abandonment of cities.

By the end of Barthelemy's second administration in 1994, however, he was again strongly criticized for his political appointments to office and his seemingly laissez faire attitude toward his job. Upon leaving office in 1994, the *Times-Picayune* remarked: "While he basked in approval ratings of 65 percent and 55 percent in 1986 and 1990, according to University of New Orleans polls, the man who has never lost an election is regarded with disapproval by something like 64 percent of voters." The mayor attributed his low popularity upon leaving office to factors beyond his control, factors such a poor city economy that forced cutbacks in city services, crime caused by a rise in the use of crack cocaine and a growing nationwide distrust of government.

The *Times-Picayune*, however, laid the blame squarely at the mayor's feet. "Analysts say [Barthelemy], once described by his sister as incapable of saying no, has been stained by a string of second-term defeats that critics charge were the result of some of his own best personal traits. Barthelemy's unfailing loyalty to family, friends and supporters, frequent beneficiaries of his influence, won him a reputation as a mayor more concerned about rewarding and sticking by friends than running an efficient government."

The newspaper produced a litany of events that clouded Barthelemy's administration. Soon after taking office, federal auditors said

the New Orleans' jobs training program was mismanaged and filled with Barthelemy supporters. The federal government dismantled the program and demanded the return of $6.4 million in job training funds. In a similar case, federal housing officials, who financed the city's embarrassing housing projects, forced the mayor to fire his own appointed Housing Authority Board and director. The mayor himself later launched a major statewide scandal when he awarded his son a $70,000, four-year scholarship to Tulane University. Under an agreement between the city, state and the university dating back to the late 19th Century, Tulane set aside a number of scholarships each year for the mayor and state legislators to award to whomever they pleased. The public eventually learned, through unrelenting news media investigations, that legislators all over the state were awarding these Tulane University scholarships to the children of their friends, financial supporters, other politicians and even to their own children. Unapologetically, Barthelemy withdrew his son's scholarship. In addition, red-faced politicians and Tulane officials greatly revised the scholarship program in the wake of public indignation and outcry.

While these events certainly blemished Barthelemy's administration, they were minor in comparison to constant news reports of staggering crime rates, corruption, and mismanagement within the New Orleans Police Department. As the *Times-Picayune* noted in April 1994: "Even as Barthelemy leaves office, two police officers, including the commander of the department's once-elite vice unit, stand trial on charges for allegedly shaking down bar owners in the French Quarter. They are among at least 16 officers arrested in the past 15 months on charges ranging from malfeasance to extortion, bank robbery, rape and most recently, murder." The paper also listed other problems, including disclosure that the department ignored reforms urged by a national police chiefs' organization, reports that a 1990 tax approved by voters to add 200 additional police officers to the force resulted in the hiring of only 65, and most new police cars purchased with the tax money went to "department brass" rather than being assigned

to patrol duty. Despite on-going criticism, Barthelemy stood by his long-time friend and hand-picked police chief, Arnesta Taylor.

Coming to his own defense, the mayor said people "will focus on what happened with the economy and projects that will come on line. [They will] judge us more fairly than we have been judged in this particular time." He pointed to the new gambling casino at the foot of Canal Street and the Mississippi River as a major accomplishment. The casino, of course, was mired in controversy and bankruptcy, and stood an incomplete shell well into the late 1990s. Barthelemy's administration worked to expand the city's tourism industry to compensate for the oil industry's collapse. To that end, his admin-istration was very successful, especially in the construction of the Aquarium of the Americas and Woldenberg Park, riverboat casinos, and the passage of special tax millages that financed expansions to the convention center and a marketing plan that eventually attracted the 1988 Republican National Convention, the 1990 Superbowl XVIV and the 1993 NCAA Final Four basketball championship.

In addition to scandals within the police department, two other major events captured the public's attention during the Barthelemy years. One was legalized casino and riverboat gambling and the other struck at the very nerve of New Orleans society—Mardi Gras. On December 19, 1991, the New Orleans City Council passed tough anti-discrimination ordinance sponsored by councilwoman and long-time civil rights activist Dorothy Mae Taylor that would deny parade permits to carnival and social organizations that did not open its ranks to all people regardless of race, gender or ethnic background. The tough ordinance was later softened, a bi-racial study commission formed, and compromises struck. Yet, three of the city's oldest carnival organizations—Comus, Momus and Proteus—refused to follow the city's mandate and cancelled all future parades. Only Rex, founded in 1872, opened its ranks to African-Americans and continued its traditional Mardi Gras day parades.

Legalized gambling, however, had an even longer-lasting impact on the city. With the spin of the Louisiana Lottery Company wheel in September 1991, legalized gambling returned to New Orleans and Louisiana in a big way. The state lottery, authorized by a popular statewide referendum and constitutional amendment, reaped a financial windfall for state government and added over $500 million to the state treasury in less than five years. Closely regulated by the state legislative auditor's office, the lottery remained scandal free. The same could not be said, however, for other forms of legalized gambling, notably riverboat gambling, a land-based casino and video poker, that were imposed upon the city and state by the state legislature. All three were, and remain highly controversial in New Orleans and throughout the state. In September 1995, fifteen men, many with connections to well-known national crime families, pleaded guilty in federal court to charges of racketeering and defrauding Bally Gaming of $10 million. Four other men were later convicted of similar charges in federal court. A month earlier, the video poker scandal reached to the highest levels in the state legislature. Payoffs allegedly were made to several top legislators to get them to kill any legislation that would give voters in each parish a chance to vote on keeping or rejecting video poker. When news of the FBI investigation broke, several powerful state senators resigned or were later defeated at the polls. The revelations later fueled statewide reform and referendum that eventually will outlaw video poker in most parishes.

Above: The Rivergate Convention Center, completed in 1968, was demolished for the construction of the land-based casino at the foot of Canal Street, despite concerted and eloquent efforts to preserve it as an archtectural and engineering landmark. Photo by John H. Lawrence

Right: The resurgence of the visual arts in New Orleans continued through the 1980s and into the 1990s with both non-profit arts organizations and a strong commercial gallery structure. A shift from the Magazine Street corridor to Julia Street and the Warehouse District focused the arts community's financial and social centers. Photo by John H. Lawrence

As to riverboat gambling statewide, the *Times-Picayune* ran constant reports of friends and relatives of high ranking politicians raking in lucrative contracts, consulting and legal fees from gambling interests while one former state senator, doing a favor for a New Orleans riverboat owner, shamelessly passed out campaign checks on the state senate floor to selected allies. Riverboat gambling in New Orleans, however, fared poorly, especially when compared to nearby Jefferson Parish and across the state in Lake Charles and Shreveport where palatial gambling boats poured tens of millions of dollars annually into city treasuries, public work projects and local economies.

Of the three forms of legalized gambling in New Orleans, casino gambling proved to be the most vexing. In June 1992, Governor Edwards signed a bill authorizing the construction of a single land-based casino in Louisiana, and that casino was to be in New Orleans. The governor and Mayor Barthelemy predicted the casino would create thousands of new jobs and generate millions of dollars for the state and city treasuries. For a year, a group of gambling companies headed by Christopher Hemmeter, who owned resorts in Hawaii and wanted the contract to build and operate Louisiana's only land-based casino, courted the governor and Mayor Barthelemy heavily. Daily newspaper articles and news shows paraded before the public glamorous artists renditions of what was to be the grandest and largest casino in the world. In 1993, however, the state gambling board, whose members were appointed by the governor, divided the contract three ways. Harrah's of Las Vegas got 53 percent ownership while 13.7 percent went to a group of Louisiana businessmen under the name of Jazzville, and 33.3 percent went to Grand Palais, Hemmeter's group.

Despite strong opposition and court challenges from preservationists and gambling foes, Harrah's plan was to open a temporary casino in the Municipal Auditorium on North Rampart Street while it demolished the Rivergate Convention Center and built a permanent casino on Canal Street near the river. The temporary casino opened in May 1995 but by August it fell well short of its projected $30 million monthly revenues. The casino laid off over 500 employees. Three months later, shock waves went through the city and state when Harrah's Jazz Company announced it had filed for bankruptcy. The company then closed the temporary casino and stopped construction of its permanent $800 million facility on Canal Street. More than 3,000 casino and construction workers lost their jobs, the city lost $23 million and the state $75 million in anticipated annual revenues from the casino. As late as 1997, what was to be the world's largest casino stood as an empty, incomplete shell at the foot of Canal Street. Gambling foes continued to point at the empty building as a warning to those who looked to gambling as a solution to the city's economic future.

Barthelemy's administration left office with a whimper while the new administration of young Marc Morial, Dutch Morial's son, came in with a roar in 1994. The 36-year-old Morial beat New Orleans lawyer Donald Mintz in what the *Times-Picayune* called "the bitterest mayoral races in recent New Orleans history." The paper went on to describe the campaign: "Morial prevailed over lawyer Donald Mintz in a campaign marked by rumors of illegal drug use by Morial and allegations that Mintz's campaign distributed anonymous fliers attacking black people and his own Jewish faith, then used the anti-Semitic fears in fund-raising solicitations." The scandal over the fliers hurt Mintz badly which was ironic since Mintz was popular in the black community for his years of work in building bi-racial coalition and launched his campaign from a black church. When the votes were counted, Morial, a black state senator, edged out Mintz with an approximately 10-point margin. The votes went along racial lines with Morial receiving only 9 percent of the white vote, while 10 percent of the black votes went to Mintz. Although a bitter campaign, Morial continued to enjoy great popularity during his early years in office.

In his June 11, 1997, "state of the city" address, Mayor Marc Morial announced: "Crime is down, jobs are up. Despair is down, hope is up. Division is down, unity is up, and we are poised to begin the new century as America's comeback city." Although crime continued to eat at the city's soul, city officials initiated new and creative programs to fight back. In his June 11 speech, Mayor Morial painfully reminded everyone that when he took office in 1994, the city had "set a record in murders, crime and police corruption."

Perhaps Morial's most popular appointment after taking office was Police Superintendent Richard Pennington, a Little Rock, Arkansas, native who had worked his way up through Washington, D.C.'s Metropolitan Police Department. Although he inherited a department riddled with scandal and mismanagement, Pennington went about reorganizing the department, raising recruiting standards, and returning community and self-respect to the department. He also instituted new and effective administrative and crime-fighting programs such as COMSTAT, an aggressive computer-driven strategy modeled on the New York City plan that monitors, analyzes and reacts to citywide criminal activity. In a 1997 interview with the *Times-Picayune*, Pennington recalled the day he took the oath of office. During the ceremony, a Federal Bureau of Investigation agent walked up to him and told him the department was filled with rogue cops, there was a drug ring operating in the department and that the FBI had a sting operation underway. Pennington said the agent ended the meeting with—"Welcome to New Orleans!"

Renaissance in the Arts

Despite the scandals, arguments over legalized gambling, staggering unemploy-ment, record crime rates and national headlines decrying New Orleans the nation's murder capital, the city, ironically, became a major center for the visual arts during these difficult years. Writers from all

Right: The growth of collections and programs at the New Orleans Museum of Art in City Park created crowding in its original Beaux Arts building dating from the first decade of this century. An addition, completed in 1995, doubled NOMA's square footage and upgraded exhibition and non-public areas. Photo by John H. Lawrence

Below: The Contemporary Arts Center recently celebrated its twentieth anniversary, with a mission to present programming of the visual and performing arts of up-to-the-minute and experimental interest. A major renovation of the facility in 1990 included interior spaces and fixtures designed by area artists. Photo by John H. Lawrence

over the country asked the question: "Is New Orleans becoming a southern version of New York's famous SoHo?" New York writer Pete Hammill suggested just that in an article for New York's *Village Voice*. He dubbed New Orleans as the "new Bohemia" and urged New York artists to give up their cramped $1,500-a-month tenements and run-down factory lofts and move to New Orleans for the good food, pleasing architecture, good bookstores, and cheap rent.

Despite the city's darker sides of life, assorted wags, reprobates and snollygosters, New Orleans awoke during these years to its own creative spirit, a spirit that lay dormant for generations. Although the city was known throughout the world for its architecture, music, food and bizarre lifestyles, it had been a backwater in the visual arts since it lost its preeminence as the South's largest and richest city. New Orleans will never be the largest city in the South again, but it reclaimed its position as a leading center for the arts. Once home to luminaries such as Tennessee Williams, Grace King, Lillian Helman, Truman Capote, O'Henry, Jelly Roll Morton, Mahalia Jackson and Louis Armstrong, New Orleans during the 1980s and 1990s laid claim to a new generation in contemporary arts and letters, including actor John Larroquette; musicians Aaron Neville, Wynton and Branford Marsalis; artists Ida Kohlmeyer, Douglas Bourgeois, Alan Flattman, John Scott, George Dureau, Auseklis Ozols, Robert Gordy, Lin Emery, Henry Casselli and Rolland Golden; and writers Walker Percy, Shirley Ann Grau, John Kennedy Toole, Andrei Codrescu, Anne Rice, Stephen Ambrose and Richard Ford.

In a 1990 newspaper interview, novelist Anne Rice of the famed vampire series claimed New Orleans had "a vintage quality …you can't duplicate. New Orleans is not filled with manufactured ideas and images. It's rich in a way that Europe was in the '20s. It has a laid-back quality. A mellowness. And an indifference to the American rat race." Existentialist novelist Walker Percy once described New Orleans as "cut adrift not only from the South but from the rest of Louisiana, somewhat like Mont Saint-Michel awash at high tide."

New Orleans artist Emery Clark spoke for most New Orleans artists in describing the influence the city has had on her work: "I think it is very accessible here. I feel what has evolved is very personal, an expression. New Orleans is a very fertile place to work. It allows

Above: The warehouse district had been for decades an area where light industry, port activities and industrial suppliers had operated. In the 1980s, conversion of these large, abandoned structures to upscale apartment buildings and condominiums created a resident population in the former industrial zone. Restaurants and other service-related businesses soon followed. Photo by John H. Lawrence

Above right: Tulane University's medical school and hospital complex exemplify a concentration of medical and research facilities along a stretch of Tulane Avenue. Photo by John H. Lawrence

you to develop in a natural way, and I don't think there are the pressures there would be in another couple of places in the country. What develops is more uniquely yours."

Internationally-famed British art critic Edward Lucie-Smith got at the very heart of New Orleans and south Louisiana art in a 1996 exhibition of Louisiana art that travelled to London. "Louisiana art," he wrote, "appears to have a distinctive character which makes it different from that produced in other parts of the South. Some links to the immediate environment are obvious: for example, artists often make use of imagery which reflects the annual festival of Mardi Gras. Other hallmarks are subtler. African-American art has a growing presence which is not always found in the southern cultural mix." He went on to write that artists in the New Orleans area "offer themselves a certain liberty to reject the fads which often sweep the New York art world. They are under less intensive pressure from both critics and their peers to conform to whatever the latest orthodoxy may happen to be."

Another major factor contributing to the city's renaissance in the visual arts came in 1993 with the $23 million renovation and expansion of the New Orleans Museum of Art, which placed the museum in the top five

art museums in the South. Located in City Park, NOMA—as it is called locally—is surrounded by an impressionist painter's dream of ancient, twisted and moss-covered live oaks, murky lagoons and hazy but intense south Louisiana sunlight. The entire project was a financial miracle at a time when the local economy had been devastated by the oil bust. Despite the city and state's dismal economy, the museum financed the project by raising over $23 million from a $5.8 million voter-approved city bond sale, $1.3 million from state government and numerous large and small private and corporate gifts. Construction broke ground in January 1991 and the new NOMA opened its doors on April 18, 1995. The renovation project expanded the museum's space from 75,000 to 130,000 square feet, almost doubling exhibition space for new shows and permanent collections, as well as space for a larger research library, staff offices, board room and storage areas for the museum's $200 million collections. Work also included major renovations and a facelift for the museum's 1971 additions and the 1911 Ionic columned Beaux Arts-style building known to generations of New Orleanians as the Isaac Delgado Museum of Art, a museum "inspired by the Greek [but] sufficiently modified to give a subtropical

New Orleans's commercial axis shifted from Canal Street to Poydras Avenue. This thoroughfare is anchored at one end by the Louisiana Superdome, and at the other by the unfinished land-based casino. Photo by John H. Lawrence

contemporary and avant-garde art in the city. At the center of that world was the Contemporary Arts Center which underwent a $5 million renovation in 1990. After its grand opening in October of that year, a New Orleans art critic described the magnificent new center as "stylish and functional and with a vengeance." Over twenty galleries opened in the Warehouse District and surrounding area between 1984 and 1990. Like the French Quarter, the district was within walking distance of major downtown hotels, the Riverwalk and Convention Center, hence it attracted tourists who were not shy about shelling out thousands of dollars for art. City officials also contributed to arts renaissance in 1986 by passing the "Percent for Art" plan that called for one percent of the cost of all city-financed construction projects to be tacked on to buy art for public places.

Changing City Skyline

The city's skyline, always in contrast to the human-scale architecture of pre-Civil War New Orleans, changed radically during the late 1970, '80s and '90s. It took on all the trappings of a Sun Belt city. The Hibernia Bank building's little white temple is almost lost among the concrete, steel and glass towers of Place St. Charles, One Shell Square and other office buildings and hotels.

While shipping and trade on the Mississippi River accounted for 19th Century New Orleans construction booms, most observers agree that tourism, oil and gas fueled the construction frenzy of the 1960s, '70s and early '80s. "The building boom in the mid 1980s was caused by the oil boom," New Orleans architect Peter Trapolin said. "We had more construction in those years than in any other period in history. There were building cranes everywhere." Trapolin disagreed with those who claimed the proposed casino and riverboat gambling were responsible for the city's construction activity. He gave full credit to the expanding Morial Convention Center during the late 1980s and '90s.

Bill Langkopp, executive director of the New Orleans chapter of the American Institute of Architects, agreed. "The oil and gas boom and general activity," he said, "created a demand for hotels and office buildings. To a certain degree, especially in

appearance." In addition, the museum purchased over 2,000 new objets d'art for the expansion, including Gauguin's "Eve Bretonne," Renoir's "Vase of Flowers" and Braque's "Still Life With Fruit." The greatly increased exhibition space made it possible for the museum to host big travelling shows such as Claude Monet in 1995 and "Faberge in America" in late 1996 and early 1997.

The city's visual arts scene also got a big boost in late 1994 when New Orleans attorney and businessman Roger Houston Ogden donated a sizable portion of his extensive collection of Southern art, valued at $13 million, to the University of New Orleans Foundation with the understanding that a suitable museum site be found. Plans call for the Ogden Museum of Southern Art to open in 1998 in the historic 1888 red sandstone building on Lee Circle that once housed the Howard Library, later known as the Taylor Library. The Romanesque-style structure was designed by famed New Orleans architect H.H. Richardson.

The rebirth of the visual arts in the city also had a staggering impact on the city landscape, especially in the Central Business District. Although the French Quarter and Faubourg Marigny have always attracted artists, the Warehouse District and surrounding neighborhoods above Canal Street became the unquestioned center for

the 1970s, favorable tax laws also helped. From the standpoint of tourism, the Convention Center, coupled with expansion of the Superdome, contributed greatly to the building boom." Both agreed that the Superdome opened an area of the city for development virtually untouched since the Civil War. "The Superdome," said Langkopp, "anchored the Poydras corridor and established it as a great commercial address."

Beginning in the mid 1960s, Poydras Avenue gradually attracted major businesses and corporations moving into the city. By the mid 1980s, Poydras outstripped Carondelet and Baronne streets which had been the city's banking and main commercial district for a half-century. Nineteenth Century brick warehouses, cafes and shops along Poydras were demolished to make way for the Federal Reserve Bank (1966), the Lykes Building (1968), One Shell Square (1972), the Hyatt Regency Hotel and the Louisiana Superdome (1975), the Hale Boggs Federal Building (1975), the Hilton Riverside Towers (1984),

Crown Plaza Hotel (1984), Rouse Riverwalk (1986), and the LL&E Tower (1987). In the late 1980s and early '90s came the glittery Equitable Center, the Entergy and Mobil buildings, Amoco Building and Energy Centre rose from the intersection of Poydras and Loyola avenues. Most of Poydras' 19th Century architectural relics are gone. Their bricks and thick cypress timbers eventually ended up in pricey new homes in suburbia. Mother's famous po-boy emporium and the once popular creole-style Maylie's Restaurant, now under new management, are among the few reminders of what the street was like before the CBD rushed head on into 20th Century business world. Over ten million square feet of Class A office space was added to the CBD market before the building boom of the 1970s and early 1980s ended.

In addition to oil and gas, the 1984 World's Fair, despite its dire financial troubles, also has had a lasting impact on the city's skyline and the CBD. Decaying Civil War-era factories and riverfront warehouses, where bananas and mahogany from Central America and coffee from South America were once stored, found new life as upscale condominiums, art galleries, restaurants and office buildings. Riverfront exposition halls became the Ernest N. Morial Convention Center and Riverwalk with specialty shops, cafes and delightful views of river traffic. For the first time in almost a century, the river was accessible once again to people. Another good example of adaptive use renovation was in the old Jackson

The modest scale of French Quarter buildings is challenged by high-rise hotels that occupy Canal Street and the Central Business District. The expansion of the convention center has created a need for more hotel rooms in the Central Business District. Photo by John H. Lawrence

Brewery facing the river and Jackson Square in the French Quarter. The old Jax Brewery was one of those turn-of-the-century architectural indiscretions committed in the name of industry, progress and a New South. By the end of the 1980s, it had become one of the glitziest tourist dining and shopping spots in New Orleans.

Canal Street also saw dramatic changes. The first few blocks of Canal Street, once filled with the city's best department stores along with flophouses, sleazy bars and other denizens, was reborn with Canal Place (1980) and the Westin Hotel, the Marriot (1973) and Sheridan (1983) hotels, the Meridien Hotel (1984), and the highly controversial and unfinished gambling casino. The Chateau Sonesta Hotel moved into renovated sections of the old D.H. Holmes Department Store building, and in mid 1997, developers announced plans for the Ritz-Carlton to occupy upper floors of the Maison Blanche building. Even the old streetcar is scheduled to make a comeback to Canal Street in the

next few years. By the late 1990s, Canal Street had become a mixed world with tee shirt shops and fast food places sitting side by side with the elegant restaurants and the world-class Windsor Court hotel.

Ironically, the CBD's biggest economic plum, the New Orleans Regional Medical Center, quietly developed during the 1980s and '90s. The expanding Center—consisting of LSU and Tulane medical schools, Charity Hospital, Veterans Hospital, University Hospital, Delgado School of Nursing, and Tulane University Hospital—has earned an international reputation for healthcare and research. Plus, it employs over 15,000 people.

Perhaps the biggest boost to the tourist industry in the French Quarter came on Labor Day 1990 with the opening of the sixteen-acre riverfront Aquarium of the Americas and Woldenberg Riverfront Park. The $40 million aquarium project, headed by the Audubon Park Commission and managed by the Audubon Institute, was funded entirely by local money—a $25 million millage approved by voters in 1986 and $15 million from the private sector. As in other city projects, the Institute spent one percent of construction costs to buy art by local artists to exhibit in public spaces. In late 1989, the Audubon Institute and Commission, which turned the city's embarrassing Audubon Zoo into a first-rate park, also announced plans to build an arboretum and natural history museum at the foot of Esplanade Avenue and the river. These projects, however, were never started. Critics of the institute's plans objected to a private organization having so much power in directing riverfront development in the French Quarter. They also feared that unplanned development, increased tourist traffic, and riverfront construction would destroy the historic integrity of the French Quarter. The Vieux Carre Property Owners, Residents and Associates Inc. fought the aquarium construction project all the way up to the U.S. Supreme Court but failed, and the National Trust for Historic Preservation placed the French Quarter on the its list of most endangered places.

"The underlying assets of downtown New Orleans don't go away," said Randy Gregson, executive director of the Downtown Development District. "We've got the convention center, hotels. We've got 80 percent of the Class A office market, which is astounding when compared to Atlanta, Houston or Dallas. We have the Superdome, the Contemporary Arts Center, the Children's Museum, the Aquarium. We're seeing the first phase of the return of the streetcars to Canal Street. What we're seeing now is new investment."

Gregson likened the economy of downtown to a four-legged stool: "We used to have a one-legged stool with oil and gas being the heavy. The port and tourism were legs two and three, but oil and gas were far and away the driving force of the economy. What we have seen now is that legs two and three have gotten stronger. Now, we have developed the fourth leg in terms of healthcare and the centerpiece of that is the teaching universities and their health centers. And those are all downtown."

With restoration tax incentives and programs like Operation Comeback and "Sellabration," the Preservation Resource Center, savvy developers sensitive to historic urban architecture, and others who refuse

to abandon the city are working hard at saving old neighborhoods from Bywater to Carrollton and Algiers Point. Even newer suburbs in eastern New Orleans that were developed in the 1960s and '70s but fell upon hard times are enjoying a resurgence. PRC director Patricia Gay remains optimistic but vigilant: "There's lots of fantastic things going on but we're still concerned about the amount of demolition. Demolishing the Whitney Young pool in Audubon Park was simply crazy. We need the state to get more involved in regional planning and for everybody to cooperate and get out urban areas rebuilt rather than building more and more causeways across the lake. Everybody needs for the city to survive."

In May 1997, a Boulder, Colorado, architect visiting New Orleans to attend the American Institute of Architects convention eloquently summed up his feelings about the city in an op-ed piece for the *Times-Picayune*: "Here, beyond the streets and buildings, there are neighborhoods and communities, people and personalities and lives and experiences that are...the very things some critics regret that modern America left behind as it paved the expressways, fled to the suburbs, protected property values and shut out the world. ...There is pride of ownership here, but this is also a city of rental property—singles, doubles, four-plexes, townhouses, carriage houses, flophouses, slave quarters. The residential buildings are tight together, close to the street, enveloped with porches and balconies, patios and courtyards. Sounds and smells drift from household to household. People visit and mingle, and truly there is cultural richness, vibrancy and diversity."

To the unknowing eye, the iridescent and chromatic highrise office buildings and hotels could be Dallas, St. Louis or any other major American city. With all its new-found glitz and troubles, New Orleans has a soul unlike any other city in our hemisphere. "New Orleans," a writer once said, "is like a heavily rouged old diva. She charms you, she manipulates you, she seduces you. She is raw emotion hiding behind a veil of gracefulness and elegance you're not likely to forget, ever."

Woldenberg Park extends along the Mississippi River from Jackson Square to Canal Street and gives pedestrians access to the riverfront. It is a site for concerts performances and fireworks displays throughout the year. Photo by John H. Lawrence

CHAPTER XI
CHRONICLES OF LEADERSHIP

In 1881, it has been reported, New Orleans had 915 factories employing 8,404 persons. That's more than a hundred years before this writing, and New Orleans was just stumbling out of the harassing years of Reconstruction that followed the Civil War, when one governor amassed a fortune of a million dollars on his $8,000 per year salary. But New Orleans can remain rich while being robbed, as attested by so many of the business biographies in this chapter.

This city can bounce back from adversity because of its number one natural resource—the Mississippi River. Folklore tells us that 75 cents of each dollar in an Orleanian's pocket is attributable to the riches of the river, and this folklore dates back before inflation.

Back in 1718, France planted New Orleans on the river because she thought it was good business. But it wasn't for France. Nor was it good business for Spain, who inherited the colony. Nor for France's Napoleon either, after he took the province back from Spain. Yet, present-day New Orleans is deeply indebted to all three of these.

Later, in the 1760s, when Spanish rule began, trade upriver became New Orleans's best business. Annually, a fleet of bateaux left the city for the Illinois Country, across the river from Laclede's Village.

Then came Napoleon. At first he tried to make Louisiana his business. Failing this, and badly in need of cash, he sold it all—more land than he had ever conquered—to the United States for 2 1/2 cents an acre, and provided New Orleans with an incredibly rich hinterland, populated by then from America's greatest folk movement that settled the Ohio Valley and reached the Pacific in a single generation.

Soon New Orleans was the greatest export port in the world, serving its great valley. The early money crop of furs soon was joined by flour and tobacco as well as cotton, sugar, rice, lumber, leather, whiskey, meats—the list becomes endless. Suddenly there were more steamboats trading on the river than all the tonnage of the British navy that ruled the seas.

Louisiana began the 20th century with the discovery of oil. Soon the treasure trove of the offshore resulted in the petrochemical industry, which has marshaled a fleet of nearly 28,000 river barges pushing petroleum products upriver to return laden with mid-western grain and Ohio Valley coal, all for Europe. Today the port of New Orleans is the second largest in the United States.

Although much turmoil has beset New Orleans—from the rule of France and Spain to Reconstruction, from ambitious politicians and merchants to the failures of Napoleon—the business community has remained strong and concerned about the quality of life in this colorful city. Side by side, old river-based companies share new futures with diversified businesses.

Today New Orleans boasts a business community committed to growth and love for their city as expressed in the following histories, biographies, and success stories. Through these pages in "Chronicles of Leadership," this book was made possible, and attests to a warm civic pride. The companies you may be employed by, services that you may patronize, the familiar places that you may see in your travels all contribute to the rich historical charm and forward-looking ideals of New Orleans.

THE HISTORIC NEW ORLEANS COLLECTION

General and Mrs. L. Kemper Williams, private collectors of Louisiana material, established the Historic New Orleans Collection in 1966 to maintain and expand their library of maps, documents, and pictures and make them available to the public through research facilities and exhibitions. In a complex of historic French Quarter buildings, the Collection operates a premier research center for southern history and a museum accredited by the American Association of Museums.

A regional landmark, the main building of the Historic New Orleans Collection is one of the oldest and most important structures in the Vieux CarrJ. The site is the house Jean Francois Merieult, a wealthy merchant-trader, constructed for his extensive commercial activities and also as an elegant residence for his family. The Merieult house survived the great fire of

The Historic New Orleans Collection at 533 Royal Street.

1794 and is one of the very few buildings that remains from the Spanish Colonial period.

In 1792, Jean Francois Merieult built his two-storied brick house on Royal Street. Surrounding a courtyard, a stable and warehouses were added to complete the complex. Following Merieult's death in 1818 the properties went through a succession of owners. Each made some alteration to the buildings. On the Merieult house, granite pillars, popular in the 1830s, gave the facade its present-day appearance. A warehouse was converted into an elegant Greek Revival business facility, and in the mid 1880s the stable was demolished and replaced with a two-storied townhouse.

In 1938, at the behest of French Quarter preservationists, General and Mrs. L. Kemper Williams purchased the Merieult House with its courtyard and surrounding structures. Following World War II the prominent couple made the surprising decision to move to their property in the bohemian French Quarter. During their 17 years of residence, the Williamses collected important Louisiana materials that grew from a personal collection to one that merited public access. With this new goal in mind the Kemper and Leila

Reading Room of the Williams Research Center at 410 Chartres Street.

Williams Foundation and the Historic New Orleans Collection were established.

The museum, headquartered at the historic Merieult House, opened its doors in May 1970. Available to the public is a gallery for changing exhibitions as well as guided tours of the founders' residence and the permanent galleries illustrating the history of the city and state. In the history galleries, period furnishings and original maps, documents, prints, photographs, and rare books, selected from the Collection's research center, reveal Louisiana's past from the earliest explorers to the 20th century. Within the Merieult complex, the 19th-century townhouse was remodeled for 20th-century living and reflects the elegant lifestyle of the Williamses. The house, together with the furnishings, creates an atmosphere of quiet elegance.

During the last 30 years the important collection of Louisiana documents, maps, and visual materials acquired by THNOC has grown to vast proportions. To accommodate these items, a nearby 1915 court house and police station on Chartres Street was restored for adaptive reuse as the Williams Research Center, which opened its doors to the public in 1996.

The structure that Jean Francois Merieult built in 1792 has evolved into a complex of seven buildings and three courtyards complemented by an impressive separate research facility. And, through the foresight and generosity of General and Mrs. L. Kemper Williams Louisiana materials will continue to be collected, preserved, and made available to all.

ABRY BROTHERS, INC.

Along with his wife and infant son, John G. Abry arrived in New Orleans from his native Frankfort, Germany, to establish this business in 1840. Already an experienced shorer, his guardian angel must have directed John G. to this city where the uncertain soil conditions of its delta land were to provide a great need for his services.

So, much like his doctor friends, he was soon making house calls all over town. By 1997, (157 years later) doctors seldom made house calls any more. But Herman Joseph Abry, who became the fifth generation president of Abry Brothers. Inc. in 1976, and his associates were still making house calls. Because, you see, this firm is in the business of fixing sick houses. Besides shoring—the word is of Old English origin and means to "prop up"—the Abry company also levels

George J. Abry, third-generation president of Abry Brothers, managed the company for more than 40 years.

houses, raises and lowers them, and installs foundations.

Ten years before his death in 1885, John G. Abry bought a small house on a large lot at 816-18 North Johnson Street. Soon after, property was acquired for the yards to stable mules and house the wagons and shoring equipment a few blocks down St. Ann Street. This was still Abry's address in 1903, when the *Daily States* carried a long article about the company. It identified Emile Abry, son of John G., as "senior member of the firm." Emile was born the year his father founded the business. The *States* further identified George J. Abry, his son, as junior partner and active manager, and went on to say, "He is thoroughly up to date in all business matters, and stands very high in business and social circles." The *States* article continued—saying George was a member of the board of directors of a homestead, a member of benevolent societies, as well as a member of the Mechanics, Dealers and Lumbermen's Exchange, where Abry Brothers had an office. In these days before telephones, it was necessary for an active businessman to have a centrally located office. As partner, George managed the company for more than 40 years. It was during his tenure that Abry Brothers acquired property on Orleans Avenue at Bayou St. John, which is still the company s headquarters in 1997. His two brothers, John and Emile Herman, were long associated with him as superintendents. In 1930, Emlie Herman succeeded him at age 51, becoming the company's third-generation head.

It was during these years that Morris (Ferdinand) Lewis, a remarkable black man who had come to work for the company in 1900 at age 13, rose to become an Abry superintendent. Following in his footsteps, his grandson Livingstone (Rudy) Lewis also played an important role in the Abry organization until his retirement in 1993.

The fourth-generation president, Herman Andrew Abry, son of Emile

Herman Joseph Abry, great-nephew of George J. Abry, is the company's fifth-generation president.

Herman. did not assume office until 1948, when he was 41 years old. As an energetic young man, Herman Andrew decided there were too many Abrys around, so he left to become a successful certified public accountant. He had advanced to comptroller and then secretary of a large manufacturing firm when his mother called him. His father had died. Would he return and head up Abry Brothers? How could he refuse? It was in his blood. He returned and gave 23 years of service before retiring in favor of his son, Herman Joseph Abry, who had been company-trained since 1959. And besides, there was the new president's younger brother, John Paul Abry, serving as superintendent. Then in 1988, Herman Greg Abry, son of Herman Joseph, came on-board after graduation from college. So once again this venerable old company that "doctors" houses was placed in expert young hands.

Since 1840, Abry Brothers, Inc., never seems to run out of brothers.

COLEMAN E. ADLER & SONS

ADLER'S

In an era where many family owned businesses seem to be all but gone, one family business in New Orleans is growing stronger. Established in 1898, the family jewelry business of Coleman E. Adler and Sons is now enjoying it's fourth generation of contiguous family ownership.

From the original Royal Street store, Coleman E. Adler laid the foundation for what has since become known as the Adler Tradition: individualized service and the steadfast insistence that only the highest quality merchandise leave the store in an Adler's box. Another distinction that makes Adler's New Orleans favorite is their tireless attention to detail. It is remarkable to note that in the true spirit of total customer service it is not uncommon to find an Adler family member personally delivering selections to customers who are unable to make it into the stores themselves. Though this practice may seem astonishing in an era when even doctor's visits at home are rare, to Adler's it's all in a days work.

Adler's moved from the original Royal Street store to their present Canal Street store in 1904, a result of rapid growth and early success. Shortly thereafter, the first appearance of what was destined to become a New Orleans landmark graced the Canal Street entrance. That landmark, of course, is the ornate street clock. This treasured symbol of the Adler's Tradition was on hand. The Adler's clock has witnessed the changes along Canal Street and the city itself, faithfully keeping track of it all and serving as a dependable timepiece for New Orleans.

Visitors to the store are greeted by long cases displaying the heart and soul of the Adler's reputation. Exquisitely crafted jewelry made with diamonds, rubies, emeralds and sapphires are dis-

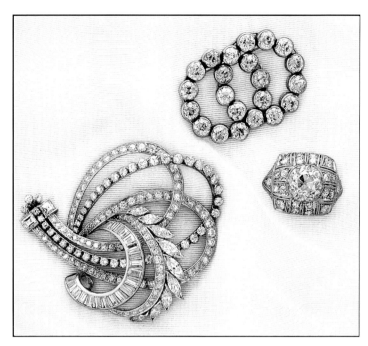

Estate jewelry from the Waldhorn & Adler collection. Left to right: platinum & diamond brooch - signed Cartier, 18kt. gold & platinum diamond brooch - circa 1915 and platinum & diamond ring - circa 1920.

played in a fascinating and seemingly endless variety. Rows of fine men's and ladies watches wait patiently to become the treasured graduation or anniversary gift of some lucky recipient. Further exploration of the store yields a veritable treasure trove of china, crystal and porcelain sculptures. Creations in silver as well as a distinguished collection of estate & antique jewelry are also waiting to be found. For over a century, debutantes, the betrothed and other fortunate recipients have anticipated the arrival of treasures like these from Adler's.

Though many family business are slowly disappearing, Adler's continues to grow. The recent acquisition of another New Orleans institution further expands the Adler's reputation for quality and distinction. In 1997, Adler's acquired the internationally renowned Waldhorn Company. This family owned antique business was started in 1881 by Moise Waldhorn, long before the term "antique" was fashionable. In poetic irony, the Waldhorn store is located on Royal Street near the original

Adler's building. Now known as Waldhorn & Adler, Adler's will carry on the Waldhorn tradition of offering fine antique furniture, porcelain, silver and antique and estate jewelry.

Since 1974, Coleman E. Adler II has guided the company to maintain and grow the Adler's Tradition. Groomed by his father and uncle, Mr. Adler was traveling abroad with them on buying trips by age 10, inspecting and grading fine gems. There are now four members of the fourth generation of the Adler family involved in the daily operation of the business: Tiffany Adler Peyton, Coleman E. Adler III, Chesley Adler and Milli Adler. Under Mr. Adler's leadership, an impressive expansion of the Canal Street store and the opening of Adler's locations in the Lakeside and Oakwood Shopping Centers have provided testament to the success of the Adler's philosophy of business.

In the jewelry business, reputation is everything. The reputation of the Adler family is firmly established and poised to grow even stronger in the century to come.

WALDHORN & ADLER

Long before antique shops were so termed, a French immigrant to New Orleans opened his shop on Conti and Royal, beginning a New Orleans tradition that helped further several more.

Moise Waldhorn arrived from Alsace-Lorraine in 1881 and opened the Waldhorn Company. Moise called his place "The People's Loan Office" in discreet reference to the shop being a sort of pawn shop for Creoles then living in the French Quarter. Discretion was necessary because the Civil War and Reconstruction had left many formerly wealthy families destitute. Though called a "loan," the transactions were actually sales to Waldhorn's, which in turn were later marketed and resold as "rare collections from Creole families." However, by the turn of the twentieth century, Moise had transformed his business into New Orleans first antique shop.

When Moise Waldhorn died in 1910, his son Samuel took over the business and over the next 61 years molded it into the New Orleans institution it is today. Samuel's generosity was well known, a trait that forever links him to yet another New Orleans tradition: the Sugar Bowl. In 1934, Samuel donated to the fledgling Sugar Bowl Committee what was to become the very symbol of the game: the shining sterling silver cup that is the Sugar Bowl trophy. The cup, which is actually an 1831 English wine cooler, was donated to the committee by Samuel with no strings attached.

Family owned and located on the same corner since 1881, Waldhorn's was acquired by another longtime New Orleans family institution in 1996. The purchase of Waldhorn's by Coleman E. Adler and Sons, Jewelers brings together two historic New Orleans businesses that have been continuously owned and operated by their respective families for well over 100 years. From the onset of the acquisition, Adler's pledged to continue the Waldhorn tradition of selling fine antique furniture, jewelry, porcelain and silver.

The marriage of Waldhorn and Adler, as the business is now known, is especially unique in that both companies were started within steps of each other. In 1898, Coleman E. Adler originally founded his store on Royal Street, before rapid expansion and strong sales prompted Adler's in 1904 to relocate to their present location at 722 Canal. In effect, for Adler's the Waldhorn and Adler store is a homecoming to Royal Street .

Waldhorn and Adler continues to be a family run store, with the involvement of the fourth generations of both families in the store. Tiffany Adler Peyton and Coleman E. Adler III, both great-grandchildren of Coleman E. Adler, actively participate in the day to day operations of the store, assisted by Nancy Kittay, a fourth generation descendant of the Waldhorn family.

Today, Waldhorn and Adler has a large and constantly changing collection of period antique English furniture, accented by lovely Chinese and English 18th and 19th century porcelain. The Sugar Bowl trophy was chosen from their well known collection of antique silver. Through the Adler's connection, a large selection of antique and estate jewelry is offered. Combining the best efforts of the Waldhorn and Adler families, the city's oldest antique store is ready for its next 100 years.

BISSO TOWBOAT COMPANY, INC.

Grenoble, in the southeastern corner of France, was the ancient capital of the former province of Dauphine, tucked between the Rhone River and the Italian border. Despite the region's alpine beauty and its opportunities for employment in the glove factories there, 10-year-old Joseph Bissot ran away from home in 1853 to go to sea.

Young Joseph has never explained, and no historian knows, how he managed to get down the 100-plus miles of the Rhone River to the Mediterranean where he signed on as a cabin boy, most likely at the port of Marseilles. But resourceful Joseph Bissot traveled light. By the time his vessel reached New Orleans in 1862, he had even dropped the extra "t" off his name. "Everybody called me Bisso," he has explained. "I didn't need the extra 't'."

Unfortunately for Bisso's ship, it reached New Orleans at the same time Farragut's Union fleet arrived to capture Confederate New Orleans and blockade the river in April 1862. A blockaded ship needs no crew, so Bisso was forced ashore to find work. We know for a time a blacksmith, in Iberville Parish, hired him to shoe horses. One historian tells us he joined the Confederate navy on the river. But

Units of the Bisso fleet of towboats range up and down the 250 miles of the New Orleans river-seaport. Between assignments they await further orders at any one of the 25 Bisso mooring stations along the river.

From his portrait on the wall of the company's executive office, the legendary Captain "Billy" Bisso, son of the founder, looks down on his daughter and her son—Mrs. Cecilia Bisso Slatten and Captain W.A. Slatten— 1981 managers of the Bisso family towboat operations.

teenaged Bisso did sign up as water tender for the Union gunboat *Albatross*. A French sailor, stranded ashore, had no side in the American Civil War. He needed a job, and work was scarce. Little is known what action, if any, 19-year-old Bisso saw before the war, and his job, ended in 1865. Suffice it to say, a gunboat in those days was any boat with a gun

(cannon) mounted aboard. Mostly the *Albatross* probably did patrol duty south of Vicksburg. So there was much time for Bisso to watch the river, study it, and learn about it.

Following his discharge from the navy, he settled at Walnut Street on the river, which has remained Bisso headquarters to this day. At first he worked for the Fischer Lumber Company, and within five years he was in the lumber business for himself and married to Mary D. Damonte. There were a number of children, five of whom grew to adulthood. It was Ol' Man River caving in the levee at Walnut Street that forced him out of the lumber business. A new levee, farther back, had to be built. Thus, in 1890, circumstance brought Bisso into the towboat and ferry business. That year he bought *The Leo*, and the Bisso Towboat Company, Inc., had its beginning.

Before his death on Christmas Day in 1907, the first Captain Bisso had sailed the river first with the U.S. Navy, then on flatboats of logs from Natchez downriver to his Walnut Street lumber mill, and before the turn of the century on *The Leo*, plus four other Bisso tugs and a river steamer. W.A. Bisso, who had been educated at McDonogh 14 on Peters (now Jefferson) Avenue and Soule Business College on Jackson Avenue, took over the business. Almost immediately he also founded the New Orleans Coal Com-

pany.

Captain Billy, as W.A. Bisso was soon generally known, was to spend 56 years piloting the company through two world wars and a Great Depression without serious mishap. However, his coal company—which had become number one in the port—could not survive the transfer of steamships and tugs to diesel power. It was shut down in 1954. At this same time, to effect the conversion of the entire Bisso fleet from steam to diesel power was a continuing capital investment for some time to come.

On shore leave, Captain Bisso appears to have found relaxation from nautical nuisances by steering a course in New Orleans city politics, with its cross currents and undertows but little less hazardous than Ol' Man River's. Nevertheless, the captain found safe harbor in election to both the city council and state legislature, as well as seeing candidates he backed successfully stowed aboard. All in all, Captain W.A. (Billy) Bisso's enterprise and accomplishments won for him respect throughout the maritime community, and for years, he was happily married to Cecilia E. LeBreton, member of an old French family. The couple had one son and one daughter.

Upon his death at age 88 in 1963, both the third and fourth generations took charge in the persons of his daughter, Mrs. Cecilia Bisso Slatten, and his grandson, Captain William A. (Billy) Slatten. A thoroughly reorganized and modernized family company entered the 1980s, a short decade before its 100th anniversary, with Captain Slatten its general manager and the other major owner, his mother, functioning as its chairman of the board. Like his grandfather and great-grandfather before him, this second Captain Billy began learning the river's secrets at an early age, completing an education at Tulane University qualifying him for leadership.

Unlike any other business is that of operating a towboat service in the country's largest seaport day and night along 250 miles of the Mississippi from Head of Passes to Baton Rouge. Besides its historic Fleet Landing Office on 800 feet of the riverfront at Walnut Street, there is a branch landing office 65 miles upriver near the Sunshine Bridge in St. James Parish, which Bisso dispatchers refer to as "St. James." Then, strung along the river from Buras to Baton Rouge are 25 Bisso anchorages, where tugs tie up momentarily awaiting reassignment. It

is unlikely one can view the river at New Orleans very long without having a familiar red and white Bisso tug, with the yellow band on its black stack, move into sight.

The dispatchers at Walnut Street and St. James know exactly each tug's schedule, as they do every unit of the Bisso fleet of some 20 units. In addition to towing, the company is organized to provide fresh water, slop, derrick, lineman, barge rental, and salvage services.

All steamship lines have contracts with its towboat services in major seaports and in the Port of New Orleans; Bisso has its share. So when a Bisso-contracted vessel enters the harbor, a Bisso towboat is there to meet it at an appointed place. Such contracts can be arranged beforehand directly with Bisso's New Orleans or New York offices, but most likely by the steamship's agency in the port.

It has been said of the Bisso company that since 1890 it has always been ready with services most needed. First there was the lumber business of the founding Bisso, then ferry service, coal service, and towboat service. And now, as the Mid-East OPEC oil cartel continues unreliable, the whole Western World is turning to coal readily available for its energy needs. In 1981, the Port of New Orleans was gearing up to export 120 million tons of U.S. coal by 1990. It is already exporting over 12 million tons. It looks like the Bisso Towboat Company, Inc., is going to be back in the coal business—towboat-wise, that is.

COOPER/T. SMITH CORPORATION

Cooper/T. Smith Corporation, one of the oldest and largest stevedoring operations in the U.S., has shared a long and interesting history with New Orleans.

Back in the early 1840s, a plucky Irish immigrant named Terrence J. Smith settled on the lower Mississippi River to ply his sail-making trade. With the invention of steam, he decided to go to work loading and unloading the growing tonnage of exports and imports along the waterfront. He called his company T. Smith & Sons. It soon became the strongest stevedoring and tugboat company on the U.S. Gulf Coast.

Nearly half a century later, an industrious Scotsman named Angus R. Cooper launched his own stevedoring enterprise in Mobile, Alabama.

This was the beginning of three generations of strong, steady growth as a multifaceted maritime service operation.

In 1983, T. Smith & Sons and Cooper Stevedoring Company merged to form Cooper/T. Smith Corporation. The combined companies operated in 26 ports on all three coasts and along America's inland waterways.

Today, the company is headed by sole owners Angus R. Cooper, II (chairman), and David J. Cooper (president)—both grandsons of the founder. Cooper/T. Smith has grown from a small enterprise into a progressive, innovative, and multiport business that employs thousands nationwide. The company now has offices in 38 ports and owns 37 affiliate companies, which include warehousing, insurance, terminal operations, barge fleeting, push-boat operations, and floating terminals.

Above: The management team at Cooper/T. Smith is pictured alongside a statue of Ervin S. Cooper at Cooper Riverside Park.

Left: Cooper/T. Smith's Crescent Towing operates 24 hours per day, 365 days per year, providing docking, undocking and towing from the mouth of the Mississippi River to Baton Rouge. Additional vessels are permanently stationed in the Industrial Canal.

Cooper/T. Smith maintains an impeccable reputation for its thorough, high quality service in New Orleans. But in true New Orleans style, there has been a tale or two that makes for great storytelling.

One such tale harks back to the 1920s, when Louisiana cattlemen were importing Brahma bulls through the Port of New Orleans.

During one of these shipments, the bulls broke loose at the Robin Street Wharf and stampeded back and forth along the riverfront. It was reported that one bull was trying its best to break into Antoine's Restaurant in the French Quarter. This seems a little unlikely, as everyone knows you can't get into Antoine's without a reservation,

or standing patiently in line. But it is true that Angus R. Cooper, Sr. did his best to physically discourage the bull from entering the restaurant, and though successful in the endeavor, spent the rest of his life trying to forget the episode!

GALLAGHER TRANSFER & STORAGE

In 1893, Mr. William Gallagher formed Gallagher Transfer & Storage with one wagon and two mules. The yellow fever season was during the warm summer months and there was very little moving in New Orleans from mid-June until mid-September. Everyone moved on the first of October when the weather had cooled a bit. And thus it became a New Orleans custom that leases on rental property ended on September 30 and everyone moved on the "first of October," All Saints' Day. On that day, the Gallagher wagons started at daybreak and were often moving people long into the night. This "first of October" custom prevailed in New Orleans until after World War II.

William Gallagher's business prospered over the years and many days were the "first of October" for the company.

Gallagher dominated the moving and storage business in New Orleans by adding storage facilities and motorized vehicles to provide service to their customers. In 1939, after 46 years of moving people and two years before his death, Gallagher sold the company to Paul Maloney, Jr. Mr. Maloney retained the company's name and continued its tradition of service and growth.

Paul Maloney, Jr. served as president of Gallagher for the next 25 years and under his leadership the company continued to prosper and expand. In 1964, his son, Robert S. Maloney, assumed the presidency. Gallagher centralized its operations in 1980 on a fifteen-acre complex located at 2401 Elysian Fields Avenue between the two interstate feeders of I-10 and I-610. This facility is geographically located in the hub of New Orleans and because of this location is able to rapidly transfer household goods from "around the block to around the world." The company is headquartered in a 24' high, dock height storage facility of 60,000 square feet. It has since added

three additional warehouses, bringing the total to over 120,000 square feet. Also located adjacent to the site is the Mardi Gras Truck Stop which includes a public truck scale and diesel-fuel facilities.

Robert Maloney and his wife Bonny, along with three of their five children are actively involved in Gallagher's operation. Jeanie Maloney, Vice President, Robert Maloney, Jr., Corporate Sales Manager and Craig Maloney, Commercial Manager are largely responsible for Gallagher's success. Another son, Kurt Maloney, successfully manages the Mardi Gras Truck Stop.

An important part of Gallagher's ability to provide quality service to its customers is its relationship with Bekins Van Lines. Founded in 1891 by two immigrant brothers, Bekins introduced the first covered moving vans to the West Coast, and later the first motor trucks to the moving and storage business. Gallagher is proud to be one of the Bekins agents. The two companies complement each other in terms of interstate transportation and storage needs. The relationship benefits not

A GMC electric van (above) and one of the first tractor trailer rigs (opposite page) ever used in the New Orleans area for moving of household goods – 1938.

only the two companies, but also the general moving public.

Gallagher, independently and with Bekins, also provides both the distribution and warehousing for various types of high-tech electronic equipment with special "air-ride" suspension trucks.

As time and communications have progressed, Gallagher's international department, under the leadership of Bonny Maloney, has continued to improve and enlarge the services it provides to their international clients. Their service area extends over the entire Southeastern region of the United States and they have sent shipments to every continent in the

world. Gallagher does not broker its shipments through a van line or a relocation service. Gallagher's membership in the best worldwide organizations has allowed the company to develop close personal relationships with the very best agents throughout the world. Gallagher is one of only 38 companies in the United States to be a member of O.M.N.I., the Overseas Moving Network International. They are also a member of F.I.D.I., Federation of International Furniture Removers, L.A.C.M.A., Latin American and Caribbean International Movers Association and H.H.G.F.A., Household Goods Forwarders Association of America, Inc.

Another focus of Gallagher's is Gallagher Records Management. This is a full-service record center that includes computerized indexing and inventory services, monthly activity reports, storage services for all media, scheduled courier services and certified destruction services.

Gallagher has over 75 years of experience with commercial cargo and can provide more than a quarter million square feet of bonded warehousing space in several locations throughout the New Orleans area. Services include storage, drayage, destuffing and restuffing, freight consolidations, transloading, bulkheading, and recoopering.

Setting the standard for office relocations, Gallagher moves delicate laboratory and computer equipment, heavy industrial equipment, office furnishing, and libraries. They maintain one of the largest and most experienced permanent employee forces in the New Orleans area.

With a third and fourth generation of experienced Maloneys presiding over a company prepared to meet the challenges of the future, and conveniently located away from the clutter of downtown city traffic, they have no fear of rush periods, such as the "first of October." Even if the "first of October" should come every day!

HIBERNIA NATIONAL BANK

Before electric streetlights or paving or city sidewalks, before jazz wafted through the streets, Hibernia National Bank was a part of New Orleans.

In 1870, a dozen men saw a window of opportunity. The economy was strengthening after the Civil War, but there were few healthy banks. On April 30, 12 Irishmen gathered in the Camp Street law office of Thomas Gilmore, the first meeting of the board of directors of a new bank to be called The Hibernia Bank & Trust Company, honoring the ancient Roman name for the land of their ancestors. Patrick Irwin was elected president, at no salary.

The bank was born in a New Orleans with a population of about 170,000, 40 percent of whom were foreign-born and 24,000 of whom were Irish. During its first year, it would accumulate about $1 million in deposits.

The oldest banking name in Louisiana, Hibernia has been characterized by innovation, creativity and reliability through 13 decades of history's flow—encompassing floods, hurricanes, two

In 1870, Patrick Irwin was elected as the first president of Hibernia.

world wars, the Great Depression, and the fluctuating economy of Louisiana and the nation. Through good times and bad, Hibernia has remained a source of financing and an engine of growth for the industries that create healthy economies and for the individuals who work hard and flourish.

For a concrete metaphor for Hibernia's leadership, we need look no further than its buildings. In 1904, Hibernia constructed a 13-story building at the corner of Carondelet and Gravier streets in downtown New Orleans that was, at the time, the tallest in the city. Only 17 years later, the bank completed an engineering and architectural marvel—a 23-story building that was the city's first modern skyscraper and the tallest building in the South in 1921. The building, still the bank's headquarters, held the record as New Orleans' tallest skyscraper for 43 years—until 1964.

The structure was topped by the Hibernia Tower, a landmark that was once the official navigation light for Mississippi River pilots and the transmission station for one of the South's first television stations. The Hibernia Tower continues as a source of delight for locals and visitors alike, thanks to the colored lights that bathe its portico in seasonal hues.

In 1918, Hibernia also established the city's first branch bank, the Industrial Branch at the corner of St. Claude Avenue and France Street. In just over five years, Hibernia had added six more branches in New Orleans—Algiers, Decatur, Dryades, Mid-City, St. Charles Avenue and the Jefferson Branch at Magazine and Gen. Pershing.

By mid-1997, Hibernia National Bank had 228 locations covering 31 Louisiana parishes, that represent approximately 80 percent of the state's population, and five counties in Texas. Hibernia has the largest banking-office network in Louisiana and is the only bank serving every major market in the state.

Hibernia has a history as a catalyst for the changes that have served as the engines for economic success in its markets. For example, in the 1930s, the bank headed the bond-holding syndicate that underwrote the building of more than 10,000 miles of new roads in

Hibernia opened in 1870 as New Orleans was recovering from the effects of the Civil War. The Hibernia name is the oldest name in Louisiana banking.

Louisiana. In 1933, Hibernia President Rudolph S. Hecht arranged financing of the first Mississippi River bridge at New Orleans, including federal funds of more than $13 million.

A decade later, Hecht became chairman of a group that founded International House, dedicated to expanding business and cultural contacts. The bank's tradition of supporting international trade continues. Hibernia was honored by the Small Business Administration in 1995 for writing the most loans to export firms in Louisiana, Mississippi and Arkansas. In winning the award, Hibernia made 107 loans totaling $14.5 million, more SBA loans than all other banks in the region combined. Recognition for export loan activity also came from the magazine *International Trade Finance Report*, which ranked Hibernia third in the nation for dollar volume to exporters in 1995 and fifth in the number of loan transactions closed. In 1996, the bank nearly tripled its number of loans to export firms over the previous award-winning year.

Community activism has helped set Hibernia apart throughout its history.

Hibernians devoted themselves to selling war bonds, were committed to helping people survive the bank crisis of the Depression and lent a helping hand in very specific ways to New Orleanians following natural disasters of all kinds. The bank supported two World's Fairs a century apart—both of which helped develop architecture and culture in the city—and most recently underwrote an exhibition of Monet paintings at the New Orleans Museum of Art that garnered international praise.

Through an annual contributions budget that totals 2% of pre-tax earnings, Hibernia assists hundreds of diverse organizations and events throughout its markets, with special emphasis on educational programs that can open doors for students of all ages and levels of achievement. Hibernia focuses on early-childhood development programs so children can begin to develop their skills as soon as possible in life, and strengthens secondary and higher education through its support of programs including Summerbridge, Teach for America, Dollars for Scholars, Partnerships in Education, Black Achievers, Junior Achievement, and research and scholarship initiatives at colleges and universities.

As times have changed, Hibernia has restructured itself to maintain a position of leadership in its industry. In 1917, Hibernia became the first large state-chartered banking institution in the South to enroll as a Federal Reserve Bank member. Following the National Bank Holiday and congressional action during the first week of the Roosevelt administration in 1933, Hibernia Bank & Trust was rechartered as The Hibernia National Bank in New Orleans.

Hibernia has been the most active Louisiana financial institution in merging with strong community banks. The 20 mergers completed or announced from 1994 through mid-1997 represent opportunities for Hibernia to offer its excellent service and innovative products to even more customers. Hibernia is first, second or third in deposit share in 27 Louisiana parishes and three Texas counties.

While providing the hometown banking that customers want, the bank continues to look for merger opportunities with

strong community banks in Louisiana and in contiguous markets in eastern Texas, southern Arkansas, western Mississippi and on the Mississippi Gulf Coast.

According to the bank's mission statement, Hibernia wants to be recog-

The Tower atop Hibernia's headquarters office in New Orleans, built in the 1920s, stands as a symbol of the company's strength and has been used as the name for many of the bank's products and services.

nized by customers, employees, and shareholders as the best financial services company in each market that the bank serves. In order to achieve that position, Hibernia is investing in technology and information, expansion opportunities, banking facilities and convenience, products and lines of business, the talents of Hibernia people, and the communities in which Hibernia is located.

After more than a century and a quarter, Hibernia is strong and on the move, and its tradition of commitment to exemplary customer service and to outstanding corporate citizenship—in every Hibernia community—remains as strong as it was with those 12 determined New Orleans leaders. By the standards of historic proof and future promise, they did indeed make a difference.

The "financial marketplace" design of new Hibernia offices goes beyond traditional consumer banking services by providing true one-stop financial-services shopping.

INTERMARINE, INC.

Intermarine, Inc., is a world leader in the carriage of "project cargo"—typically heavy and cumbersome equipment associated with major construction projects, power generation plants, mining operations, oilfield developments, chemical plants, and other industrial concerns.

Founded in 1990 by marine transportation veteran Roger Kavanagh, Intermarine is headquartered on the 47th floor of One Shell Square in Downtown New Orleans. The world's fastest growing carrier of project and breakbulk cargo, the company's annual revenues now exceed $175 million, up from $5 million during its first full year of operation.

Since its founding, Intermarine has earned a reputation for performing time and cost efficient voyages of overdimensional, hard-to-handle equipment to all corners of the world. With most of its business focusing on deliveries to the Caribbean, South America, the Far East and now the Middle East,

Pakistan and India, the company constructs over 250 voyages a year carrying in excess of 2 million revenue tons.

Intermarine acts as the managing agent of two vessel operating companies; Industrial Maritime Carriers (USA), Inc., and Industrial Maritime Carriers (Bahamas), Inc. Together the compa-

M/V Industrial Advantage, a 17330 DWT multipurpose vessel capable of lifting 150 metric tons.

nies form one of the world's largest charterers of multipurpose vessels. Ships chartered by the companies range from small 3,000-ton coaster vessels to 24,000-ton multipurpose heavy-lift ships.

Intermarine has at its disposal the largest and most flexible fleet of multipurpose, heavy lift, project cargo carrying vessels in the world. Together the companies control 45-50 vessels with cargo capacities ranging from 3,500 to 35,000 cbms and heavy lift capacity up to 650 metric tons. Thirteen vessels have lift capacity of more than 150 metric tons; an additional twenty have 100 to 150 ton capacity. No other company can provide the scope of vessel capabilities that is available through Intermarine or spends as much time and money maintaining the quality of their fleet. As a matter of fact, the company recently concluded long term charters on six newbuildings to further expand its Americas service. Five of the ships are sister ships, 4,900

225 Ton Gas Turbine being loaded aboard one of Industrial's vessels.

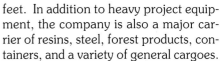
Hovercraft ready to load onto an Industrial vessel at New Orleans, LA.

DWT, 15.5 knot vessels with twin 60 metric ton cranes, combinable for 120 ton lifts. They will be known as the Alliance Class vessels. The remaining newbuilding is a 300 metric ton heavy/lift/container ship, 9,000 DWT, 650 TEU ship with 16.5 knot service speed.

Intermarine manages Industrial Maritime Carriers (USA) Americas service, which specializes in transporting project and liner cargoes from the United States and Mexico to Latin America and the Caribbean Islands. Featuring weekly sailings to Venezuela, Colombia, and Trinidad as well as fortnightly sailings to both East and West coasts of South America, Intermarine is the leading carrier of breakbulk, containerized and project cargoes to the area.

Intermarine manages Industrial Maritime Carriers (Bahamas) Far East service, which offers four to five sailings per month from the U.S. Gulf and East coasts to the entire Pacific Rim range. This line operates from loadcenters at Houston and Philadelphia in the United States; Busan, Shanghai, Xingang, Dalian, Qingdao, Kaohsiung, Hong Kong in the Pacific North Range; Manila, Singapore, Jakarta, Surabaya, Port Kelang, Bangkok, Map Ta Phut, Laem Chabang in the Pacific South Range. Earlier this year the line started offering service once monthly to the Arabian Gulf, Pakistan and India. This service is also the leading carrier of project and breakbulk cargo in the trade.

Intermarine's quick ascent in the shipping world is largely credited to its expertise in safely and quickly transporting individual pieces of cargo as heavy as 640 metric tons and as long as 200

M/V Industrial Harmony, one of five new Alliance Class vessels.

feet. In addition to heavy project equipment, the company is also a major carrier of resins, steel, forest products, containers, and a variety of general cargoes.

Flexibility and personal attention to client's special needs are company hallmarks. Instead of confining customers to a rigid shipping schedule and a set fleet of vessels, Intermarine addresses their project cargo needs on a case-by-case basis. Upon learning of the cargo job at hand, Intermarine will find exactly the type of vessel to meet the specific need. If the vessel type is not available within Industrial's fleet of approximately 50 vessels, they will charter the appropriate vessel to accommodate the customer's schedule and technical needs. Once the cargo arrives at its port of call, Intermarine oftentimes arranges land-based or barge services to complete the movement to final destination, no matter how remote.

Intermarine employs about 90 individuals with 60 in its headquarters in New Orleans and 30 in Houston, its largest cargo loadcenter. Industrial Maritime Carriers (USA and Bahamas) is the U.S. largest and most frequent carrier of breakbulk, heavy-lift and general cargo to South America and the Far East.

J. CALDARERA & COMPANY, INC.

When Joseph Caldarera matriculated at Louisiana State University in the fall of 1973, as a stop-gap occupation during his four years of formal study he looked to his father as a pattern and chose carpentry. He hardly realized while pouring foundations, erecting structures, repairing, restoring, painting, or doing whatever the immediate project demanded that he was gaining practical hands-on experience that would stand him in good stead for a lifetime. As a master carpenter employed by T.L. James & Co., Inc., the elder Joseph Caldarera not only passed on to his son an appreciation for the skills demanded of his craft, from finishing residential interiors to designing and constructing the labor-saving concrete forms for highway and bridge work, he also handed down a respect for the fundamental ethics of the profession: deliver a quality product and do it efficiently and on-time.

By the time the younger Joseph graduated from LSU in May 1977, he had decided on construction for his career, and before the month was out he had established J. Caldarera & Company at Kenner in Jefferson Parish, with

Entryway to River Parish Hospital, one of many company projects.

two full-time employees. He purchased his first tractor in 1974 and did jobs with this single piece of equipment, as well as remodeling work and custom homes, which helped put him through school. Not long after, he procured the Jefferson Parish maintenance and clearing contract which his company held for a number of years. He got his first two commercial construction jobs after college graduation through the influence of his father and mentors at T.L. James and Co., Inc, such as Mr. George D. Williams. Finishing the work professionally and on schedule won him the trust of his customers and a reputation for integrity that quickly led to a sweeping series of contracts blanketing the general contractor's field.

J. Caldarera & Co. has built houses, apartments, multi-unit government housing, retail stores, and controlled-temperature warehouses, such as those for Dixie Tomato Company and Crescent Distributing, distributors for Miller Beer products.

The firm has constructed shopping centers, office buildings, banks, funeral homes, and restaurants for national chains, including a Kentucky Fried Chicken franchise that was serving customers during its grand opening only 50 days after Caldarera workers first stepped onto a bare, grassy lot. Such efficiency in fast-track construction has drawn multiple contracts from

Joseph Caldarera founder of J. Caldarera Company, Inc.

McDonald's, Pizza Hut, Popeye's, Rally's, Slammers and other proprietors for whom time literally means money. It has also made the company a major player in metal-building construction for offices, warehouses, and manufacturing, packaging and fabrication plants—as a certified ARMCO Metal Buildings dealer, as a select Golden Eagle Dealer for American Building Company, and as the region's exclusive dealer for Varco-Pruden Buildings.

Its capacity to place radio-dispatched teams in the field immediately during and following natural and accident-caused emergencies has put J. Caldarera in the quick-dial systems of global insurers and claims services such as AIG, Allstate, Cigna, CNA, Crawford, GAB, Hartford, Lloyd's of London, Reliance, State Farm, Travelers, and USF&G. As an illustration, when a massive explosion devastated the Shell Oil refinery in Norco on May 5,1988, J. Caldarera experts quickly and accurately evaluated the destruction, allowing for a rapid start toward getting the refinery back in operation.

Joseph Caldarera expanded his equipment fleet, warehouse, and set-up yard in 1980, and again in 1984, when he moved his operation to the intersection of Interstates 55 and 10 in LaPlace, and once more in 1986 as business continued to grow. Construction of hazardous waste containment facilities, water purification and waste water treatment plants, municipal utility and drainage systems, hurricane protection and environmental reclamation levees, fire stations, libraries, schools as well as sev-

eral prison facilities including the state-of-the-art juvenile detention facility in Robert, Louisiana which features an electronically controlled monitoring center allowing for maximum control with minimum personnel.

Educational facilities include the $4.1 million Ethel Schoeffner Elementary School in New Sarpy built in 1992. The following year the firm began work on a $1.4 million school and gymnasium at Albert Cammon Middle School in St. Rose and a $3.5 million restoration-expansion of the John L. Ory School in LaPlace. Built in 1909 and deserted to weeds, creeping vines, and mildew, in 1994, the blonde-brick structure received a foundation-to-roof renovation along with 18 new classrooms. When fire destroyed an entranceway and two classrooms of the La Place Elementary School, the School Board of St. John the Baptist Parish declared an emergency and immediately called on J. Caldarera's experience to deal with the disaster and fast-track the construction so the board could return 145 displaced third graders to permanent classrooms as quickly as possible.

The company also builds highways and bridges which link one end of the state to the other and does interstate work in neighboring states where they are also licensed. Their success on these bridge projects is based, in part, on the experience Caldarera's father passed on to his son, as well as to their deep equipment base and personnel which affords the company the ability to do their own concrete, base and piling work in-house.

A Natural Resource Division headquartered in Woodville, MS encompasses oil, gas, timber, aggregate and wildlife conservation.

Executive Vice President Ray Caldarera, referred to by his brother as "my right hand" and "the best estimator I've ever seen," oversees the computerized estimating systems that allows the company to project costs and set firm schedules, benefiting both customer and contractor. Of late, Ray has applied his systems to increasingly technical projects as various as installing industrial and technical electrical systems,

New Orleans Zephyrs baseball park in Metarie built by J. Caldarera Company, Inc.

building heliports, and work on professional and medical complexes, such as a $5.11 million renovation-expansion of the intricate Cardiovascular Center of East Jefferson General Hospital.

Careful financial management combined with the continuing procurement of equipment and the growth of a skilled work force, now numbering more than 130, has given J. Caldarera the financial base to take on jobs of unprecedented proportion, jobs that have forced Ray to upgrade his software exponentially.

In November 1996 the Louisiana Superdome Commission awarded J. Caldarera a $13 million contract to build a multipurpose center in Bayou Segnette State Park near Westwego. The 75,000-square-foot Olympic regulation arena holds four courts with a seating capacity as high as 3,400 for basketball and volleyball games, wrestling meets, other sporting events, and concerts. It also contains three versatile 1,500-square-foot rooms, including a gallery capable of feeding the multitudes. The main auditorium can also be configured to accommodate programs ranging from Mardi Gras balls to high school graduations.

In May 1996, a J. Caldarera crew began shaping the grounds of the $20 million New Orleans Zephyrs baseball park in Metairie. The state-of-the-art triple-decked stadium, complete with

air-conditioned suites, evokes memories of the classic baseball stadia of the Babe Ruth era, and anticipation of its splendor led Zephyr fans to set a record in the purchase of season tickets. The 10,000-seat stadium contractually required an August 1997 completion date, but was ready for play when 10,366 spectators appeared for the opening home game on April 11, 1997—4 months ahead of schedule. Fans dramatically gave the park their stamp of approval seven weeks later on May 31 when 9,256 ticket holders pushed the young season's attendance past the 1996 full-season tally of 180,485, making the Zephyrs the sixth best drawing team in all of minor league baseball. Their overall attendance exceeded 500,000 by August 31, 1997.

Throughout his fruitful two decades as a builder, Joseph Caldarera has remained faithful to what he calls his "Old School" credo of integrity based on a strict code of ethics that emphasizes completing work under all conditions on schedule and beyond customer expectations. As a result, by September 1997, the firm is listed in the top 10 of general contractors in the state. His desire for the future is as simply expressed—to continue honoring that code and to provide prosperity, security and an ethical model for his five daughters.

MEMORIAL MEDICAL CENTER

Memorial Medical Center is a blending of two historic medical institutions and their integration into Tenet Louisiana HealthSystem, the largest provider of healthcare delivery in the greater New Orleans area.

The foundation for Mercy Hospital can be traced back to Dublin, Ireland and the early 1830s. It was there that Catherine McAuley, an orphan and founder of the Sisters of Mercy, inherited a sizeable fortune from her guardian. Sensitized by her own life experiences, she used her inheritance to respond to the needs of the sick and the poor. Her organization, the Community of the Sisters of Mercy, spread to the United States and New Orleans in 1869 with the opening of a school for children and a local clinic. In 1924, Mrs. Leonce Sonait donated her estate on Annunciation Street to the Sisters of Mercy where the hospital originally began.

Mercy Hospital moved to the present location at the corner of North Jefferson Davis Parkway and Bienville Street in 1953. Over the coming decades Mercy added the convent and expanded the hospital to include the adjacent Medical Office Building.

The roots of Southern Baptist Hospital reach back to the turn of the century. In 1917, a young Baptist missionary raised an important question at the Southern Baptist Convention II —"What about a Baptist hospital in New Orleans?" From this question grew a commitment of the Convention to build a hospital. In fact, it is interesting to note that a fund was established with the help of the Archbishop of New Orleans and individuals of all denominations.

In 1926, a 248 bed hospital opened. Throughout the decades, numerous wings were added and the hospital grew to become a 533 bed tertiary facility. The 1980s also brought the addition of the Women's Pavilion, a cornerstone of local healthcare for many women in the greater New Orleans area.

Memorial Medical Center's Baptist Campus, located at 2700 Napolean Avenue, in the Uptown section of New Orleans. Photo by Bevil Knapp

But perhaps the greatest challenge for both institutions was about to occur in 1994, when Mercy Hospital and Southern Baptist Hospital merged to become Mercy+Baptist Medical Center. This merger created the largest private hospital in the metropolitan area, with 726 beds and a dual-campus geographic advantage. The management of the facilities also merged to become Christian Health Ministries and two medical staffs became one.

While the merger helped to strengthen the position of the institution in the volatile market, the leadership of Christian Health Ministries began to see the evolution of large healthcare systems or partnerships developing in the market. These partnerships were combining multiple hospitals and using this leverage to negotiate managed care contracting. Additionally, pressures to reduce healthcare costs and reduce charges also caused concern among hospital leadership.

By 1995 it was decided that Mercy+Baptist Medical Center could not stand alone in the New Orleans market. It needed a partner that could place the

medical center at the center of a growing network, while providing capital for continued improvement and important cost controls. After a review of three alternatives, including a partnership with a group of non-profit hospitals in New Orleans, or acquisition by one of two for-profit chains including orNda and Tenet, Christian Health Ministries decided to sell the facility to Tenet Healthcare Corporation. As an additional condition of the sale, the hospital was required to change its name, becoming Memorial Medical Center in August of 1996.

Today, Memorial Medical Center is the tertiary flagship of the Tenet Louisiana HealthSystem and is one of the premier facilities of the national Tenet Health-System. Memorial Medical Center continues to remain a market leader and a hallmark for quality healthcare, as it has been for generations of New Orleanians. Since the acquisition, Memorial Medical Center capitalized on the unique opportunity to acquire the adjacent acute care and outpatient surgical facility known as Eye, Ear, Nose & Throat Hospital.

With the recent expansion of the solid organ transplant program, and the addition of bone marrow transplantation, Memorial Medical Center, as part of the growing Tenet Louisiana HealthSystem, is poised to become the premier healthcare facility in the highly competitive New Orleans healthcare market.

The Mercy Campus of Memorial Medical Center is located in the Mid-City section of New Orleans at 301 North Jefferson Davis Parkway. Photo by Bevil Knapp

NEW ORLEANS MUSEUM OF ART

The story of the New Orleans Museum of Art, the third oldest fine arts institution in the South, began in 1910 when Isaac Delgado, a local sugar broker and philanthropist, donated $150,000 to build a "temple of art for rich and poor alike." On December 16, 1911, the Museum, a beautiful neo-classic building then known as the Isaac Delgado Museum of Art, presented its first exhibition.

In 1971, the Museum underwent a major expansion, adding the Wisner Education Wing, the Stern Auditorium, and the City Wing, which included the Ella West Freeman Gallery. Recognizing the City of New Orleans' long-term support, the Board of Trustees, in turn, voted to change the name of the institution to the New Orleans Museum of Art.

With the new addition, the Museum increased the size and diversity of its collection and attracted international exhibitions such as the *Treasures of Tutankhamen* (1977-1978), *The*
Search for Alexander (1982), *The Precious Legacy* (1985), and *Carthage: A Mosaic of Ancient Tunisia* (1988-1989).

In 1993, NOMA completed a major $23 million expansion and renovation project that doubled its size and ranked it among the top 25 percent of museums nationwide. Besides increased space for exhibitions, art storage, library, and educational activities, the expansion also included a new Museum Shop and Courtyard Café.

The added space allowed for a more thorough display of the Museum's 45,000 objects and enabled it to attract such blockbuster exhibitions as *Monet: Late Paintings of Giverny from the Musée Marmottan* (1995), *Fabergé in America* (1996-1997), *Andrew Wyeth: The Helga Pictures* (1997), and *Sacred Arts of Haitian Vodou* (1998).

Visitors to the Museum today encounter a comprehensive survey of Western and non-Western art from the pre-Christian era to the present. Reflecting the city's cultural heritage, the Museum's collection is particularly strong in French art, including works by such beloved masters as Monet, Renoir, Gauguin, Degas, Picasso, and others. Objects from the great Mayan culture of Mexico

Whisperings of Love, French (1825-1905), oil on canvas, gift of Mr. and Mrs. Chapman H. Hyams

and Central America, works from the Cuzco School in Peru, and Haitian and American painting and sculpture are among the highlights of the Museum's Art of the Americas collection. One of the most popular attractions in the Museum is the special gallery containing three *Imperial Easter Eggs*, the *Imperial Lillies of the Valley Basket*, and numerous other treasures of Peter Carl Fabergé on extended loan from the Matilda Geddings Gray Foundation Collection. The Museum also has nationally recognized collections in sub-Saharan African Art, photography, Japanese painting of the Edo period (1615-1868), and glass works from ancient Egyptian vessels to contemporary glass sculpture. A specially-designed orientation gallery known as *the stARTing point* introduces visitors to the world of art and to the Museum's collection through the use of interactive computers, films, and videos.

New Orleans Museum of Art

WALDEMAR S. NELSON AND COMPANY, INCORPORATED

Waldemar S. Nelson and Company, Incorporated has grown from a partnership of three engineers employing a single draftsman in Louisiana in 1945, to a professional engineering, architectural and environmental science practice employing four hundred engineers, architects, scientists, designers, drafters, secretaries, technicians and support personnel on projects throughout the world.

It is rated number 182 out of the top 500 engineering firms in the United States, according to the latest Engineering News-Record report of such statistics.

The company practices in many disciplines, including civil, structural, electrical, mechanical, chemical, process, instrumentation, control and environmental engineering; industrial, commercial and institutional architecture; project management, procurement, and inspection of construction.

The firm started in New Orleans, Louisiana at the close of World War II, when the pent-up demand for infrastructure projects, construction of which was prohibited during the war, gave impetus to the fledgling company's development. Early work included a series of airport and seaport projects, design of manufacturing plants, and expansion of the Grande Ecaille, Louisiana sulphur mine for Freeport Sulphur Company.

This last project started the company on a series of mining projects for Freeport Sulphur Company, including ten sulphur mines in the Louisiana and Texas coastal areas and the first offshore sulphur mines. This work culminated in the development of Freeport's Main Pass Sulphur mine in water 206 feet deep 17 miles off the mouth of the Mississippi River, a half billion dollar project, completed in 1991.

The relationship with Freeport also resulted in major mineral processing projects, including design and development of a nickel mine at Moa Bay in Cuba, 1956-1959; design of the world's largest phosphoric acid plant at Convent, Louisiana processing phosphate rock brought from

Corporate Officers: left to right: Richard J. Cabiro, P.E., Treasurer; Waldemar S. Nelson, P.E. ,Chairman of the Board; Charles W. Nelson, P.E., President; Thomas G. Ehrlicher, P.E., Secretary; and James D. Cospolich, P.E., Executive; Vice President

Florida; and continuing expansion of P.T. Freeport Indonesia Company's copper and gold mine, plant and shipping facility on the island of Irian Jaya, Indonesia.

Experience onshore in the design and commissioning of oil and gas production and processing facilities, and over thirty years of experience offshore in the adaptation of such facilities to marine operation on fixed platforms has resulted in recent years for Waldemar S. Nelson and Company, Incorporated becoming experts in designing offshore deep water production installations in water depths of 3,000, 4,000 and 5,000 feet and more. These are monster projects, with costs of three-quarters of a billion to a billion and a quarter dollars each. They are justified by the discovery of tremendous reservoirs of oil and gas beneath the ocean bed making possible production rates from a single installation of 100,000 to 200,000 barrels of oil and 100,000 to 400,000 million cubic feet of gas per day. Waldemar S. Nelson and Company, Incorporated and its associates have completed work on five such platforms and are starting on two more as this is being written.

Several factors have contributed to the company's success. Its location in New Orleans, Louisiana, a port city with a very cosmopolitan population has helped. One finds persons of English, Scotch, Irish, French, German, Italian, Scandinavian, Latin, Slavonian, African, and Asian heritage contributing their native talents and technology to the city's commerce and culture. The Mississippi River from the Gulf of Mexico through New Orleans to Baton Rouge is the greatest port in the world, a major driving force in the economy of the area. The availability and economy of marine transportation is a strong attraction for industry.

The supply of fresh water from the Mississippi River, a minimum of 100,000 cubic feet per second, and the ample supplies of natural gas, oil, salt and sulphur from the coastal and offshore deposits has been an incentive for a host of industries to locate in the area, and these have a continuing need for engineering, architectural and environmental services.

There are more than eight universities or colleges in Louisiana offering engineering, architecture, and technical programs making it easy to find and develop good staff members. The pleasure of living in New Orleans, with its friendly spirit, mild climate and year round opportunities for fishing, sailing, boating, golf, tennis, and hiking, its low cost of living, and excellent food and music, have made it easy to attract and maintain good staff members.

There are forty staff members who have been with the company twenty years or more, and their accumulated knowledge and experience is invaluable.

From the beginning, the company has insisted on conducting its work as a professional practice, where the aim is to provide the highest quality professional service. This has been a strong factor in attracting clients and maintaining their use of its services. This philosophy has also been instrumental in inducing top quality professionals to join the company in its practice.

For the first ten years of its existence, the company operated in a building at 840 Union Street, a former cotton factor's office. The cotton sampling room offered a broad open space, with good natural light for a drafting room. The location in the downtown business district was convenient for access to clients, banks, governmental offices and commercial services such as blueprinting.

In 1956, the company purchased an office building at 1200 St. Charles Avenue which had been occupied by IBM for the previous seventeen years.

This office, fronting on St. Charles Avenue, backed up to three large office buildings used by the telephone company, aggregating 300,000 sq. ft. of excellent office space. Over the years, the company acquired these buildings and, with their large capacity, is able to establish project offices for major programs, accommodating the company's engineering staff, the clients and frequently the clients' con-struction contractors in a single location, thus making for very efficient operation.

Computation is an essential part of engineering design, and when Waldemar Nelson entered the Tulane University College of Engineering in 1932, he was required to purchase a ten-inch Mannheim slide rule. At that time, the slide rule was a mark of distinction for engineering students.

Mechanical calculators were developed in the nineteenth century. One such machine, in use in the 1930s, was the Monroe Calculator and, when the company began its professional practice in 1945, they proudly acquired one.

As the demand for computing capacity in the company's office continued to increase, WSNCO recognized that computers had come of age. In 1956, the company purchased its first modern computer!

The development of personal computers and the reduction in the cost of these through improved design and market demand made it feasible for the firm to place computer stations throughout the office. In fact, computer stations are located at the desks of every engineer, architect, scientist, designer and secretary. The uses seem to multiply as fast as the services become available. At the present

Bottom, left: Shell Offshore, Inc.- MARS Tension Leg Platform in 3,000 ft. water depth, Gulf of Mexico

Bottom, right: P. T. Freeport Indonesia Company Copper and Gold Mine Project, Irian Jaya, Indonesia

Freeport Sulphur Company's Main Pass Sulphur Mine, 17 miles east of the Mouth of the Mississippi River, Gulf of Mexico

time, there are over two hundred fifty Nelson-owned and over three hundred fifty client-owned CADD and engineering computing stations throughout the company's building complex, all connected via a network to the company's central computer.

In 1996, to further enhance the company's communication with its clients, Waldemar S. Nelson and Company, Incorporated implemented a Microsoft Exchange e-mail system on a DEC Internet Alpha Server 1000. With this system, the company is capable of sending and receiving drawings, letters, purchase orders, and other documents which will help to facilitate client interaction while shortening the time of completion of a project.

Waldemar S. Nelson and Company, Incorporated is on the World Wide Web, and the Universal Resources Locator, or URL, for the company is: http:// www.wsnelson.com.

THE TIMES-PICAYUNE

Following the Louisiana Purchase a new generation of wealth and aspiration sprang up in New Orleans. Despite yellow fever epidemics, the city literally rose up out of the swamps and bayous. Trade in the port of New Orleans and sugar and cotton production soared. By the 1830s, a bustling new American mercantile class had built a new sector of the city and rivaled the established Creole and European cultures. The boisterous social scene often flared up in the illicit but common practice of dueling.

Arriving with $700 in gambling winnings, a couple of northern journalists decided to test their fortunes in New Orleans. On January 25, 1837 while rains and flooding kept state government offices closed, a sixth daily newspaper hit the streets of New Orleans. Named for the 6 1/4 cent Spanish coin it cost, *The Picayune* launched a history of innovation in journalism and raised a new voice in New Orleans.

The newcomers, Francis A. Lumsden and George Wilkins Kendall, thought it possible the city had a market for a new

"Sunday Amusements" a New Orleans-Duel at the half way house—sketched by A.R. Waud.

type of newspaper. From a 12 by 14 foot office on Gravier Street with a small staff, they printed 1,000 copies per edition and, like the wave of penny presses in the East, sought a broad readership.

The Picayune was the first New Orleans paper to sell for less than a dime. It was smaller than the mercantile papers and lighter in spirit and tone, publishing fiction and often flippant commentary. The price and local appeal brought the paper quick popularity.

Lumsden's civic-mindedness led him to serve on the Municipal Council, in the Louisiana Legislature, on the Board of Administrators of the Public Schools and as a member of the House of Refuge, the city of New Orleans boys' orphanage.

Kendall's pioneering spirit took him west to explore Mexico. Later a Texas county was named for him. When the Mexican War erupted in 1846, Kendall set up a system of coverage, using couriers and steamboats. He consistently delivered news ahead of the military messengers, enabling *The Picayune* to scoop its competitors. A copy of the peace treaty reached *The Picayune's* offices by chartered steamer, beating the government's boat and that of the paper's competition.

The Mexican War was the first war covered daily by the newspapers and Kendall was one of journalism's first

famous war correspondents. *The Picayune* became one of the most quoted newspapers, and later initiated one of the earliest newspaper wire services.

In New Orleans, *The Picayune's* editorial voice addressed more local conflicts. Early editorials spoke out against the commonplace practice of dueling. Editorials also warned of the perils of women's suffrage and the fashion of bloomers, which might later encourage women to start wearing trousers.

In the 1870s one of the South's first female journalists, Eliza Jane Poitevent, became *The Picayune's* publisher. Colonel Alva Holbrook had succeeded Lumsden and Kendall before the Civil War. Holbrook met Poitevent in 1870. She began publishing poetry under the name Pearl Rivers, and later married Holbrook.

Holbrook sold the paper to a consortium of 225 merchants during difficult economic times during Reconstruction. They struggled to succeed, but sold it back to Holbrook, who died, leaving the paper to Eliza Jane Poitevent Holbrook with a debt of $80,000.

As the first woman publisher of a major metropolitan daily, Mrs. Holbrook brought the paper out of debt with the help of business manager George Nicholson, whom she later married. In the following years she expanded its pages in new directions, adding a society column, greatly increasing the number of illustrations and introducing the popular weather prophet, a sophisticated, potbellied frog.

As Eliza Nicholson settled into her role as publisher she became a leading social advocate, though not for women's suffrage. She lobbied for education programs in night schools, for a Children's Annex in a hospital for the severely ill and against cruelty to animals. New Orleanians affectionately referred to her as the "old lady of Camp Street," where *The Daily Picayune*, as it was then called, was headquartered. She wrote about a woman's world and work. A series labeled the "Cherry Wood Desk" stories attracted more women readers.

Nicholson recruited a neighbor, Elizabeth M. Gilmer, to work for the paper in the 1890s. Writing under the name Dorothy Dix, she became the first syndicated advice

Ashton Phelps, Jr., Publisher, The Times-Picayune.

columnist, dispatching tips to lovelorn readers around the world well into the 1940s.

The Daily Picayune changed its name as it combined with several papers created in the wake of the Civil War. *The Democrat*, founded in 1875, annexed *The Picayune's* bitter rival, *The Times*, in 1881 to form *The Times-Democrat*. *The Daily Picayune* merged with it in 1914 to become *The Times-Picayune*. Ashton Phelps, who had risen from the ranks of *The Times-Democrat* for his authoritative cotton market review and his writings on finance and economics, was named president.

Many famous literary writers have worked for *The Times-Picayune* over the years. William Faulkner wrote for the paper while he wrote his early novels and lived in the French Quarter. And William Sidney Porter assumed the name O. Henry while working for *The Times-Picayune*, using the synonym to avoid legal problems in Texas, where he had lived.

The Times-Picayune later joined with two other post-Reconstruction era newspapers. In 1933, *The Times-Picayune* purchased the afternoon *New Orleans States* and in 1958 bought *The New Orleans Item*, which was founded in 1877. The two newspapers were com-bined to form *The States-Item*. S.I. Newhouse bought both papers, The *Times-Picayune* and *The States-Item*, in 1962. In 1980 the publishing company combined *The States-Item* and *The Times-Picayune*, dropping the name of T*he States-Item.*

Through the years, *The Times-Pica-yune* has maintained a strong profile as it fought for good government in New Orleans and Louisiana. This was especially true during the regime of Huey P. Long, when Long became a virtual dictator while serving as governor, and later as the de facto governor while a United States senator.

In January of 1933 during the national banking crisis, the newspaper stood steadfast for freedom of the press by refusing to bow to the wishes of Long, who ordered it not to publish news about bank closings. Long had Adjutant-General Raymond Fleming call up some dozen Guardsmen and order them to "march down to that paper...and break every machine they got." Cooler heads prevailed upon Long, however, and the assault was thwarted.

The Times-Picayune championed the cause of the people in the summer of 1934, when Long had more than a hundred Guardsmen camped to duty because of Long's allegations that the Old Regular political organization was tampering with the voting rolls. The Long forces took over the registration office, and for a time it appeared there would be violence as the Guardsmen stood ready. Again, cooler heads prevailed and not a shot was fired even though the crisis lasted a month.

In the Louisiana Scandals that followed the demise of the Huey Long machine, *The Times-Picayune* played a leading role, especially with its daily Page One "Pertinent Questions," which struck at the core of public corruption. A massive prosecution by the federal government led to one governor's (Richard W. Leche) resignation and the election of a reform governor, (Sam H. Jones.)

Leadership of *The Times-Picayune* has maintained continuity. Ashton Phelps, first president of The Times-Picayune Publishing Company, was later succeeded by Eliza Jane Nicholson's son, Leonard K. Nicholson, and later by his grandson Ashton Phelps, Sr.

Today Ashton Phelps, Jr. is publisher of *The Times-Picayune* and works with President Linda Dennery. The newspaper has established bureaus throughout the metropolitan area and prides itself on intensive coverage of local news. Ventures in new media are connecting New Orleans to the world. An extensive web site delivers a daily sense of the city.

In the 1990s, *The Times-Picayune* has been recognized as one of the country's leading newspapers. Editor Jim Amoss was named editor of the year by the National Press Foundation in 1997, the year the paper captured two Pulitzer Prizes.

"Oceans of Trouble," a series which grew out of regular reporting on marine-life issues in the Gulf of Mexico, received the Pulitzer for public service for reporting on threats to the world's fisheries. As with several special series in the 1990s, reporting on local issues has led to more coverage of global subjects and trends. The newspaper's Walt Handlesman won the Pulitzer Prize for editorial cartooning.

Relating local issues to global concerns embodies the bold vision of a leading newspaper. *The Times-Picayune* in 160 years of service to New Orleans has established itself as a vital force in journalism.

Linda Dennery, President, The Times-Picayune.

WHITNEY NATIONAL BANK

Known for its famous clocks that now spread across the Gulf Coast, the Whitney has been serving its hometown of New Orleans for more than a century. By virtue of being the only New Orleans bank that didn't close its doors during the Great Depression, the Whitney can boast of being the city's oldest continuously operating bank. The bank got its name from three of its founders: George Q. Whitney, Charles M. Whitney, and Marie Louise Whitney. George Q. Whitney and 11 other original stockholders, including future U.S. Chief Justice Edward Douglas White, Jr., signed the Articles of Association and received their charter

George Q. Whitney—one of the founders and president of the Whitney National Bank from 1905-1907.

certificate in October of 1883. With James Hayden serving as its first president and White as its first legal counsel, Whitney National Bank opened its doors on November 5, 1883.

In 1888 the Whitney moved into its first permanent home, a landmark on Gravier Street that still serves as the bank's safe deposit department. The 1919 addition of the Common Street Annex provided St. Charles, Gravier, and Common Street access to the classic structure. This structure now serves as the bank's Main Office.

Early on, the bank earned a reputation as a staunch supporter of local business and civic endeavors. It offered an atmosphere where hometown entrepreneurs could close loans with a handshake and where organizers of local promotions such as the city's first world's fair (the 1884 Cotton Centennial Exposition) could rely on prompt and substantial backing.

The Whitney clock, a fixture on many Whitney branches, has been the symbol of the bank for more than 70 years.

The Whitney underwent significant geographic expansion in the early 20th century, acquiring the Germania National Bank in 1905 and six other local banks by 1930.

The buildings that were among the bank's early acquisitions—such as the old Pan American Bank building at the corner of Poydras and Camp Streets—became the Whitney's first branches. Soon enough, though, the Whitney began building branches from the ground up, beginning with the Margaret Place, Canal Street, Broad Street, and St. Roch Market branches in the mid-1920s. Since 1972 the bank has maintained a branch in the Cayman Islands to serve Louisiana's offshore petroleum interests. In the 1990s, while many banks have been closing branches, the Whitney has opened numerous branches in the city and along the Gulf Coast.

The 1990s have seen the Whitney spread throughout Louisiana to Baton Rouge, Lafayette, Morgan City, Iberia Parish, Houma, Covington, Mandeville, and Slidell. The Whitney expanded to Alabama in 1994 and

1996 acquisitions in Pensacola and Gulf Port made it the first Louisiana bank to enter Florida and Mississippi.

Support for the New Orleans community is still considered a matter of responsibility and pride at the Whitney. As proof, the bank established the Cabildo Fund when fire damaged Louisiana's most important landmark in 1988, and supports many economic development, cultural, and educational organizations.

In 1990, when William L. Marks became CEO of the bank, New Orleans and most of the city's financial institutions were struggling due to the petroleum industry's collapse and real estate market fluctuations in the 1980s. Since then the turnaround at the Whitney has been dramatic.

While maintaining its tradition of experienced bankers delivering personalized service, the Whitney has anticipated changing customer needs. As a result, the bank greatly expanded its consumer banking operations in the mid 1990s. Introducing competitive and innovative products along with state-of-the-art computer systems helped strengthen Whitney's consumer banking presence.

The bank offers a comprehensive line of products and services for consumers including a convenient Loan By Phone service and a 24-Hour Account Information phone line. Building off the strong tradition of relationships, the bank offers "Whitney SELECT" an all-in-one package that attracts financially sophisticated customers. Another unique product, "Check & Save Banking," targets younger customers who may be beginning their banking relationships. Understanding the value of convenience to its customers, the Whitney also offers a VISA® Check Card, an ATM card that also works like a check. It is one of the fastest growing financial products nationally.

For the small business customer, the bank created "Business Edge Banking" the core of which is an easy-to-understand checking account that works like a personal account and even includes an ATM card. As a result of introducing this product, Whitney received national recognition from *Entrepreneur* magazine as a bank that "creates new partnerships with small business."

Well known for the quality of its commercial account relationship managers, the Whitney offers valuable services for commercial customers. The bank has been a leader in International Banking Services, which are very important in a port city such as New Orleans. It is expanding its operations in Latin and South America

Whitney's growing International Department is headquartered in the Barnes Building. The bank recently renovated this historic building which was built in 1884.

and throughout the Pacific Rim. Services for commercial customers include Employee Benefits Programs, Merchant Credit Card Services and Treasury Management Services.

The Whitney's expansion into Alabama, Mississippi, and Florida was an important strategic decision. Many other businesses cover this market area, and many families and companies do business from Acadiana to the Florida Panhandle. They can find the Whitney's unique blend of old-fashioned service and the modern convenience at over 100 branches and 140+ ATMs as they travel across the Gulf South.

Thanks to the Whitney's expert blending of tradition with modern banking concepts and technology, New Orleans's oldest continuously operating bank remains a financial cornerstone of the community today and promises to hold that position in the future.

A new Whitney branch showing the new corporate signs including the image of the traditional clock.

SELECTED BIBLIOGRAPHY

Articles

Drew, Christopher. "Hard Times Were Hardest on Blacks." New Orleans *States-Item*. October 27, 1929.

_____ and Pope, John. "Nightmarish Memories of Crash Still Haunting Orleanians." October 27, 1979.

Dufour, Charles L. "The Fall of New Orleans." *Louisiana History*, vol. 2, no. 2 (Spring 1961).

Haas, Edward F. "New Orleans on the Half-Shell: The Maestri Era, 1936-46." *Louisiana History*, vol. 13, no. 3 (Summer 1972).

Heleniak, Roman. "Local Reaction to the Great Depression in New Orleans, 1929-1933." *Louisiana History*, vol. 10, no. 4 (Fall 1969).

Jackson, Joy J. "Prohibition in New Orleans: The Unlikeliest Crusade." *Louisiana History*, vol. 19, no. 3 (Summer 1978).

Kemp, John R. "Politics and the Depression." New Orleans *States-Item*, November 2, 1979.

Kurtz, Michael L. "Earl Long's Political Relations with the City of New Orleans: 1948-1960." *Louisiana History*, vol. 10, no. 3 (Summer 1969).

Pope, John. "New Orleans Danced as Market Fell." New Orleans *States-Item*, October 24, 1979.

Reinders, Robert C. "A Wisconsin Soldier Reports from New Orleans." *Louisiana History*, vol. 3, no. 4 (Fall 1962).

Roland, Charles P. "Louisiana and Secession." *Louisiana History*, vol. 19, no. 4 (Fall 1978).

Schweninger, Loren. "A Negro Sojourner in Antebellum New Orleans." *Louisiana History*, vol. 20, no. 3 (Summer 1979).

Tansey, Richard. "Prostitution and Politics in Antebellum New Orleans." *Southern Studies*, vol. 18, no. 4 (Winter 1979).

Books

Asbury, Herbert. *The French Quarter; An Informal History of the New Orleans Underworld.* New York: Alfred A. Knopf, 1936.

Carter, Samuel III. *Blaze of Glory: The Fight for New Orleans, 1814-1815.* New York: St. Martin's Press, 1971.

Caughey, John Walton. *Bernardo De Galvez in Louisiana, 1776-1783.* Berkeley: University of California Press, 1934.

Chase, John. *Frenchmen, Desire, Good Children.* New Orleans: Robert L. Crager and Company, 1949.

Christovich, Mary Lou; Toledano, Roulhac; Swanson, Betsy; and Holden, Pat. "The American Sector (Faubourg St. Mary). New Orleans Architecture," vol. 2. Contains essays by Samuel Wilson, Jr., and Bernard Lemann. Gretna: Pelican Publishing Company and The Friends of the Cabildo. 1972.

Clark, John G. *New Orleans, 1718-1812; An Economic History.* Baton Rouge: Louisiana State University Press, 1970.

Costa, Myldred Masson, trans. *Letters of Marie-Madeleine*

Hachard, Ursuline of New Orleans, 1727-1728. New Orleans: 1974.

Davis, Edwin Adam. *Louisiana; A Narrative History.* rev. ed. Baton Rouge: Claitor's Publishing Division, 1971.

Dufour, Charles L. *Ten Flags in the Wind: The Story of Louisiana.* New York: Harper and Row, 1967.

Giraud, Marcel. *A History of French Louisiana.* vol. 1. Translated by Joseph C. Lambert. Baton Rouge: Louisiana State University Press, 1974.

Haas, Edward F. "The Southern Metropolis, 1940-1976." *The City in Southern History.* Edited by Blaine A. Brownell and David R. Goldfield. Port Washington, New York: Kennikat Press, 1977.

————. *DeLesseps S. Morrison and the Image of Reform; New Orleans Politics, 1946-1961.* Baton Rouge: Louisiana State University Press, 1974.

Hair, William Ivy. *Bourbonism and Agrarian Protest; Louisiana Politics, 1877-1900.* Baton Rouge: Louisiana State University Press, 1969.

Jackson, Joy J. *New Orleans in the Gilded Age; Politics and Urban Progress, 1880-1896.* Baton Rouge: Louisiana State University Press, 1969.

Kemp, John R. *Martin Behrman of New Orleans: Memoirs of a City Boss.* Baton Rouge: Louisiana State University Press, 1977.

Kendall, John Smith. *History of New Orleans.* 3 Vols. Chicago and New York: Lewis, 1922.

Kirk, Susan Lauxman; and Smith, Helen Michel. *The Architecture of St. Charles Avenue.* Gretna: Pelican Publishing Company, 1977.

LaBree, Ben, ed. *The Confederate Soldier in the Civil War, 1861-1865.* Louisville, Kentucky: 1895.

Liebling, A.J. *The Earl of Louisiana: The Liberal Long.* New York: Simon and Schuster, 1961.

Macdonald, Robert R.; Kemp, John R.; and Haas, Edward F. *Louisiana's Black Heritage.* New Orleans: Louisiana State Museum, 1979.

Mclure, Mary Lilla. "Development of Political Parties and Factions to 1860." *Readings in Louisiana Politics.* Edited by Mark T. Carleton, Perry H. Howard, and Joseph B. Parker. Baton Rouge: Claitor's Publishing Division, 1975.

Nolte, Vincent. *50 Years in Both Hemispheres.* New York: Redfield, 1854.

Olmsted, Frederick Law. *A Journey in the Seaboard Slave States with Remarks on Their Economy.* New York: Dix, 1856.

Reed, Merl. "Boom or Bust—Louisiana's Economy During the 1830's." *Readings in Louisiana Politics.* Edited by Mark T. Carleton, Perry H. Howard, and Joseph B. Parker. Baton Rouge: Claitor's Publishing Division, 1975.

Reinders, Robert C. *End of an Era, 1850-1860.* Gretna: Pelican Publishing Company, 1964.

Reynolds, George M. *Machine Politics in New Orleans, 1897-1926.* New York: Columbia University Press, 1936.

Rightor, Henry. *Standard History of New Orleans, Louisiana.* Chicago: Lewis Publishing Company, 1900.

Robin, C.C. *Voyage to Louisiana.* Translated by Landry O. Stuart, Jr. New Orleans: Pelican Publishing Company, 1966.

Rose, Al; and Souchon, Edmond. *New Orleans Jazz; A Family Album.* rev. ed. Baton Rouge: Louisiana State University Press, 1978.

Samuel, Ray; Huber, Leonard V.; and Ogden, Warren C. *Tales of the Mississippi.* New York: Hastings House Publishers, 1965.

Siegel, Martin, ed. *New Orleans: A Chronological and Documentary History.* Dobbs Ferry, New York: Oceana Publications, Inc., 1975.

Sindler, Allan P. *Huey Long's Louisiana: State Politics 1920-1952.* Baltimore: Johns Hopkins University Press, 1956.

Taylor, Joe Gray. "The Warmoth Administration." *Readings in Louisiana History.* Edited by Glenn R. Conrad. New Orleans: Louisiana Historical Association, 1978.

————. "The Kellogg Era." *Readings in Louisiana History.* Edited by Glenn R. Conrad. New Orleans: Louisiana Historical Association, 1978.

————. *Louisiana Reconstructed, 1863-1877.* Baton Rouge: Louisiana State University Press, 1975.

Tindall, George B. "The Emergence of the New South, 1913-1945." *A History of the South,* vol. 10. Edited by W. H. Stephenson and C.M. Coulter. Baton Rouge: Louisiana State University Press, 1967.

Wilds, John. *Afternoon Story: A Century of the New Orleans States-Item.* Baton Rouge: Louisiana State University Press, 1976.

Williams, T. Harry. *Huey Long.* New York: Alfred A. Knopf, 1969.

Wilson, Samuel, Jr. *Benjamin Henry Boneval Latrobe: Impressions Respecting New Orleans.* New York: Columbia University Press, 1951.

————. and Lemann, Bernard. "The Lower Garden District." *New Orleans Architecture,* vol. 1. Compiled and edited by Mary Lou Christovich, Roulhac Toledano, and Betsy Swanson. Gretna: The Friends of the Cabildo and Pelican Publishing Company, 1971.

Exhibition Catalogues

Hardy, D. Clive. *The World's Industrial and Cotton Centennial Exposition.* New Orleans: The Historic New Orleans Collection, n.d.

Louisiana Purchase. Louisiana State Museum, n.d.

Manuscript Collections

Louisiana State Museum. Beebe Papers.

————. Kenner Papers.

————. Nathaniel Cox Letters.

————. Webb Diaries.

Unpublished Papers

Douthit, Leo Glenn. "The Governorship of Huey Long." Unpublished M.A. thesis, Tulane University, 1947.

Frazar, Luther E. "The Constitutional Convention of 1921." Unpublished M.A. thesis, Louisiana State University, 1935.

Bibliography Chapter 10
Articles
Bourg, Gene. "Gastronomical Putdown." *The Times-Picayune*, July 3, 1990

Button, Graham; Koselka, Rita.. "Gambling Gumbo." *Forbes*, January 17, 1994

Dawson, Victoria. "Authors writing new chapter in N.O. literary life." *The Times-Picayune,* February 2, 1990.

Eggler, Bruce. "Living's easy in N.O." *The Times-Picayune,* August 24, 1989

Finn, Kathy. "Development plans loom." *City Business*, January 29-February 11, 1990

Jackson, Connie. "Poll: Food in N.O. the best." *The Times-Picayune*, November 7, 1994

Judice, Mary. "Energy stocks rise on N.O. good news." *The Times-Picayune* April 8, 1997

Katz, Allan. "Morial: Mayoral legacy clouded by personality." *The Times-Picayune*, April 27, 1986

Kemp, John R. "New Orleans Reborn." *The New Orleans Vignette.* 1989

    "Art in a Goldfish Bowl." *New Orleans Magazine*, June 1989.

    "The Rise and Arrival of Contemporary Art." *New Orleans Magazine.* April 1991 .

    "Thirty Years of Changes in the Skyline." *New Orleans Magazine.* January 1986.

    "New Orleans: Welcome to their world...Exposition." *Travel-Holiday,* April 1984

    "The New Bohemia." *New Orleans Magazine*, July 1990.

King, Wayne. "Bad Times on the Bayou." *The New York Times Magazine*, June I I, 1989

Larando, Mark. "Simpsons take a shot at Crescent City." *The Times-Picayune*, October 1, 1992

Mullener, Elizabeth. "Richard Pennington: Top Cop." *The Times-Picayune* March 16, 1997

Remnick, David. "The Crime Buster." *The New Yorker.* February 24, 1997

Ruth, Dawn. "Mayor gets low marks in job." *The Times-Picayune* May 10, 1992

    Warner, Coleman; and, Theim, Rebecca. "It's Morial." *The Times-Picayune*, March 6, 1994

Sancton, Thomas. "Why the Good Times Still Roll." *Time*, November 4, 1991.

Scott, Liz. "Opening Day at the Fair." *New Orleans Magazine*, May 1994

Thiem, Rebecca; Finch, Susan; and, Cooper, Christopher. Series on New Orleans Mardi Gras, *The Times-Picayune* January-August 1992

Thomas, Greg. "Back in Business." *The Times-Picayune,* March 9, 1997

Woodbury, Richard. "Down in the Big Queasy." *Time*, February 28, 1994

Books
Wall, Bennett H.; Cummins, Light Townsend; Schafer, Judith Kelleher, Haas, Edward F., and Kurtz, Michael. *Louisiana: A History*. Third Edition. Wheeling, Illinois: Harlan Davidson, Inc., 1997.

ACKNOWLEDGEMENTS

This history of New Orleans is not the work of any single individual, but is the product of the dedicated efforts of many people and organizations.

Innumerable services and great encouragement have been proffered by several New Orleans historical groups and their staffs, especially the former Historic Collection's Director (and former Preservation Resource Center President) Stanton M. Frazar, and Curator John H. Lawrence. John was tireless in locating, selecting and captioning the hundreds of old and new illustrations appearing in this volume. I also wish to thank the Louisiana State Museum Historical Center, particularly former Curator Edward F. Haas and staff members Rose Lambert and the late Joseph Castle and the book's original sponsor, the Preservation Resource Center of New Orleans. I would especially like to single out three members of that organization: Patricia Gay, Ann Masson, and of course Mary Lou Christovich, who wrote the excellent chapter on preservation. Contributions from William Trufant, former President of the Louisiana Historical Society; D. Clive Hardy, Archivist at the University of New Orleans; and Suzanne Ormond, also were appreciated.

I am deeply indebted to the late Samuel Wilson, Jr., architect and architectural historian, and the late Charles "Pie" Dufour, historian and longtime columnist for the *States-Item*, for reading the manuscript and making helpful suggestions.

Finally, I want to thank my wife, Betty, and my daughter, Virginia, for their patience throughout.

John R. Kemp

The illustrations in this volume came from many sources—obvious and obscure, public and private. The following individuals and organizations contributed greatly toward the visual content of this book. Their assistance is greatly appreciated.

Stanton M. Frazar, former Director of the Historic New Orleans Collection, allowed great freedom of access to the pictorial holdings of that institution, which immensely simplified my task of selecting appropriate illustrations. The Collection's Chief Curator Dode Platou, and Curators John A. Mahe II and Rosanne McCaffrey were also very helpful in suggesting pieces for illustrating this book. Robert R. Macdonald, Director of the Louisiana State Museum offered his assistance and that of his staff, notably Vaughn Glasgow, Chief Curator; John Burton Harter, Curator; and Amy Husten, Registrar, in locating important illustrations from the museum's holdings. Colin Hamer, Head of the Louisiana Division of the New Orleans Public Library, and Wayne Eberhard of the same division were helpful in providing information and illustrations concerning recent political history. John Bender, Director of the Public Information Office of the City of New Orleans, provided access to the vast pictorial holdings relating to the operation of the mayor's office over the past 30 years. Charles Ferguson, Managing Editor; Jack Davis, City Editor; and Warren Nardelle, Librarian of the *Times-Picayune/States-Item* made available to me the photographic files of the newspaper. Their assistance is deeply appreciated. Pat Aymard of the Louisiana Historical Association's Confederate Museum permitted access to the holdings of that institution. William Slatten, President of the New Orleans Levee Board, was extremely cooperative and supportive of this project.

Robin Boylan, who did nearly all of the contemporary color photography that appears in this book, deserves special recognition for the zeal and enthusiasm he displayed in undertaking this assignment.

I also wish to thank Ann Masson and Patricia Gay of the New Orleans Preservation Resource Center for their confidence in me and their wholehearted support. John Kemp, author of the text, never failed in his encouragement and helpful suggestions for illustrations.

In addition to all of those who lent assistance during the picture selection process of the first edition, I would like to recognize the following for their assistance and support in the revised, updated edition.

John Kemp's lucid and specific text of the final chapter, permuted a selection of pictures that was both natural and informative of the last 15 years of New Orleans's history.

The Historic New Orleans Collection offered both tangible and intellectual support in this project. Special thanks are due to Jon Kukla, Executive Director; Jan White Brantley, Head Photographer and Dustin Booksh, Assistant Photographer; John T. Magill, Curator. The Collection's rich holdings and informed staff make a project such as this both a delightful and productive undertaking.

Other individuals and organizations who were especially helpful in this revised edition are: Marc Morial, Mayor of New Orleans; Ann Masson, editor, *New Orleans Preservation in Print,* The New Orleans Preservation Resource Center; Christmas in October; Operation Comeback.

My wife, Priscilla, provided *good* counsel and good cheer through this process. Her presence and advice were important factors in the successful illustration of the revised edition

John H. Lawrence

INDEX

Chronicles of Leadership Index